SHAKESPEARE'S
FESTIVE TRAGEDY

In Shakespearean studies, the category of the festive has been applied by critics only to the comedies. In this groundbreaking and provocative work, Naomi Conn Liebler introduces the category of festive tragedy. Shakespearean tragedy is, she argues, a celebration of communal survival, demonstrating what happens when a community violates or neglects the ritual structures that define and preserve it.

Liebler's highly original argument focuses upon tragedy as the formal representation of real social action and conflict. She views the community, not just the protagonist, as the real subject of the drama. Festive tragedy is concerned with ritual practice whose function is, as *King Lear*'s Tom O'Bedlam put it, 'to prevent the fiend and to kill vermin', that is, to protect and purge. The violation of this ritual practice jeopardizes the survival of the entire community.

Into her argument Liebler weaves the work of cultural anthropologists such as Clifford Geertz, Victor Turner and Mary Douglas and theories of drama by Aristotle, Brecht, Artaud and Girard. The result is a powerful, elegantly written work which extends the study of Shakespeare's tragedies into whole new areas of anthropological criticism and dramatic theory.

Naomi Conn Liebler is Professor of English at Montclair State University, where in 1990 she was named Distinguished Scholar. She is the author of a variety of articles on Shakespeare and, with John Drakakis, is co-editor of a forthcoming reader on tragedy.

SHAKESPEARE'S FESTIVE TRAGEDY

The ritual foundations of genre

Naomi Conn Liebler

London and New York

First published 1995
by Routledge
11 New Fetter Lane, London EC4P 4EE

Simultaneously published in the USA and Canada
by Routledge
29 West 35th Street, New York, NY 10001

© 1995 Naomi Conn Liebler

Typeset in Baskerville by LaserScript, Mitcham, Surrey
Printed and bound in Great Britain by
TJ Press (Padstow) Ltd, Padstow, Cornwall

British Library Cataloguing in Publication Data
A catalogue record for this book is available from the British Library

Library of Congress Cataloging in Publication Data
Liebler, Naomi Conn
Shakespeare's Festive Tragedy: The Ritual Foundations of Genre/
Naomi Conn Liebler.
p. cm.
Includes bibliographical references and index.
1. Shakespeare, William, 1564–1616 – Tragedies. 2. Literature and
society – England – History – 16th century. 3. Literature and society –
England – History – 17th century. 4. Rites and ceremonies in
literature. 5. Community life in literature. 6. Festivals in
literature. 7. Ritual in literature. 8. Literary form.
9. Tragedy. I. Title.
PR2983.L5   1995
822.3′3 – dc290   95-9687

ISBN 0–415–08657–4 (hbk)
ISBN 0–415–13183–9 (pbk)

For John,
sine quo multo minor

and dedicated to the memory of my mother,
Anne Conn

For when the morrow . . . upon a time quarrelled with the festivall day which went next before it, saying, that herselfe was busied and tooke a great deale of pains, preparing & providing with much travel those goods which the feast enjoied at her ease, with all repose, rest, and leisure: the Festivall day made this answer: Thou saidst true indeed; but if I were not, where wouldst thou be?

Plutarch, The Romane Questions 25

CONTENTS

ACKNOWLEDGEMENTS

This book emerges from more than a decade of starts and stops, during which time the encouragement of mentors and friends sustained both me and the work. Chief among these are Richard L. Levin, Rose Zimbardo, Martin Stevens, Inga-Stina Ewbank, Anne Paolucci, and Maurice Charney, who first suggested the book's title. I am grateful to them all, and also to Vance Adair, Michael Bristol, Ed Hack, Milla Riggio, and Peggy Samuels for listening, reading early versions, suggesting improvements, listening again, propping me up, cheering me on, and still listening. In the collegial settings of several Shakespeare Association of America seminars, many of the ideas in this book had their first exposures to and their first critiques from a learned and generous community of scholars. I thank Janice Price and Talia Rodgers of Routledge for their abiding faith in this project, and Michael Bristol and Diane Purkiss, readers for Routledge, for their detailed and helpful critiques. My greatest debt is to John Drakakis for his patience, generosity, uncompromising argument, and equally uncompromising support.

I would like to acknowledge as well the material forms of support I have received from the following: the Folger Shakespeare Library for a Junior Fellowship in the spring of 1982; the National Endowment for the Humanities Summer Seminar Program (1979, 1984, and 1991), whose work and fellowship contributed much to the development of this project; Dean Rachel Fordyce of the School of Humanities and Social Sciences at Montclair State University for technical support; and the President and Trustees of Montclair State University for a Distinguished Scholar Award which released me from teaching duties during the fall semester of 1990 and enabled me to write the first draft, and for a sabbatical leave in 1993–94 which enabled me to write the last.

ACKNOWLEDGEMENTS

Permission to reprint the following material under copyright is gratefully acknowledged: Jacques Derrida, *Dissemination* (1981), reprinted with permission from the University of Chicago and Athlone Presses; Antonin Artaud, *The Theater and Its Double* (1958), reprinted with permission from Grove/Atlantic, Inc.; Wole Soyinka, *Myth, Literature and the African World* (1976), reprinted with permission from Cambridge University Press; and Gerald F. Else, *Aristotle's Poetics: The Argument* (1967), reprinted with permission from Harvard University Press. Early versions of parts of this book have appeared in the following publications; I gratefully acknowledge their permissions to reprint revised versions of those essays: *Shakespeare Quarterly* (14: [1994]) for the section on *Titus Andronicus*; *Shakespeare Studies* (45: 3 [1994]) for the section on *Julius Caesar*; *Cahiers Élisabéthains* (45 [April 1994]) for the section on *Hamlet*; and the University of Illinois Press for the section on *Richard II* which originally appeared in *True Rites and Maimed Rites: Ritual and Anti-Ritual in Shakespeare and His Age*, eds Linda Woodbridge and Edward Berry (1992).

1

FESTIVE TRAGEDY

How to prevent the fiend and to kill vermin

"Festive tragedy" is not an oxymoron. The conjunction of "festive" and "tragedy" as parameters for a discussion of genre expresses complexity rather than contradiction. Apart from obvious genre-driven differences in plotting, Shakespeare's tragedies perform social and communal concerns similar to those C. L. Barber examined more than thirty-five years ago in *Shakespeare's Festive Comedy* (1959).[1] Barber's initiative in referring the study of Shakespearean comedy to the ordinary and recurrent social life of its original audiences has been widely and deservedly acknowledged. By situating the study of Shakespearean drama in a social and anthropological context, he and others of his generation, notably Northrop Frye (1957; 1965; 1967),[2] made a permanent difference in the ways subsequent generations have read and seen Shakespeare's plays, especially the comedies. They contributed much more than just another critical perspective; they literally launched a new awareness, a new field of inquiry for Shakespeareans whose work had been, until the late 1950s and early 1960s, restricted to printed and authorized "literature," to the "literary."

Since then, influenced by the writings of Mikhail Bakhtin (1968; 1981), René Girard (1977), Robert Weimann (1978), and others, the study of Shakespearean drama has ventured excursions into social and cultural anthropology. These excursions have found support in the work of anthropologists such as Victor Turner (1969; 1974; 1982), Mary Douglas (1966), Jack Goody and Ian Watt (1968), and Clifford Geertz (1973; 1983), who have provided information about the study of cultural dynamics as well as models for relating those dynamics to literary production. Constructs that were once thought simple and univocal – like each of the three words of my title – disclose upon examination a complexity that

1

summons new definitions, and sometimes seems to defy definition altogether. The first word, "Shakespeare's," belongs to this latter group, and its meanings have been energetically and competently investigated, notably by Michael D. Bristol (1990) and Margreta de Grazia (1991). The two remaining terms, "festive" and "tragedy," modified and contextualized by the first, are the subject of this book.

In appropriating two-thirds of Barber's famous title, I mean to acknowledge his work and move on, to explore the ways in which Shakespearean tragedy is "festive" in a sense broader, deeper, and more complex than the one Barber intended for comedy. Since the 1960s, Shakespearean critics have increasingly recognized that plays are sites of contestation where a multiplicity of constituencies (patrons, audiences, readers, actors, playhouse managers, printers) collaborate and compete in constructing a variety of meanings (Bristol 1985; Kastan and Stallybrass 1991). In print and in performance, the plays themselves confirm this; as William Gifford observed more than a century ago, Renaissance dramatists were "the most clear-sighted politicians of those troubled times" (quoted in Knights 1937: 175).

Barber's study was undertaken in and reflected the motif-hunting and pattern-seeking interests (the "lit-crit" equivalent of what anthropologists call "butterfly-collecting") that characterized much of literary criticism in the late 1950s, emerging from what was then known as "New Criticism." As such, it offered a valuable springboard to subsequent studies that in one sense or another have acknowledged their indebtedness. In marking communal festivity as inherent in the comic genre, Barber applied the pattern he found in popular English seasonal rites – May Day, Twelfth Night, Midsummer Eve, Harvest Home – whose dynamic is expressed as a movement "through release to clarification" (1959: 4). What is released is a saturnalian energy of celebration and mirth, clarifying "a heightened awareness of the relation between man and 'nature' – the nature celebrated on holiday" (1959: 8). Order restored after mishap, disaster averted, marriages appropriately settled, disruptive behavior chastized: these and similar plot arrangements mark the occasions for comic festivity, for celebrating individual and communal survival over those mishaps, disasters, mismatches, and disruptions. In the last thirty-five years, however, the large field in which Shakespearean scholars labor has increasingly resisted these and other definitive kinds of enclosure; its boundaries have expanded to encompass the crops of many other fields: social and political anthropology, history, and the reflexive revelations of critical theory itself.[3]

Newly acquired knowledges, however, are costly. These expanded arenas have obliged us to debate, negotiate, and sometimes reluctantly choose between, the comfortable satisfactions of reading hermeneutically, that is, of reading reiterative "patterns," and the often combative rigors of reading locally, of historicizing as much as possible within the limits of present knowledge the specific significations of any artifact's various representations (Marcus 1988; Pecora 1989). Two very recent, meticulously empirical works (Duffy 1992; Hutton 1994) chart the shifting character of ritual practices in Reformation and post-Reformation England; in so doing, they also demonstrate how overemphasis on exceptional or idiosyncratic instances can undermine the project of historicizing ritual practice in the early modern period, especially when the project is made to depend entirely on the survival of specific documentation.[4] As E. C. Cawte sagely observed, "the absence of a record does not mean the absence of a custom" (1978: 10). The importance of mapping the contestational and variant nature of early modern ritual is unquestioned, but at the same time there is a danger in rendering popular ritual practice almost completely indeterminate. It is also important to notice what is retained, and under what circumstances, and also to notice the anxiety that results when long-held practices are jettisoned by interdiction or by gradual slippage, as in Hamlet's threnody for the forgotten hobby-horse. Performance, like memory, is itself a kind of record, although not necessarily the kind that can be preserved. It is a Foucaultian "subjugated knowledge," "*le savoir des gens*" or "popular knowledge" (1980: 82). Moreover, discourses *about* ritual in plays performed on London stages are distinct from specific local ritual performance across rural England. As such, performances of both early modern plays and ritual practices can never be completely historicized. In the discussions of Shakespearean tragedies that follow, I have therefore tried to balance applications of "local knowledge" with theorized connections between discrete and disparate but nonetheless relatable texts. Implicit in the very concept of "genre" is the possibility of such connections.

The traps inherent in attempts to define, to pin down in some unarguable formulation, such terms as "tragedy," "ceremony," "ritual," and "festive" are to be recognized and respected. Because

3

it sets boundaries for interpretation, definition *is* a kind of enclosure, but the material practices and significations implicit in
these terms, like the theater itself, are hermeneutically unstable,
and thus vigorously resist such enclosure. Festive tragedy is, I
repeat, not an oxymoron. It is, in the Derridean sense, a dialectic,
a "mutual questioning and self-examination . . . through the
detour of the language of the other" (1981: 121). In tragedy, "self"
and "other" take various forms. They occupy the horns of a situational or characterological dilemma, represented by protagonist
and context or community, fictively constructed to embody simultaneously identical and opposing aspects of each other. The drama
does not *en*close social operations, which are not fixed or finite but
dynamic, fluid, shifting, alternating, at once dialectical and dia-
logical. Instead it *dis*closes them, with attention to the warrants of
tradition, precedent, and similar identifiable coordinates. These
operations occur in gesture or utterance, as Bourdieu explains,
and "reproduce in a *transformed form*, inserting them into the
structure of a system of symbolic relations, the oppositions and
hierarchies which actually organize social groups, and which they
help to legitimate by presenting them in a misrecognizable form"
(1977: 97). That "misrecognizable form" is nonetheless recoverable,
re-memberable, as ritual, and as tragedy. It can be excavated carefully
from beneath the overt significations of dramatic plot and social
action. In so doing, we can recover what Derrida calls the "*economy*,
the investment and deferred benefit behind the sign of pure renunci-
ation or the *bidding* of disinterested sacrifice" (1981: 120).

The performance of this critical excavation ideally requires
what Geertz, appropriating Gilbert Ryle's term, calls "thick description" (1973: 6): the patient and careful representation of the
contextual and circumstantial ground of any human activity. By
the meticulous relation of a particular action or practice to both
motivation and situation, *in so far as these may be known*, "thick
description" attends to the sedimentations of culture that com-
prise an integrated organism, and that in turn can be analyzed
synchronically. "Relativists" see every cultural activity discretely,
producing a check-list of unrelatable data; they reject efforts by
"essentialists" to obscure specific contexts in favor of similarities
and patterns held in common by disparate groups. "Thick description" attempts a useful compromise by respecting both pattern
and displacement. Although Geertz's anthropological project has
been challenged recently (Crapanzano 1992: 45–6, 60–9) on the

4

grounds that it fails in its own stated intentions, both those intentions and their arguable failure are nonetheless important caveats for those of us who would try to recover the contextualized resonances of Shakespearean tragedies in their original performative settings. Geertz reminds us that "Looking at the ordinary in places where it takes unaccustomed forms brings out not . . . the arbitrariness of human behavior . . . but the degree to which its meaning varies according to the pattern of life by which it is informed" (1973: 14). "Thick description" thus tries to recognize and accommodate not only the differences between separate and disparate cultural groups, but also the subtle and overt hierarchies of value systemic within a particular group.

In what has become a classic text in undergraduate courses in both anthropology and literature, Laura Bohannon's essay, "Miching Malecho: That Means Witchcraft" (sometimes reprinted under the title "Shakespeare in the Bush") illustrates particularly well the problematics of "thick description." Bohannon, an American anthropologist studying the Tiv people of West Africa, was given by a friend at Oxford a copy of *Hamlet* to take with her in the hopes that she would "by prolonged meditation, achieve the grace of correct interpretation" (1956: 174). To honor their "guest," on successive nights the Tiv narrated for her one or another representative legend. After many such nights and narratives, she was asked to share the "paper" that she had been seen reading. She summarized the plot for her auditors, who responded with a mixture of shock and derision. Hamlet, they told her, was quite wrong to disrespect and disobey his father's brother, even to save his own life. As for killing Claudius, Hamlet must have been mad! They explained that in their country, "also," a younger brother customarily married his elder brother's widow and became the "father" of his children. If the uncle is the father's "full brother," then he would be a "real father" to his nephews and nieces. Thus it was important to know whether Hamlet's father and Claudius had the same mother. Since she did not know these crucial genealogical details, Bohannon was urged to "ask the elders" about them when she returned home (1956: 178). And who, the chief elder asked, had married the other wives of the "dead chief"?

"He had no other wives," I told him.

"But a chief must have many wives! How else can he brew beer and prepare food for all his guests?"

I said firmly that in our country even chiefs had only one wife, that they had servants to do their work, and that they paid them from tax money.

It was better, they returned, for a chief to have many wives and sons who would help him hoe his farms and feed his people; then everyone loved the chief who gave much and took nothing – taxes were a bad thing.

(1956: 179)

Moreover, he continued, no young man should challenge his elders, and certainly not under the influence of witchcraft, which was the only logical explanation for the "ghost." For Hamlet to seek revenge against his uncle who had become his father was a terrible and wicked thing. If retribution was required, Hamlet should have appealed to his father's age-mates, the only ones empowered to avenge an elder's murder: "No man may use violence against his senior relatives" (1956: 185). Furthermore, as the chief elder explained,

> it is clear that the elders of your country have never told you what the story really means . . . . We believe you when you say your marriage customs are different, or your clothes and weapons. But people are the same everywhere; therefore, there are always witches and it is we, the elders, who know how witches work . . . . [You] must tell us some more stories of your country. We, who are elders, will instruct you in their true meaning, so that when you return to your own land your elders will see that you have not been sitting idle in the bush, but among those who know things and have taught you wisdom.

(1956: 186–9)

Lacking "thick description," Bohannon and her Tiv interlocutors had no choice but to misrecognize each other's narratives. Curiously, Bohannon's essay is sometimes taken as "proof" that Shakespeare can be understood only by a Western audience (perhaps only by a British one, as Bohannon's Oxford colleague thought her "American" perspective lacked the "grace of correct interpretation"); such a view inaccurately privileges a specific Western reading. Bohannon's narration of Hamlet's story in fact spoke loudly to the Tiv, and told a tale that resonated with the values and practices of Tiv culture. Indeed, it told a tragic tale of a protagonist caught in a web of cultural violations. The Tiv heard the story in a context perspectively different from that of Western audiences, but it was for them a story no less powerful, no less morally weighted, and no less tragic.

The same kind of structural, binary misrecognition applies to the relation of tragedy and comedy. Certain parallels and con-versions of the comic "pattern" can be seen in tragedies where, simply stated, individual and community are threatened by more powerful versions of comedy's disturbances. Comic ripple inten-sifies to a tragic rupture whose resolution, unlike comedy's, moves beyond the bounds of human redress and becomes an irrational and sometimes apocalyptic "promis'd end / Or image of that horror" (*King Lear* V.iii.264–5). However, despite the invitation of innumerable "definitions" of tragedy, beginning with over-simplified abstractions from Aristotle's and those in Renaissance dictionaries, it is a mistake to read "tragedy" as the mere inverse or obverse of established comic patterns. The "restoration of order" in tragedy amounts to much more than burying the dead and patching up the wounded (persons and kingdoms alike); it reflects, among other things, the (over)determined and driven choices that people in communities – collectively and individually – make towards survival, and the price, again collective and indi-vidual, of those choices.

The syntax or context of these actions involves every political and social institution at work in a given community. Contestation and confrontation result in the serious violation of all agreements implicit in the term "civilization," itself always a dialectic of control and resistance (Freud 1961), and wreak irreparable losses beyond the mere correction or elimination of bad behavior. The licensed misrule of comedy (Barber 1959: 36–57) is intensified in tragedy to eruptions of chaos; comic forms such as masquerade and oath-breaking (Barber 1959: 87–92) are magnified in tragedy to the denial or obliteration of significant human connections. What in comedy occurs as happy celebration is replaced in tragedy with appeals to solemn ceremony and other strategies for containment and order that reflect political and social operations. Comedy performs a "breaking out" of the social restraints imposed by necessary labor, prescribed or proscribed behavior, or seasonal obligations, followed by a return to a socially and politically viable stability. Tragedy performs an uncontrollable breakage at great expense, despite human efforts, either inevitably or accidentally

7

inadequate, to contain its repercussions. It, too, "celebrates," by reconstructing, re-membering, what is lost.

Thus, both comedy and tragedy are festive genres. The former (as Barber demonstrated) recognizes, negotiates, and celebrates the social operations that reaffirm and revitalize social institutions, while the latter discloses the consequence of misrecognizing or debasing those operations by diverting or disjoining them from the structures through which a society normally derives its meaning. The term "festive", applied to tragedy, signals, as it does when applied to comedy, the celebration of a community's survival, although that application entails an alternatively focused view of both celebration and survival. Tragedy "celebrates" by anatomizing its community's claims and constructs, how they work, what threatens them, how to preserve them, and at what cost. In both comedy and tragedy, the constructed cultural values of the fictive community are invariably reaffirmed and reconsecrated, but in tragedy the management, alteration, or manipulation of those values is put to question. That question interrogates not only the capability of representative human communities to act for their own continuing good, but also what *constitutes* "the good," the "common weal" in each dramatized case.

At one level, tragedy participates in what Barber described for comedy as the movement "through release to clarification" (1959: 4). In tragedy this release is closely related to Aristotle's claim for catharsis; it is also a release of the powerful and destructive energy unleashed when the bonds that identify and protect a collectivity of individuals as a community are severed. Because their focus is upon human rather than natural creation (and indeed upon what sometimes appears to be most "unnatural" in human creation), we do not find in the tragedies the same close correlations between ritual and seasonal festivity that Barber and Frye asserted for the comedies. What is clarified is not, as Barber thought, the "relation between man and nature" but that between human beings and their own creations, the values that inform and sustain a civilization.

It is the business of ritual to protect and reaffirm those values. This is the function identified when Edgar, disguised as Tom o' Bedlam, answers Lear's question, "What is thy study?" Edgar replies, "How to prevent the fiend and to kill vermin" (III.iv.159), in other words, prophylaxis and purgation. Edgar's line masquerades as a quip tossed off by a pretend lunatic whom Lear recognizes as the "poor, bare, forked animal," "unaccommodated man." But "unaccommodated man" is a fiction, just as Tom o'Bedlam, Edgar, and the play itself are fictions. "Man" is very much "accommodated" (Bourdieu 1977: 82–3; Foucault 1986: 23). "Thou art the thing itself," says Lear, in an errant attempt to ascribe a particular materiality and definition to what he sees before him. Lear's tragedy springs in part from his belief not only that he can reify and redistribute the meaning of abstractions such as kingdom, love, and loyalty, but that he knows what they are in the first place, and that he can legislate their operations. What he is to learn through the tragedy (among other things) is that these abstractions are labels for certain kinds of human relations that are negotiable and fragile, and that these relational "bonds" are protected and insured by ritual action that wards off both spiritual harm and physical disease, prevents the fiend and kills vermin.

This is as much the aim of ritual action in Shakespearean tragedy as it is in traditional cultures. As Mary Douglas explains in a well-known formulation, defilement or dirt is "matter out of place . . . . It implies two conditions: a set of ordered relations and a contravention of that order"; "dirt is that which must not be included if a pattern is to be maintained . . . . It involves us in no clear-cut distinction between sacred and secular" (1966: 35, 40). No communal structure has permanent immunity from such danger: "We are not free. And the sky can still fall on our heads. And the theater has been created to teach us that first of all" (Artaud 1958: 79). In tragedy, when the ordered relations of a community are disrupted, the hero draws to herself or himself all of the ambiguity and crisis present in the community, just as an organism fighting a disease localizes antibodies at the site of infection. This is the operation of Artaud's analogy of theater and plague. There are moments in each drama, sometimes sustained through several scenes, in which this localization takes on the forms and echoes of rituals known to the community within the play (and often to the community watching it). Stephen Booth calls these moments "ceremonies of safety" in "the emergency measure that the word *tragedy* is itself" (1983: 85).

At another level, tragedy problematizes communal relations by responding to the breaking, not the sustaining, of rules and order, to what Hamlet refers to as time wrenched "out of joint." Tragedy represents the consequences of perverting, inverting, or neglecting the ordering, containing properties of civic and social rituals, understood as required for the preservation and functioning of a

9

community. Such exemplary representations of festive comedy as the lunatics, lovers, and poets of *A Midsummer Night's Dream*, "observe / the rite of May" (IV.i.132–3) and the requirements of time (I.i.1–11), however carelessly they neglect their own human relations. Inversely, those of festive tragedy, like the characters caught up in the confused celebration of the Lupercal that opens *Julius Caesar*, all interrogate, undermine, or violate seasonal and social forms of order.

Seeing such disclosures as "festive" requires that we unfasten the idea of celebration from its traditionally comic moorings. Celebration, as the opening conflict in *Julius Caesar* so clearly demonstrates, depends upon who is doing the celebrating, and perhaps to an even greater extent, upon whether and by whom that celebration is authorized or legitimated. As political constructs, both "community" and "individual" are interdependent terms. Similarly, the idea of "festivity" admits to what François Laroque has called a "profoundly ambivalent" meaning (1991: 5).[5] In this regard, the "ambivalence" of festivity is inseparable from the "ambivalence" of the practices that mark festivity, that is, of ritual practices themselves, and these in turn both ratify and are ratified by the prevailing social system (Bourdieu 1977: 98). The ambivalence (more precisely, the complexity) of ritual inheres precisely in its very nature: ritual sets boundaries. Operating in time and space, it marks alterations in time and space, as well as in status, condition, and identity. As an integral in the calculus of past and present, or of one status and another, a boundary is itself a site of ambivalence, or rather, of multivalence. Because they distinguish margins, boundaries are liminal,[6] and thus both dangerous and vulnerable. As Douglas writes, "all margins are dangerous. If they are pulled this way or that the shape of fundamental experience is altered. Any structure of ideas is vulnerable at its margins" (1966: 145). Transitional states are structurally dangerous, she argues, because transition itself is undefinable; the person in transit from one status to another loses the defining identity attached to either status and thus is both in danger and dangerous to others. Ritual controls that danger by precisely separating old from new status, segregating the subject for a time, and then publicly declaring the transformation completed. In Douglas's terms, "the whole repertoire of ideas concerning pollution and purification are used to mark . . . the power of ritual to remake a man" (1966: 116–17).

Because rituals are ontologically and functionally *trans*versive, they are thus open to the uses of the *sub*versive. These embedded alternative applications give some perspective on the complexity of ritual operations in practice. For instance, Laroque notes that the practice of "beating the bounds" at Rogation-tide provided an orderly representation of ritualized space and the consecration of communal property. But on other festival occasions – Palm Sunday, May Day, and Midsummer Day – the same practice devolved into misrule, "affording people license . . . to steal flowers, timber and trees from the forests and their adjacent parks." He does not say why Rogation-tide should have been less susceptible than other sacred occasions to abrogation, but finds the difference "a particularly striking illustration of the ambivalence of the festival: sometimes it served as a solemn ratification of boundaries, points of reference and dividing lines; at other times, it gave a community license to transgress those boundaries and abolish those dividing lines" (Laroque 1991: 13–14).

It could be argued that licensed transgressions are no transgressions at all, but are instead alternative forms of permissible behavior that serve to reinforce the status quo. Interpretation depends upon the uses to which ritual practices are put, because their inherent multivalence articulates complex cultural formations whose strands are often difficult to tease out even by members of the participating group. Keith Thomas's detailed discussion of "beating the bounds" may explain the exception of Rogation-tide: it consecrated specifically the protection of parish property-lines from encroachment during the year by interests competing for land-use, and it afforded a special opportunity outside church walls to pray for good weather and a fruitful harvest (1971: 62–4). Thomas's remarks imply a real contestation between material and doctrinal interests over the management and import of the ritual, and also suggest that in the case of such a contest, material interests prevailed in determining popular behavior. Moreover, both popular and clerical activities change over time in response to doctrinal and economic alterations (Hutton 1994: 85, 175–6).

In considering the function of a festive agrarian calendar, Bourdieu notes that it distinguishes "practical time" made up of "incommensurable islands of duration" whose rhythms depend upon the demands and functions of necessary activities, from "linear, homogeneous, continuous time." A calendar sets *"guide-marks* (ceremonies and tasks) along a continuous line," and thus "turns them into *dividing marks* united in a relation of simple succession, thereby creating *ex nihilo* the question of the intervals and correspondences between points which are no longer topologically but metrically equivalent" (Bourdieu 1977: 105). It is important to remember that such calendrical distinctions are neither inevitable nor entirely arbitrary. Festive occasions and practices result from highly complicated agreements between constituencies regarding the specific events and activities to be sustained at regular intervals within and by a group or community. As Bourdieu explains, "those which are socially recognized as the most representative and successful, those worthiest of being preserved by the collective memory . . . are themselves organized in accordance with the structures constituting that system of classification" (1977: 98). Therefore, at any given moment of performance, they already encode a deliberate selection and ratification of the prevailing social structure, and are capable of being "read" for "codified references and strict guidelines" (1977: 98).

"Festive" means something more socially complex than "merry." The Latin root, *festum* ("feast") incorporates the sacramental, patterned, and entirely serious functions and meaning of ritual as communal activity. In this sense, the meaning of the word "festive" expands to include "ceremonial," "solemn," "celebratory," and "consecrative." In fact, in its early use, the term "feast" incorporated ritual, and especially sacrificial ritual. Bede's *Ecclesiastical History* (I: 30) cites the well-known instructions from Pope Gregory to the mission at Canterbury in 601:

> the temples of the idols of the people should on no account be destroyed. The idols are to be destroyed, but the temples themselves are to be aspersed with holy water, altars set up in them, and relics deposited there . . . . And since they have a custom of sacrificing many oxen to demons, let some other solemnity be substituted in its place . . . and celebrate the solemnity with devout feasting. They are no longer to sacrifice beasts to the Devil, but they may kill them for food to praise of God . . . .
>
> (Bede 1968: 86–7)[7]

"Feast" or *festum* thus etymologically signals at once doctrinal and sociopolitical control and communal consecration beginning in sacrificial ritual (Bynum 1987; Douglas 1982: 82–124; Lincoln 1989:

75–88). A solemn feast – a state dinner or a ritual meal – is therefore nonetheless festive, for all its gravity of form and purpose. Through the communal breaking of bread, the event marked by the banquet is validated and affirmed. Shakespeare explores this connected function in the formal banquet scene in *Macbeth* (III.iv); the banquet implodes with Macbeth's guilt-driven collapse, leaving his kingship in fact unconfirmed.

"Festive" thus carries a great deal of meaning available to tragedy. It recognizes that, like comedy, tragedy consecrates and celebrates something. That something varies insignificantly from play to play. Shakespearean tragedy *seems* to magnetize its audiences to a focus on the individual; indeed, the titles of Shakespeare's tragedies all point to their protagonists. Traditional critical discussions that focus obsessively on individual protagonists have led to a notion that tragedy is about discrete personae with important personal histories and complex psychologies (or psychological complexes). Such discussions tend to occlude the fact that tragedy is at least equally interested in the *agon* of the community, and that protagonists along with all the other characters are representations of component positions or institutions within a community.

Even that construction must be carefully considered: what is represented in a play is not a "real" community, any more than the characters are "real" people. They are representational models designed to express the complex relations of an exemplary society whose story is frozen for examination purposes at a particular moment in its fictionalized history. Institutions or estates, component social–political structures, are *embodied* in tragedies in order to explore their composition and their respective cooperative or conflicting operations. The institution of monarchy, for example, not the monarch, is the real subject of tragedies of state. As Moretti observes, "the one who, himself in equilibrium, provides the point of equilibrium for the social body, the sovereign is the missing person, the impossible being in Shakespearean tragedy" (1982: 30). There is in that sense no sovereign in *Titus Andronicus, Julius Caesar,* or *Coriolanus;* there is none in *Othello,* nor, effectively, in *Romeo and Juliet.* After the first act, there is none in *Macbeth* or *King Lear.* If we look from the protagonist's point of view in *Hamlet,* there is none there either. The oriental/feminine construction of the Egyptian queen in *Antony and Cleopatra* problematizes the ways in which a Jacobean audience might have received that play's image of "monarchy."

The required distinction is effaced by the absence of a stable, communally acknowledged, supreme, i.e., "sovereign" center of authority. "Sovereign" is a term whose application requires acceptance by the governed. It implies efficacy and potency. The characters who represent authority in a given play inhabit their offices: it is not so much their "personae" with which tragedy is concerned, as it is the ways in which these representations manage the offices they inhabit and the consequences of that management in a larger arena. Such concerns are in fact very traditional ones whose contours obtain in a wide variety of cultures, both modern and early: it is the action, not the fictive personality (although that personality may influence action), of a leader or a king *as* authority that determines the stability or the survival of the community. Thus neither Hamlet nor Lear nor, ultimately, Richard II is sovereign, despite their unquestionable royalty. Tragedy manifests the decentering of authority; it is the image of authority in crisis. The problem of sovereign (central, supreme, ordering) authority is enacted in the crisis faced by the tragic protagonist whose behavior reflects a disruption or discontinuity, both producing and produced by that behavior.

To put the case a little differently, the office of sovereign is a construct of custom, tradition, continuity, and law. In plays where sovereign authority is at stake, the *agon* reproduces the process and context by which that office is generated and sustained. The process is dramatized as a decentering, a conflict, an imbalance that threatens the ecology of the larger community, but it is at base the larger community's survival *as it knows itself* that is at issue in these plays. Whether or not the protagonist is royal, his or her action in the tragedy serves as the interface between systemically inscribed structures of order and the disruptive nature of the action, making the real focus of that action communal rather than individual, and macrotemporal, long-term, and connected, rather than local, momentary, or isolated to the specific circumstances represented.

In so far as a play is arranged around ideological questions (Whose play *is* this? What ideological issues are represented in the action and in the dialogue? Who "wins" the contest?), we must bear in mind that the protagonist has been designed specifically to demonstrate particular qualities that a certain interest defines as representing the ideal, the best and the brightest embodiments of its society's values. These qualities, with remarkable consistency, are cited in the eulogies given at the protagonists' deaths: "The noblest Roman of them all" (Brutus); "the oldest [who] hath borne most" (Lear); "a noble heart" (Hamlet); "the most noble corse that ever herald / Did follow to his urn" (Coriolanus): these Shakespearean eulogies describe the heroic nature of the Aristotelian tragic protagonist, "a man held in high opinion and of good fortune," who is preeminently, as in S. H. Butcher's gloss, "composed of mixed elements, by no means supremely good, but a man 'like ourselves' (ὅμοιος) . . . a man of noble nature, like ourselves in elemental feelings and emotions; idealised, indeed, but with so large a share of our common humanity as to enlist our eager interest and sympathy" (1951: 316–17). Whatever the fictive society celebrates, it celebrates in and through the *agon* of the tragic hero. Macbeth appears to be the notable exception, but at the beginning of his play he too embodied the highest form of military valor and feudal loyalty to his king. Hamlet is "Th'expection and rose of the fair state, / The glass of fashion and the mould of form" (III.i.152–3). Titus epitomizes *romanitas* by bearing with pride the deaths of twenty-one sons for Rome's defense. Brutus and Coriolanus, at times, are seen as pivotal figures in the survival of their respective communities. Lear and Richard II are anointed kings by birth, thus they are microcosmic kingdoms; their bodies and the state are reciprocal symbols (Greenblatt 1981; Kastan 1986; Tennenhouse 1986). In each of the tragedies, the subject–body, whether perceived as discrete, individual or collective state, is fragmented, divided, dis-integrated.

The metaphoric relation of body and state was never accidental: both are hierarchically arranged; both require a large degree of internal homeostasis in order to survive, let alone to thrive; and both exist by a fragile interdependence of tensions and conflicts among their component parts. This relationship is complex, as evidenced by the identification in Renaissance texts of various parts of the human body with their social "counterparts" in the state. By general agreement, the prince was the "head," but the belly's role, depending upon the attribute emphasized, was assigned by William Averell (*A Mervailous Combat of Contrarieties* 1588) to the aristocracy, by Francis Bacon ("Of Seditions and Troubles" [1625] [1985: 103]) to both a deprived populace and a troubled aristocracy, and by Edward Forset (*A Comparative Discourse of the Bodies Natural and Politique*, 1606:14 [A2r]) to the sovereign as the governor of a healthy digestive system.[8] The point is that the metaphor cannot be read simplistically; everything in the equation depends upon the purpose for which it is generated, and by whom. The "human experience of body tends to sustain a particular view of society, the latter in turn constraining the way in which the body itself is regarded" (M. James 1983: 6). These individual "observ'd of all observers" (*Hamlet* III.i.154) who draw our gaze are both protagonists and antagonists of their communities; each is dramatically constructed as bi-valent. Moreover, as representations (both pro and contra) of their respective community's power structures, its hierarchy, and its internal or introduced disruptions and anxieties, each also represents the conflicts, ambiguities, contradictions, and fears that threaten the community, and for that reason must be destroyed. Tragic heroes are their communities' *pharmakoi*, constructed by and at the same time constructing their communities. Because they constitute the site of all that the community stands for, including its conflicts and crises, they must be removed, taking, if only temporarily, those conflicts and crises with them. Their removal, or sacrifice, in turn reconfirms or reinscribes the community in the image it has chosen for itself, or more accurately, in the image chosen by its particular surviving structures of authority. In the often eulogistic final lines of each play we can read how the ways in which protagonists are remembered authorize what is retained from their actions as the "moral" or "lesson" of the play. This is invariably a partial, not a universal, representation, as indeed official structures, institutions, and social values encode only selections within a full range of "tensions, contradictions, superficial stability, and potential fluidity . . . that circulates at any given moment" (Lincoln 1989: 7) in any broadly complex society.

In order to reinscribe those selected values and institutions, it is in the community's best interest that the tragic heroes appear to "fail"; and yet their defeat and death represents a huge loss to the community. In some instances the hero turns against the community (Romeo and Juliet, Lear, Macbeth, Coriolanus); in all, or nearly all, the represented community (and, I will argue, through a process of misrecognition, members of the audience as well) turns against the hero. One way or another, in each case, the entire fictive sociopolitical organism, a unit incorporating both hero and community, in turning against a representation of itself, turns against itself. The image of humanity devouring itself is often deployed in Shakespearean tragedy to express chaos, the uncreation of order through inversion or perversion. In *Lear*, "Humanity must perforce prey on itself, / Like monsters of the deep" (IV.ii.49–50); in *Coriolanus*, communal as well as individual self-consumption is similarly imagined three times (I.i.85; III.i.288–92; IV.ii.50–51). The transformation of the protagonist from hero to the locus of crisis displaces communal self-annihilation onto a valid scapegoat.

René Girard's discussions of the hero as *pharmakos* (1977: 39–67, 250–73; 1978: 178–98), and especially his claim that scapegoating requires an artificial or assigned differentiation (marginalization, misrecognition, demonization) for the community to exact its violent penalties, are particularly useful in this context (despite the totalizing circularity of his argument that such "reciprocal violence" is the irreducible foundation of all human societies). In his view, violence is that "excess" which threatens to break through the surface of community. The *pharmakos* localizes "the very real (though often hidden) hostilities that *all the members of the community feel for one another*" (1977: 99); sacrificial ritual imitates and reenacts this "spontaneous collective violence" which, he says, "*operates without reason*" (1977: 46) and is "eminently communicable" (1977: 30) in an endless cycle of differentiation, sacrifice, and reincorporation. Sacrificial ritual, or "good" violence, channels otherwise random slaughter into an act of purification ratified by the structure and the membership of the community.

Girard's "endless cycle" diminishes the role of interested and partisan human agency; his emphasis on "randomness" obscures the important and meaningful specificity of the *pharmakos*'s selection. Because the relation of body and state is more than metaphoric or metonymic, the hero becomes *pharmakos* through the objectification of the protagonist's body *as* the body of the state. By a process of mystification requiring ritualistic redress, the protagonist literally *embodies* the sociopolitical taint, disease, or disruption that produces political anxiety and destabilizes the *polis*. The deaths of tragic protagonists at the ends of their plays represent a kind of self-surgery by the community (as Coriolanus is called "a disease that must be cut away" [III.i.293]), which accompanies a ritualized effort to restore some semblance of order and to clarify and reclaim the culture's primary values. This order cannot be exactly the *status quo ante* – too many characters are swept away with the hero – but it is potentially order of a new kind, or at the very least a clearing for such order, out of which the community can attempt to heal itself.

It is precisely because the protagonist's body mystifies real social relations in the body politic that the redress constructed by the protagonist's death is only temporary. It may or may not be in the nature of human communities to enact violent sacrifices of their designated doubles, but it is unarguably the practice of human communities to organize themselves hierarchically, and therefore politically. Thus, the conflict between (or within) the protagonist and the *polis* releases alternative forces that cannot both be suppressed at the same time. This bivalent, or paired, energy is represented in the Aristotelian idea of *dilemma*, on whose equivalent horns both the protagonist and the community are gored. It is also because of this bivalence that the dramaturgical endings of Shakespeare's tragedies resist closure: no matter which force has been, for a time, suppressed, the other still ranges unchecked: Aaron and Iago, to cite obvious examples, remain alive at their respective plays' ends; Aufidius is extensively acknowledged as Coriolanus's surviving double, and the hero's death has done nothing, in any case, to relieve the threat of starvation that forms one of the play's contestational premises. Fortinbras, also sometimes recognized as Hamlet's double, is designated king of Denmark, *faute de mieux*, but his Norwegian birth and his prior aggression against his newly acquired kingdom raises questions about what, if anything, is restored at the end of *Hamlet*. In some plays the "restoration" of order results from somewhat arbitrary, and therefore contestable, designations: Malcolm, as the nominated Prince of Cumberland, promises to heal Scotland at the end of *Macbeth*; his brother Donalbain is noticeably absent from the celebrations. The same problematic implications may be noticed at the ends of most, if not all, of Shakespeare's tragedies if we look just beyond the formal and formulaic language of their respective closures to see who among the represented populace is listening or absent. Those formulaic rhetorical closures can be heard as anxious, willful or wishful assertions of resolution against the structural implications of renewed conflict and unresolved estrangements. Among the questions that resonate at the ends of Shakespearean tragedies are these: what exactly has been contested in the play, how is the represented community's anxiety assuaged by the semblance of resolution at the end, how are the play's ritual elements molded to confirm that resolution, and whose version of what restoration or healing does the closure serve?

Representing the preservation of the sociopolitical organism is as much the end or aim of tragic action as it is of comic. Comedies, in Michael Long's eloquent comparison, are plays "in which the wayward vitality of the non-socialized world is something which men, without fear, may take into themselves as nourishment. The plays thus celebrate the adaptability of culture and . . . the capacity of human structures to bend and not break under pressure from nature" (1976: 2); whereas in tragedies,

> the structure of a human culture is seen as built upon a raw chaos of the contradictory and the unpredictable – a vulnerable thing. What we see in the tragedies is the fatal inadaptability of cultures and . . . minds trained in and adjusted to a given set of civilized mores . . . . [Beneath is] a volatile, kinetic world of the destructive and the absurd to which accommodation is nearly impossible. This is the journey from culture into trauma, the tragic counterpart of the journey from Law into release.
>
> (Long 1976: 7–8)

His claim for tragedy's volatility comes very close to Artaud's analysis in *The Theater and Its Double*:

> Like the plague, the theater is a formidable call to the forces that impel the mind by example to the source of its conflicts
> . . . .
> The theater, like the plague . . . releases conflicts, disengages powers, liberates possibilities, and if these possibilities and these powers are dark, it is the fault not of the plague nor of the theater, but of life.
>
> (1958: 30–1)

Inspired in large measure by Jacobean tragedy, Artaud's manifesto is, as I will argue in chapter 2, a profoundly important document for readers and audiences of Shakespeare's plays. For the moment, in this brief selection, it directs us to see tragedy as a discourse of danger as well as of redress, whose representation locates conflict in the mind of the population (that is, of the audience as well as of the community represented on stage). The "double" of the theater implicated in the title of his manifesto is life as it is lived in a blended state of conscious and unconscious energies, disturbing, terrifying, and finally regenerating. Artaud's construction of theater as a "plague" is insistently celebratory and optimistic of the theater as an agency of change – first in itself and then, consequently, in its producing culture.

19

And the question we must now ask is whether, in this slippery world which is committing suicide without noticing it, there can be found a nucleus of men capable of imposing this superior notion of the theater, men who will restore to all of us the natural magic equivalent of the dogmas in which we no longer believe.

(1958: 32)

In the drama of the seventeenth century, including Shakespeare's, Artaud saw a vital and constructive social catalyst. Like Foucault's "subjugated knowledges" (1980: 82), Artaud's views have been ignored by modern critics of Shakespearean tragedy to an extent perhaps inversely suggesting their importance. Artaud intuitively opposed the enduring and erroneous critical commonplace that tragedy represents the hero's failure. No matter how admirable the tragic protagonist, or how difficult or impossible the protagonist's task, critics persist in identifying his or her *hamartia* as a failure to do something. As Leslie Fiedler put it, "The image of man in art – precisely when it is most magnificently portrayed – is the image of failure. There is no way out" (1960: 7). But the charge of failure properly belongs only to efforts that are themselves inadequate, which the audience recognizes as poor choices they themselves would not have made in the same circumstances, seeing the same alternatives. The wholly or partly fictive situations of tragic heroes dramatize extremities beyond the experience of real human beings; they are enlarged versions of what is possible, but not probable, in real life: representation as distinct from mimesis.

The fact that the tragic heroes' chosen actions "miss the mark" (the literal meaning of Aristotle's 'αμαρτια) does not make those actions or those heroes failures. The precise circumstances of tragedy involve situations in which the task to be done is itself impossible. Tragedy does not represent the failure to do noble, difficult, necessary things; it represents the attempt to do them in a context that will not permit them to be done. That context varies from play to play, and from one producing culture to another, and therefore so do the particular circumstances or actions represented. If we remember that the protagonist is selected and shaped to represent specific aspects of the communal situation, we can avoid the interpretive trap of "blaming the victim." A *pharmakos* is a victim of a very special kind. To see the tragic protagonist as essentially "flawed" is to erase the intense identification of hero and community that is central to the workings of tragedy. The heroes of Shakespearean tragedy are admired for a reason, or for several reasons, and those reasons are not anchored in some major inadequacy in the character. To say this a century after Bradley first published the lectures in which he cautiously extended Hegel's idea that the "fundamental tragic trait" in Shakespearean heroes is their "greatness, which is also fatal to [them]" (Bradley 1904: 27), may appear to be the unnecessary reinvention of a critical wheel. But even Bradley came to rest in the comfortable notion of the protagonist's responsibility for calamity through some "error," thereby placing the onus of the situational conflict squarely and exclusively on the protagonist's shoulders.

The extraordinary shelf-life of the notion of a "tragic flaw" reveals a persistent critical misrecognition of *hamartia* that characterizes the way tragedy is received by modern audiences. Tragedy presents the contestation of a range of social and political values in conflict in a fictive but recognizable community. The protagonist is constructed to embody all of those values, constructive and destructive, which in the course of the play become polarized. The fictive community, in turn, is constructed as a recognizable version of the audience for whom it is performed; by reproducing familiar values, the drama both produces and is produced by its audience's culture. To the extent that the critical audience is led by this recognizable representation to identify more with the fictive community than with the protagonist, the resultant victimization of the protagonist on account of a "flaw" or "error" simply replicates within the audience the situation represented in the play. In other words, tragedy works upon its audience in very much the same way that it works upon its characters: by an inevitable misrecognition of the relation between protagonist and community, the protagonist is demonized as "other" and the audience/fictive community ratified as "us." The alternative view of the protagonist or *pharmakos* as a microcosm of the generative community is indeed very disturbing, and that disturbance is one of the principal affects of the genre.

The "failure," if any, that tragic heroes "commit" is the one committed by their society. Their *hamartia* is their community's *hamartia*. Their crises concentrate their community's crises. In the context of the body–state nexus briefly discussed earlier, given the interdependence of tensions and conflicts among the component parts of the equation, the protagonist both internalizes and objectifies the communal crisis. Like Rome, Brutus is "with himself at war"; "the state of man, / Like to a little kingdom, suffers . . . / The nature of an insurrection" (*Julius Caesar* II.i.67–9). Richard II weeps for his "wounded" kingdom when he lands in Wales (III.ii.4–26). Even Macbeth, in his brief but focused moment of remorse, asks his wife's doctor to "cast / The water of my land, find her disease, / And purge it to a sound and pristine health" (V.iii.50–2). Each of these protagonists conflates the subjective body with that of the state.

If failure is represented in the play, it is that of the community convened therein to be better than it is at doing the impossible. The communal nature of *hamartia* is embedded in each tragedy, and is recognized in the rhythm and echo of ritual patterns that run understage like Old Hamlet's ghost. Through ritual action, communities sometimes invoke supernatural forces – divine or demonic – to explain or subsidize their determinate social limitations. In tragedy those limitations are seen ultimately as manmade, despite the occasional notice of "cosmic forces," and we seem to be stuck with them.

Tragedy is a meditation on social and political order, on hierarchy, the differential structure that embeds conflict, tension, or anxiety in its very existence. In a deliberate oversimplification, we might say that if the structure is "good" its preservation produces anxiety; if it is "bad" it must be overturned. But the moment that is said, the terms are immediately betrayed by their moral qualifiers ("good" and "bad"), which are themselves not only arguable but artificially constructed and thus radically limited. The question of who determines such moral values underlies all such distinctions. In Laurence Michel's formulation of Shakespeare's "enormous capacity for the negative," the plays exhibit "not only overt evil-versus-good but misgivings, qualms, about the vision of good itself . . . . [It] is the critique from the inside: not a flaw in an otherwise good thing, but the corruptibility of the apparent good itself" (1970: 40).

Ritual, likewise designed towards the "good," is subject to the same interrogation: not only by whom and for what is it constructed, but how fragile or corruptible is that construction? Ritual, like the community it serves, is inherently hierarchical, orderly, in both the shape of its action and in its enactment by a designated performer. Like the heroic subject, hierarchy is therefore both the cause and the cure of conflict. Other genres besides tragedy, of course, represent the endless permutations of conflict and violence. Tragedy locates them precisely, crystallizes them in order to represent and express them, and thereby interrogates the issues and ideas upon which a society is founded. In the course of that interrogation, tragedy releases energies that hierarchy is designed to contain but cannot, and those energies, as Artaud argued, are themselves both the overt and the latent content of the drama. Implicit in the resolution of conflict at the end of a given play is its resurgence at another moment. These energies, whether radical or reactionary, follow the laws of entropy: they are never dissipated; they are only transformed, and only temporarily. Simultaneously, they are contained and resist containment.

The symbiotic and contingent relation of the represented community to its protagonist interrogates a model of social existence by positioning its components in terms of their respective, and often competing, interests. The audience is invited to "look closely at how men attach themselves to a social structure and shape their identities thereby, and at how this attachment creates habits of perception, behaviour, and evaluation, which are radically delimiting" (Long 1976: 8). That is, Shakespearean tragedy foregrounds an openly artificial but credible set of social constructions and anatomizes the consequences of destabilizing those constructions. Communities tend collectively to be conservative in regard to their social structures and customs: thus we see in the tragedies "minds in fear of ambiguity, in fear of flux, chance, and change, . . . for which the volatilities of unstructured experience hold terror, not release" (Long 1976: 9).

In every Shakespearean tragedy the status quo of the community is at risk from the first moments of the play. The community, like the protagonist, undergoes an *agon*, a crisis, as Nietzsche (1967: 33–41), Freud (1961), and more recently Girard (1977) recognized in different ways, that positions a process of individuation against the collective or aggregate requirements of the larger social construct. In each case, a change or the threat of change is already occurring from the moment the play begins, and the threat of alteration, a fissure in the familiar social structure, initiates the possibility of calamity. *Titus Andronicus* opens with a transfer of rule; *Julius Caesar* begins with a transformation of the Lupercalian celebration that exposes it as a site of contestation and proceeds to the matter of a significant change in the nature of government. In *Hamlet* and *Coriolanus*, the state is under attack from outside as well as from its internal self-division; in *Romeo and Juliet* the family feud overruns communal life; in *Macbeth, King Lear,* and *Richard II* the source of fissure is within the kingdom.

In each case restorative action should begin with an appeal to the central heroic figure through whom the community seeks its survival. But the community faces a paradox, in fact several paradoxes. One occurs because the hero, by embodying the very same conflicts, contradictions, and ambiguities that plague the community, re-presents the communal crisis. Heroic subjects mirror their worlds, and thus reflect the limitations of those worlds. To preserve itself, the community must efface the image of itself, like Richard II shattering his mirror. Another paradox emerges because the hero represents simultaneously both the subjection of the community and the agency for overturning that subjection; this double representation is the function of the *pharmakos*. This in some measure accounts for the highly problematic situation in *Macbeth*: until he murders Duncan, Macbeth is an unambiguous hero, supporting by violence the status quo, punishing the former Cawdor's rebellion, serving his liege lord, and sustaining the cycles of violence through which feudal values are articulated in the play. The profoundly disturbing difficulty of "explaining" how a community incorporates in its own values the potential to destroy itself is handled in this play by displacing the "cause" onto the feminine, in the demonization of the Weird Sisters and Lady Macbeth (Eagleton 1986: 2–4). But ultimately the play demands a recognition that Macbeth himself has become the "monstrous double" (to use Girard's term) of the violent community itself. The relation of hero and community is understood as reciprocal: they have nurtured each other, and now threaten to destroy each other. The same kind of paradoxical crisis governs *Coriolanus*, and in a different but related manner, *Othello*. The community, through its designate (e.g., Macduff, or in another paradox of contradiction and identification, Aufidius and also Volumnia, or even more problematically, Othello himself in a division of the self that contests the "outside" threat from Cyprus), "wins" by destroying the hero. It achieves a needed stability by removing for a time the dangers of ambiguity and change, but in so winning it loses its epitome.

The resolution of each play's imagined crisis is either accompanied or brought about by a specific kind of action, that of an initially clear ritual that becomes in the course of the play ambiguated or perverted. Properly performed ritual actions disclose their self-serving or conservative functions. In and through them the members of the community remind themselves of the fundamental grounds and armatures of their respective societies, whether empire, kingdom, or republic, and each play ends with some narrated expression of that lesson. Societies need moments to examine, in the anthropologist Barbara Babcock's terms, "a breach in social relations, a discontinuity in customary process, a gap or an aporia in discourse, or the deliberate paradox or disordering of liminal symbols"; only in such moments, she says, quoting her mentor Victor Turner, "do we truly reflect on the order of things . . . . '[Any] society that hopes to be imperishable must carve out for itself a piece of space and a period of time in which it can look honestly at itself'" (Babcock 1987: 43). In traditional cultures,[9] actual ritual practice provides the necessary space and time. In England, the transfer of that function to crafted drama began with the medieval cycle play, especially the Corpus Christi performances (M. James 1983: 26). By Shakespeare's time and in his plays, ritual actions or their abrogations are embedded in secular representations. The sacrifice of the hero promises a period of calm to the play's fictive community that will hypothetically permit assessments of gains and losses and the reaffirmation of social values. In its vicarious relation to the situation represented, the audience is afforded the same opportunity in regard to its various constitutive values.

The absence, misconstruction, or perversion of a necessary ritual is a hallmark of Shakespearean tragedy. It is neither the cause nor the consequence of the tragic patterns of these plays; rather it is an accompaniment, part of the tragedy's representation of what happens when crisis threatens to disintegrate a social or political organism. What these tragedies celebrate, what makes them "festive," is the heroic effort of the protagonist, involving some recognition of ritualistic action at some point in the play, to hold the edges of the world together, to keep Nature's molds from cracking and all germains from spilling at once, to set right disjointed time. This attempt is represented variously, through specific language, the shape of the play's action, or its resonant imagery. In tragedy, of course, the attempt does not work, and the crisis is not averted. Tragedy is not ritual; ritualistic elements in tragedy are not themselves actual rituals. In theater we are always in the realm of "as if," of semblance or resemblance. Ritual and theater do not share similar efficacies, but they do share similar intents. In tragedy as in "real life," ritual action is an effort at containment; it is controlled, dispassionate, ordered, and impersonal. It is the community's, not the subject's, well-being, its organizational pattern, that is at stake in the drama.

The homology of "play" (*ludus*) and "play" (*theatrum*) is scarcely accidental. Cultural anthropologists have wrestled over time with the distinction between "ritual" and "play" (in both senses), a distinction which continually threatens to blur because both ritual and play are performances (Huizinga 1955; Caillois 1959; V. Turner 1987; Schechner 1988). Turner attempted to distinguish ritual (as traditional, axiomatic, authorized actions and words) from play which permits greater flexibility and creativity in behavior, thought, and feeling than is normally permissible in either everyday life or the ritual frame (1987: 48). But he concluded that the distinction is idealized and in practice unstable, and settled on the metaphor of a "frame" for "the rules that set off, establish and channel the flow of the performative process. But the process transcends its frame in various ways" (1987: 50).

In a related sense, "frame" describes the ordered and ordering ideas upon which a given community predicates both its survival and its identity: its laws, structures, practices, and behavioral norms. Regardless of whether the breach in those structures is expressed in kinds of performative genres or in ambiguous or anomalous behavior by one or several within a community, the resultant disruption is a potential threat to the stabilizing order on which the community relies. In tragedy, an audience's perception of frame-breaching depends upon the degree to which it takes seriously or identifies with the situation represented in the play's action and recognizes the anomaly created by the hero's *agon* and removal. This is the mode in which tragedy re-presents ritualistic performance. An attack upon the state, the violation of a time-honored sociopolitical practice, a murder, pollution, or boundary-breaking of any significant kind constitutes the initial dis-order or dis-ease which necessitates some kind of re-ordering action.

Performance assigns meaning to events (Turner 1987: 50). Hamlet knows this:

> I have heard
> That guilty creatures, sitting at a play,

Have by the very cunning of the scene
Been strook so to the soul that presently
They have proclaim'd their malefactions . . .

(II.ii.588–92)

To catch the conscience of a king requires something more powerful than what we normally understand by "play." The "Mousetrap" seems to operate effectively only for Claudius and Hamlet; the rest of the courtly audience, arguably ignorant of Claudius's crime, see a performance they take to be entirely fictional, entirely a "play" in the usual sense of the term. Claudius sees something that drives him to his knees in a futile attempt to pray. In tragedy, ritual is always present in a perverted, inverted, or aborted form, or is suggested to the audience's mind by a reminder of its absence. At Elsinore, where a king has been killed by his brother and "the time is out of joint" in a variety of other ways, "play" and decontextualized gesture replace ritual. Appropriate performances are confused or conflated: funeral-baked meats supply wedding feasts, and "the hobby-horse is forgot." Hamlet's concern to "set it right" by means of the most appropriate and effective action is itself most appropriate in the context of ritualistic, i.e., purifying, redress.

Shakespearean tragedies refer to their respective communities' ruptures as the impetus for ritualistic actions. Sometimes the protagonist himself makes the reference, as in the cases of Brutus, Hamlet and, eventually, Richard II; sometimes the reference is made by other figures who emerge as survivors and scavengers of order, as in the cases of Marcus in *Titus Andronicus*, Prince Escalus and the bereaved fathers of *Romeo and Juliet*, *Macbeth*'s Malcolm, *Lear*'s Albany, and *Hamlet*'s Fortinbras at the ends of their plays. When these references occur, they are signposted in certain unmistakable ways, usually by a reference to the nation, the community, or the synechdoche of the land occupied by the community, and to its wounds, its illness, or its putrifaction, as in Macbeth's request to the doctor to find out his land's disease, or in Richard II's apology to the ground at Pomfret Castle.

There is yet another less obvious context for ritualistic action in Shakespearean tragedy. It is a moment often attributed to the protagonist's self-conscious theatricalism, in which the speaker seems very much aware of having an audience, whether by breaking the "fourth wall" in soliloquy or by certain startling formalities and isolated gestures (as performed by both Hamlet and Richard

27

II at several points). Brecht noticed such gestures as part of the "alienation effect" and identified them specifically as ritualistic action in his 1935 essay "Alienation Effects in Chinese Acting."

> The artist's object is to appear strange and even surprising to himself. He achieves this by looking strangely at himself and his work . . . . The audience identifies itself with the actor as being an observer, and accordingly develops his attitude of observing or looking on.
>
> The Chinese artist's performance often strikes the Western actor as cold. That does not mean that the Chinese theatre rejects all representation of feelings. The performer portrays incidents of utmost passion, but without his delivery becoming heated . . . . [This] is *like a ritual*, there is nothing eruptive about it . . . . The coldness comes from the actor's holding himself remote from the character portrayed . . . . [and from] the spectator. Nobody gets raped by the individual he portrays; this individual is not the spectator himself but his neighbour.
>
> (1966: 92–3; emphasis added)

What marks this kind of performance as ritualistic is, first of all, its deliberate formality and discipline. These serve to objectify or depersonalize the action so that it is deflected back upon the audience, significantly, "not the spectator himself but his neighbour." The implication of this deflection is therefore communal rather than individual. The actor represents not me but my neighbor, someone *like* me in that we share in a community. From my neighbor's point of view, the actor has represented me too. In this sense the "alienation effect," instead of cutting the spectators off from the action's reference, includes them by the fact that within the boundaries of the theater, all in the audience are each other's neighbors. Brecht's *Verfremdungseffekt* does not preclude or obscure the recognition of represented emotion; it rejects *personal* identification with "character" and therefore draws attention to the situation or condition within which "character" is produced.

Excessive focus upon the protagonist, Brecht wrote, upon "the great individual experience," results in "a drama for cannibals" (Heinemann 1985: 205). He was referring specifically to Shakespeare as performed in the 1920s on the German stage; he found it irrelevant to modern spectators "who unlike Lear or Hamlet are small people, whose destinies are controlled not by fate or their own personal characters or actions but by the behaviour of collectives, large masses, social classes" (Heinemann 1985: 205). Until he could describe during the late 1930s to about 1950 in the dialogues known as *Der Messingkauf* (Brecht 1966: 169) a theater for the Shakespeare he *read* that could speak to those modern spectators, Brecht had to find his model in the performance of Mei Lan-fang's company of Chinese actors whom he saw in Moscow in 1935 (1966: 99). In the Chinese theater Brecht found the kind of production that could be realized in both Shakespeare and his own plays. One of the things he saw was an alignment with ritual, for both ritual and the Chinese theater privilege formulaic and collectively recognizable gestures or analogues. The Chinese actor does this by means of basic stylized movements whose meaning does not depend on individual interpretation and does not vary significantly with repetition.

These too are the movements of ritual, which depends upon communal agreement about its meaning in order to promise effectiveness. The dramatist who deploys such movements in telling stories from the stage counts on the audience's collective understanding of the words and gestures the actors use. For example, the impact on Elizabethan audiences of *Richard II*'s images of the king reversing his coronation ceremony and handing over the crown to Bolingbroke, or York's description of dust and rubbish thrown on the deposed king's head, must have been profoundly disturbing, no matter what views they held of the transfer itself, if only because these representations debase the way such transfers occur. The imagery of this treatment of an anointed monarch subverts the system of belief that dominated the subjects of the later monarch, Elizabeth I. As Brecht himself noted about another of Shakespeare's histories, "If I want to see Richard III, I don't want to feel like Richard III. I want to see this phenomenon in all its strangeness and incomprehensible quality" (Heinemann 1985: 215). This "seeing" must be done at a distance; at the remove of stylized action, representation works precisely because it does not rely upon this or that specific identification.

What Brecht found in the Chinese theater, Artaud found in the Balinese theater. There are differences, of course: the "unheated" performance of the Chinese actor becomes in the Balinese theater the energized gestures and sounds of the actor-in-costume, whom Artaud, writing in 1938, called the "double" of the actor himself, a kind of *gestalt* in which the whole *mise en scène* finds its own voice and expression, unsubmissive to any language of mere words:

29

through the labyrinth of their gestures, attitudes, and sudden cries, through the gyrations and turns which leave no portion of the stage space unutilized, the sense of a new physical language, based upon signs and no longer upon words, is liberated. These actors with their geometric robes seem to be animated hieroglyphs . . . . [These] spiritual signs have a precise meaning which strikes us only intuitively but with enough violence to make useless any translation into logical discursive language. And for the lovers of realism at all costs, who might find exhausting these perpetual allusions to secret attitudes inaccessible to thought, there remains the eminently realistic play of the double who is terrified by the apparitions from beyond. In this double – trembling, yelping childishly, these heels striking the ground in cadences that follow the very automatism of the liberated unconscious, this momentary concealment behind his own reality – *there* is a description of fear valid in every latitude.

(Artaud 1958: 54)

In the space between Brecht and Artaud, it does not matter that the Chinese actor is virtually immobile whereas the Balinese is precisely animated, for like Brecht, Artaud found in his chosen model "a whole collection of ritual gestures to which we do not have the key and which seem to obey precise musical indications" (1958: 57). The same powerful affect of ritual action that Brecht found in the Chinese actor's performance occurred for Artaud in the "regulated and impersonal" Balinese expressions:

A kind of terror seizes us at the thought of these mechanized beings, whose joys and griefs seem not their own but at the service of age-old rites, as if they were dictated by superior intelligences. In the last analysis it is this impression of a superior and prescribed Life which strikes us most in this spectacle that so much resembles a rite one might profane. It has the solemnity of a sacred rite – the hieratic quality of the costumes gives each actor a double body and a double set of limbs – and the dancer bundled into his costume seems to be nothing more than his own effigy.

(1958: 58)

For both Brecht and Artaud, Eastern theater at its best offers the West a kind and a means of expression that encompasses an idea much larger than individual character, indeed, one that subordinates both character and the actor portraying it to a force and a mysterium too large for any single medium, especially the anchoring definitions of spoken language, to encompass or express it. That mysterium is what elicits the terror that both Brecht and Artaud, and Aristotle as well, locate at the center of significant theatrical performance. Artaud's aphorism bears repeating: "We are not free. And the sky can still fall on our heads. And the theater has been created to teach us that first of all" (1958: 79). For the two modern theorists, and for Shakespeare, ritualistic action offers an economical analogue and an effective reminder of the volatile contexts surrounding social, political, and spiritual life.

Ritual works within a shared cultural context. Without explanation, without in fact "thick description," the precise references of Balinese or Chinese or any ritualized actions cannot be understood by someone outside the contextual culture as they would be by a native of that culture. But they can have an analogous impact once understood as rituals of a particular type. For example, the transition from adolescence to adulthood is marked by a rite of passage whose function is the same everywhere, regardless of whether the form of that passage is a week's solitary survival in the wilderness or a fifteen-minute Haftorah reading in the presence of family and community. A Native American male might not recognize the form of the Jewish Bar Mitzvah as a passage to manhood, but he would recognize the significance of the rite once it was identified as such.

Conceptual systems theorists, along with many anthropologists, argue that all human beings are capable of this kind of cognitive translation, which is general enough to allow for differences in details of signification.[10] Although the highly problematic issue of universals in human experience is now the subject of serious and heated debate, it seems worth the risk of setting off theoretical or ideological alarm systems to acknowledge, with Brecht and Artaud, the plausibility of a claim for widely similar affects of tragedy within differences of cultural production. Wole Soyinka adds a persuasive argument to the debate over "universals": the very notion that irreconcilable differences preclude intercultural recognition of specific creative expressions is itself a Western construct, even at times a Western obsession; questions of transferability are "largely artificial" (1976: 6).

31

The question therefore of the supposed dividing line between ritual and theatre should not concern us much in
Africa, the line being one that was largely drawn by the
European analyst. Groups such as the Ori-Okun Theatre in
Ife, and Duro Ladipo's company, also of Nigeria, have
demonstrated the capacity of the drama (or ritual) of the
gods to travel as aesthetically and passionately as the gods
themselves have, across the Atlantic . . . . If civil servants
(beginning with the colonial administrators) and even university entrepreneurs who are most often responsible for
bringing our Cultural Heritage out of its wraps to regale
foreign delegations, Institute [sic] of African Studies con-
ferences etc., retain the basic attitude that traditional drama
is some kind of village craft which can be plonked down on
any stall just like artifacts in any international airport
boutique, it should not surprise us that the spectator sums up
his experience as having been entertained or bored by some
"quaint ritual". Such presentations have been largely responsible for the multitude of false concepts surrounding the
drama of the gods; that, and their subjection to anthropological punditry where they are reduced, *in extremis*, to
behavioural manifestations in primitive society. The burden
on a producer is one of knowledge, understanding, and of
sympathetic imagination.

(Soyinka 1976: 7)

This argument exactly opposes what many ideology-centered critics
condemn as "essentialism," because it allows for recognition,
supported by "knowledge, understanding, and . . . sympathetic
imagination," of differences that enlarge rather than foreclose
dramatic experience. If discrete cultural experience were so ghet-
toized as to prevent access by all but native inhabitants, then none
of us would have useful access even to the culture that produced
Shakespearean tragedy, separated from it as we are by four centuries of history and change. Blinkered relativism has no greater
purchase on accuracy than does reductive essentialism. The kinds
of rigorous and diligent efforts that are now made by theoretical
laborers in historicist, materialist, anthropological, and other
fields of inquiry allow informed and "sympathetically imaginative"
access to cognitively analogous representations in tragic drama.

In fact, Soyinka makes a strong case for what he calls "essentiality"

32

as a framework for performing and relating culturally specific constructions outside of their producing cultures. This does not in any way fail to acknowledge the operations of "economics and power" in the constructions of the narratives, whether discursive or performative (1976: 11–12). By way of example, he summarizes the story of the "tragic fall" of the god Sango as told in Yoruba myth and re-told by the modern playwright Duro Ladipo.[11] His description is strikingly similar to Plutarch's version of the death of Romulus, which Shakespeare subsequently imbricated in *Julius Caesar* (see chapter 3 below); Soyinka himself finds Ladipo's version somewhat analogous to Euripides's *Bacchae* (1976: 12). These connections do not efface cultural specificity; they permit recognition of meaning through structural homologies. They enable us to re-cognize the *agon* of Oedipus, Prometheus, and Medea, the Chinese actor, the Balinese dancer, Sango, Lear, Macbeth, and Coriolanus. Their violent outrages (done by and/or upon them) are analogues of ritual events, that is, events calling for ritual redress, embedded in the structure of particular acculturations.

The violations of *comitatus* and of the rules of hospitality that occur in *Macbeth* and *King Lear*, the breaches of governmental agreements in *Julius Caesar* and *Richard II*, the ruptures of kinship and community in *Romeo and Juliet*, *Hamlet*, and *Coriolanus* likewise show horrific acts that culminate in various kinds of murder. It may be difficult for modern Westerners to think of violations of hospitality as equivalent to murder or communal annihilation. But all communities depend for both immediate survival and perpetuation upon contractual arrangements for the management of personal and material interests. As Philip Brockbank observed,

> What we may take to be remote, pagan and even barbaric rites persist and flourish in complex urban civilizations and in finely tempered urbane communities .... Our primordial selves are a present as well as a past reality; ... and some of the most powerful dispositions of human consciousness continue to manifest themselves in ways that certainly would not have surprised Aeschylus, and probably would not be wholly strange to the Neanderthals either.
>
> (1983: 11)

A threat to any categorical social arrangements, whether it involves the transfer of rule or real estate or the social agreements of marriage contracts, challenges the definition and thus the integral survival of the community within whose boundaries they occur. Such violations are perversions of sociopolitical formalities that, when properly observed, function to protect society. These abrogations shake the structures and stabilities of the world of civilized human beings. Lear's vivisection of his kingdom, for example, and his rejection of Cordelia, Gloucester's blinding in his home by his guests, Edmund's plot against his father and brother, and Edgar's disinheritance are not simply "wrongs" against persons; they are violations of the bonds that identify a culture. Similarly, Duncan's murder is at once a regicide, a kin-killing, and a violation of hospitality, as Macbeth himself recognizes: he "should against his murtherer shut the door, / Not bear the knife" himself (I.vii.15–16). Moretti argues that the political subject of tragedy is not so much the displacement of power as it is the investigation of "whether a *cultural foundation* of power is still possible" (1982: 26), and concludes that the answer is negative. Although he examines several overt manifestations of early modern "culture," he in fact neglects the matter of "foundation." The ritual underpinnings of Shakespearean tragedy locate the question Moretti rhetorically poses. The "cultural foundation of power" is disclosed in cultural rituals, perpetually renewed against the threat of stagnation and stasis, which is far greater than the threat of one power structure over another. "The ideal order of society is guarded by dangers which threaten transgressors . . . . The whole universe is harnessed to men's attempts to force one another into good citizenship" (Douglas 1966: 3).

The cultural rituals with which Shakespeare's tragedies are concerned are primarily those that foreground the community at large rather than those that refer to personal or familial rites of passage such as birth and initiation or courtship and marriage. Personal and family rituals are often noted in the course of the plays, but not to the extent and degree that they are in the comedies (Berry 1984) and always in the context of their impact in the larger social arena. Ritualistic action is incorporated in tragedy to show that matters of the greatest communal urgency are investigated by the specific drama. The hero in tragedy, like the performer in ritual, is less the subject than the agency or the surrogate through whom those concerns – which *are* the subject – are expressed (Moretti 1982: 25–6; LaFontaine 1985: 13). Ritualistic performance in tragedy points to the larger unit: the *polis*, the state, the community. The material elements of celebration, such as costume or other significant clothing, masks, feasting and drinking, and mythic or historical narratives of continuity indicate the communal rather than the individual importance of such markers. "Festive" tragedy, then, is the drama of communities in crisis and of the redress available to them, in which the protagonist is both priest and *pharmakos*, victim and villain, actor and acted upon, in the reciprocal relations of a community and its individual members.

2

SEEKING DEFINITIONS
Aristotle, Brecht, Artaud, and others

As Stephen Booth astutely observes, "The search for a definition of tragedy has been the most persistent and widespread of all nonreligious quests for definition" (1983: 81). Most modern commentaries and theoretical formulations about tragedy are root-bound in those of the nineteenth century: the familiar voices of Hegel, Nietzsche, Coleridge, Hazlitt, and their immediate heirs are still heard. Critics who have in recent years shifted and altered the ways in which we understand Shakespeare's work seem, with few exceptions (Dollimore 1984; Moretti 1982; Tennenhouse 1986) to have neglected the question of what Shakespearean tragedy, as *tragedy*, said to its original audience. The noted exceptions recast the genre of tragedy into a specifically political discourse. Tennenhouse, for example, attempts to collapse the generic differences between a history play and a tragedy on the grounds that such distinctions "had more to do with the vicissitudes of political conflict than with any cultural logic intrinsic to a particular dramatic form" (1986: 5). But that intrinsic cultural logic is a crucially important consideration. Tennenhouse rightly claims that Renaissance drama simultaneously idealizes and demystifies specific forms of power (1986: 6). For this reason among others, the "cultural logic intrinsic to" any one genre can be only partly revealed through analysis of its political framework. That "cultural logic" may indeed emerge as a partisan polemic, but it should not be assumed without careful disclosure of its various and complicated premises.

The difficult matter of definitions must be addressed. Derrida grappled rigorously with the ambiguity, the plasticity, of the concept of the *pharmakon* in Plato's *Phaedrus*, which discusses the origins of writing. In this text, the word *pharmakon* signals "remedy," "recipe," "poison," "drug," "philter," simultaneously "through skewing, indetermination, or overdetermination, but without mistranslation" (Derrida 1981: 71).

> It will also be seen to what extent the malleable unity of this concept, or rather the rules and the strange logic that links it with its signifier, has been dispersed, masked, obliterated, and rendered almost unreadable not only by the imprudence or empiricism of the translators, but first and foremost by the redoubtable, irreducible difficulty of translation. It is a difficulty . . . situated less in the passage from one language to another . . . than . . . in the tradition between Greek and Greek; a violent difficulty in the transference of a nonphilosopheme into a philosopheme.
>
> (1981: 71–2)

The "malleable unity" of the word *pharmakon* signals not so much an untranslatable indeterminacy as it does an important complexity, an etymological/mythological ambivalence or double strength (literally, "strength on both sides," derived from *ambi*: "on both sides" and *valere*: "to be strong"); the *pharmakon* acts as both toxin and cure, an operational and functional rather than a characterological distinction. This kind of distinction is centrally important to any discussion of the genre of tragedy, whose analytic terminology is plagued with ambivalence. Too often, confronted with ambivalent or seemingly ambivalent (for Derrida, "indeterminate") words such as *hamartia, hybris,* "hero," even "tragedy" itself, analysts feel compelled to select one univalent or "overdeterminate" meaning, and thus choke off the multiple resonances inherent in the words for the sake of definition, of clarity. Far from defining or clarifying anything, the selection betrays its subject through oversimplification, or "skewing." Although Derrida's nominal subject, Plato, had something to do with this "violent difficulty," it is most often Aristotle – the quintessential empiricist – to whom we turn in seeking definitions of tragedy.

It is possible to locate in Aristotle's *Poetics* the coordinates of politics and tragedy in a way that permits a focus on "cultural logic" without restricting it as topicality. For Plato, literature and especially drama undermined the strict designation of rules and identities that he thought necessary to a thriving republic. In contrast, Aristotle sought to

discover a series of limits in order to guarantee the integrity
of the city and to protect citizens from both outside and
inside violence . . . . Tragedy presents the city with its political
and ethical flaws in an act of clarification and self-definition,
and it is this all-too-human nature that the population both
fears and pities. Tragedy focuses on the political dimension
of ethics. It reveals that standards of justice are the products
of political decisions and not of ideal forms, thereby making
it possible to debate those standards of justice.

(Siebers 1988: 22)

The Brazilian playwright-in-exile, Augusto Boal (1979), with a
much more specific political platform, comes to similar conclusions about Aristotle. He assumes first of all, as he states in his
foreword, that "all theater is necessarily political, because all the
activities of man are political and theater is one of them." In a long
chapter entitled "Aristotle's Coercive System of Tragedy," he assesses
catharsis (using the Butcher translation) as implicitly about the
removal not of pity and fear but of "something contained in those
emotions, or mixed with them," some "non-social or socially forbidden instincts . . . . In this case, pity and fear would only be part
of the mechanism of expulsion and not its object. Here would
reside the political significance of tragedy" (1979: 29). He argues
that since "Pity and fear have never been vices or weaknesses or
errors, and, therefore, never needed to be eliminated or purged,"
what is purged must be some other kind of emotion or passion:

> The impurity to be purged must undoubtedly be . . . some-
> thing that threatens the individual's equilibrium, and
> consequently that of society. Something that is not virtue,
> that is not the greatest virtue, justice. And since all that is
> unjust is foreseen in the laws, the impurity which the tragic
> process is destined to destroy is therefore something *directed
> against the laws* . . . . This extraneous element is . . . a social
> fault, a political deficiency . . . .
>
> (1979: 31–2)

Taken on its own terms, Boal's logic is clear, at least in this part of
his discussion, shaped as it is by his view of tragedy as a state-
governed tool for social and political repression. *Hamartia*, which
he calls "the only 'impurity' that exists in the character . . . that can
and must be destroyed, so that the whole of the character's ethos

38

may conform to the ethos of society" (1979: 34), is punished by the death or bereavement of the protagonist. Catharsis occurs when "the spectator, terrified by the spectacle of the catastrophe, is purified of his *hamartia*" (1979: 37). All of this makes sense in the context of Boal's assumptions about the nature and process of catharsis, and also about the identification of the spectator's and the protagonist's respective *hamartia*. But it also constructs tragedy as not much more than a state-sanctioned morality play for an easily frightened and easily controlled populace. Indeed, he concludes that Aristotle's kind of tragedy serves "only more or less stable societies, ethically defined," and that during "cultural revolutions" when "the social ethos is not clearly defined, the tragic scheme cannot be used [because] the character's ethos will not find a clear social ethos that it can confront. The coercive system of tragedy can be used before or after the revolution . . . but never during it" (1979: 47).

Boal's argument is thoughtful, but it overdetermines not only what all tragedy is and does, but perhaps even more problematically, it assumes without exception how an audience must respond to what occurs on stage within the neat constructs of an undisturbed political ecology. If he is correct, then either Shakespeare wrote during a time of such political stasis (as indeed Tillyard argued in *The Elizabethan World Picture* [1948]), or else he did not write tragedy, at least not tragedy that is amenable to Aristotelian analysis. In fact, that is Boal's conclusion in his next chapter on "Machiavelli and the Poetics of *Virtu*": Shakespearean tragedy "serves as documentary evidence of the coming of the individualized man in the theater . . . . The character was converted into a bourgeois conception" (1979: 63).

Tragedy is indeed a political genre, though not quite, or not always, in the ways Boal imagines. As Bristol (1985) in particular has argued, regardless of who survives at the ends of specific dramatic contestations, the contestants have had reciprocal impacts on each other. There are in fact no winners in the tragic contestation, and there is no resolution of its conflicts. There is only closure, a stop in the action represented, at the edge of which (at the point of closure, at the end of the play) another rupture or disruption already threatens. In such instances the partisan or local formulations implicit in the term "politics" are an affect, a vehicle for the expression of another, deeper, movement than what is represented by specific persons (characters in a play or those outside the play whom they are understood to signify) or specific structures of authority in the extradramatic domain. "Historicist" readings such as Stephen Greenblatt's (1981; 1982; 1985) tend to localize these signifying persons and structures very specifically, but they do so by overdetermining the play's social referentiality.

As Siebers (1988) reminds us, it is time to reassess some of what Aristotle had to say about the nature of tragedy. He rightly emphasizes Aristotle's concern with the relation of protagonist and community. It is always the tension, the conflict, the contestation between the two that is in focus in tragedy, usually but, as Heilman (1968) argued, not always because there is something wrong, in moral terms, with either one. The focus on moral conflict in tragedy has been urged upon us, perhaps, by translations of Aristotle's citation of the "good" man as the hero of tragedy. To a great extent, the sixteenth century was responsible for this skewed emphasis on the didactic moral function of tragedy, but it is important to realize that it was not the dramatists of that century but the theorists (Robortello, Castelvetro, the so-called "pseudo-Aristotelians") who were, in Stephen Booth's terms, "only lip-servants of their masters," and who created "a tradition of debasement – phrased in Aristotelian echoes – not of Aristotle but of the Horatian doctrine of sweetened instruction" (1983: 82). This tradition has for centuries chained our grasp of the formalist principles laid out in the *Poetics* to a distracting and unresolvable debate about the meaning of "good." The *Poetics* "became not so much a table of commandments as a sign of the covenant between literature and the ultimate values of the universe" (Booth 1983: 83).

Booth correctly argues that reliance on Aristotle for the keys to tragedy has been an automatic reflex throughout the last four centuries. The reflexive spasm that has created the greatest difficulty occurs when we are hooked by that most flexible and variable of concepts, the "good." Butcher's translation (1951) uses the word often but spends intermittently nearly 100 pages glossing it. In Telford's translation (1961), the word "good" appears only in reference to the poet's skill or to "good" fortune. Telford avoids the word as an identifying characteristic of the hero. Even in Butcher's more meticulous version the hero is explicitly "the man who is not eminently good and just, yet whose misfortune is brought about not by vice or depravity but by some error or frailty. He must be one who is highly renowned and prosperous . . . "

(1453a). The most recent translation I have seen, by Halliwell, gives the line this way: "Such a man is one who is not preeminent in virtue and justice, and one who falls into affliction not because of evil and wickedness, but because of a certain fallibility (*hamartia*)" (1987: 44).

The meaning of *hamartia* hinges upon these distinctions about the ethical nature of the hero; they are important distinctions not because of an arguable "goodness" but rather because of the hero's design as a representation of humanity that is cast in terms of a debate about what constitutes "goodness." Halliwell thinks that Aristotle was compelled to equivocate in his attempt to define the hero's character: "Aristotle has a clearer idea of what he believes does *not* belong in tragedy than of what does . . . . Although [he] does not share all of Plato's ethical ideas, he is close enough to him to be disturbed by (though not actually to deny) the idea of a person of *outstanding* qualities coming tragically to misfortune" (1987: 124). Gerald Else's monumental commentary offers both the most persuasive and the most thoughtful exegesis:

> Another source of confusion has been the temptation to equate Aristotle's ideal hero with the ethical Mean, which has nothing whatever to do with the case . . . . Even more pernicious has been the misintepretation of τουτων . . . so that the ideal hero comes out statistically average man, halfway between good and bad . . . . It is not merely a question of a kind of man but of a man suffering a certain fate. . . . If he were *merely* ὁμοιος ("average") his fate would not be significant one way or the other. Hence the hero must fall somewhere within the range, not between good and bad, but between good and average: high enough to awaken our pity but not so perfect as to arouse indignation at his misfortune, near enough to elicit our fellow-feeling but not so near as to forfeit all stature and importance. The formula defines a range of values (not a single point), within which various degrees and combinations of pity and fear are possible.
>
> (1967: 376–8)

Unlike Halliwell's, Else's Aristotle does not equivocate; he struggles for precision about a matter that is nearly impossible to define. Else's commentary is especially important for its emphasis on action even in the discussion of character. Aristotle is moved by certain kinds of persons "suffering a certain fate," that is, in the specific context of events or situations in which their stories are told, and characterized by one or another shading of behavior (that is, action) along "a range of values." The problem of interpretation is attached crucially to the meaning of *hamartia* (*Poetics* 1453b10 and b16), generally read as an error or a moral failing. "Unfortunately the issue has been beclouded by the almost habitual use of the terms 'intellectual error' or 'error of judgment' on the one side and 'moral flaw' on the other. All these phrases . . . are misleading and beside the point" (Else 1967: 378–9).

Although translators seem to feel compelled to assign some idea of the "wrong" in their semantic choices for *hamartia* ("mistake," "error," "failure"), they are nonetheless careful to explain in commentaries and glosses that it means "a missing of the mark . . . an action, not a suffering or a flaw of character" (Telford 1961: 23n.). To the extent that we become distracted by a romantic conception of what "good" and "right" (and consequently, "evil" and "wrong") mean, we lose sight of the primary contestation (*agon*) inherent in tragedy. As Else argues, the location of Aristotle's discussion of *hamartia* in the context of action makes it clear that it must be a constitutive element of plot or situation rather than of "character" (1967: 379). Else cites related discourses in the *Nichomachean Ethics* and the *Rhetoric*, where Aristotle discusses the differences between voluntary and involuntary actions. Only involuntary "acts caused by ignorance of general principles [and] . . . of particulars . . . win *pity and forgiveness* . . . . [For] we remember that the preferred tragic recognition is of the identity of persons" (1967: 380–1).

The crucial distinction, then, is in the "general principles" and "particulars" of the mark that is missed and in how it is missed; i.e., in the operation of misrecognition. This is not a matter of morality, of flawed character, stupidity, naivete, or any of the usual inculpations to which tragic heroes have been subjected by a long march of critics. Nor is it essentially a matter of local politics, except in the sense that groups of real people tend to function with as little accuracy and awareness as dramatic characters do. Else's commentary works toward this distinction:

> It follows that the tragic *hamartia* is . . . a "big" mistake
> (1453a16) . . . [which] will have to do with the identity of . . .
> a blood relative [who will be] slain or wounded. As a component
> or cause of the complex plot, such a *hamartia* is
> inherently fitted to arouse our pity – and our "fear," that is,

42

our horror that a man should have killed or be about to kill a "dear one." The discovery is then the counterpart and reverse of the mistake. Here the emotional charge which is inherent in the mistake (not in the ignorance *per se*, but in the horrible deed to which it stands in causal relation) finds its discharge. The *hamartia* represents the reservoir of emotional potential, the recognition is the lightning-flash through which it passes off.

(1967: 383)

Hamartia is specifically an act of misrecognition and is linked to *anagnorisis*. The reason this connection has itself been misrecognized is, according to Else,

the myopia with which the sequence of Aristotle's argument has been regarded, so that *hamartia* was thought of as a part of the hero's character . . . while recognition was purely a technical device, a part of the plot. . . . *Hamartia* also is a part of the plot . . . [and] must be brought out of its isolation and seen as an integral part of a single edifice of thought.

(1967: 385)

Hamartia, then, is a deed, an action; it is something protagonists *do*, not what they *are* intrinsically. It is not a flaw in the character, nor is it the result of one. Aristotle is both consistent and insistent upon action, not character, as the essential consideration in tragedy, and what the tragic hero does is extrinsic to moral or psychological makeup, which in any case are modern concerns that completely deflect Aristotelian principles. For Aristotle, the basic "goodness" of the hero is a given; tragedy arises when "good" is problematized by plot or circumstance. As Halliwell argues, the factor that problematizes "goodness" is ignorance of particular matters in a given situation (not ignorance as a characteristic); ignorance of specific kinship bonds, for example, exculpates the agents, while allowing them to "move by their own unwitting choices [towards] . . . the execution of an 'incurable' deed" (1987: 125).

Missing-the-mark is required for recognition-and-reversal; without it there is no tragedy. The shape of the action performed is dictated by the genre. *Hamartia* is unavoidable in tragedy. There is no question of superior or inferior "morality" in this doctrine. Halliwell's note on the "incurable" deed suggests the basic function of ritual, the redress of an actively dangerous situation,

43

whether potential or realized. Focusing on some "flaw" in the protagonist, as so many have done, effaces the tragedy's relation to its audience, excludes the audience completely from its implications, and makes the drama itself irrelevant. There is, then, no such thing as a "tragic flaw." *Hamartia* is misrecognition not only by the protagonist, which could still be interpretable as a "flaw" or an "error," but also *by the community* of the identity and social function of the protagonist. Further, the construction of *hamartia* as a "flaw" or "error" is itself a misrecognition. By the operation of a kind of Althusserian (1971) "ideological state apparatus," what begins as an "action," an *agon*, is converted into a characteristic. An external and objective operation is attached to a subject, and the deed becomes internalized as a "mark," not unlike the internalizing of Original Sin, the "mark of Cain," and similar Western constructions that transform an outward and singular action into an internal and totalizing characteristic of identity.

This emphasis upon morality has clouded tragic exegesis for at least the last century and a half; it is a narrow view from the inside, from within an imagined community through a close-up lens focused on the hero. Such a view arose from reading Aristotle through the lens of Horace (Booth 1983: 82; also Weinberg 1965; Steadman 1971; Dollimore 1984). Theorists from the Renaissance to Boileau in the eighteenth century, Weinberg argues,

> came to the text of Aristotle with habits of textual interpretation, habits of fragmentation and methodological anarchy, which made it impossible for them to understand this closely constructed and tightly argued document. [They] . . . reduced all aspects of literary documents to considerations stemming from the audience . . . and they insisted on reading Aristotle as if he were a kind of Ur-Horace. And finally, they tried to "modernize" Aristotle . . . in a manner scarcely authorized by the Aristotelian text. The result was one of the strangest misunderstandings of a basic text in the history of ideas.
>
> (1965: 199–200)

Such thinking, says Weinberg, still persists (1965: 200), rooted in a minimal evolution from late-Renaissance debates over what constituted the "beautiful and instructive" and what emotions tragedy elicits to the nineteenth century's focus on the hero positioned against society.

44

Romantic critics (Hegel, Coleridge, and their contemporaries) and their immediate heirs (Bradley, Eliot, and others of the early twentieth century) were magnetized to an idea of tragedies as representations of protagonists, often admirable but nevertheless doomed to some magnificent inadequacy, whose personalities conflicted with those of their compatriots. Dollimore characterizes this view of the heroic *agon* as an "essentialist humanist" reduction in which "the forces destructive of life . . . paradoxically pressure it into its finest expression . . . . [In] defeat and death 'man' finds his apotheosis" (1984: 49–50). Or, to quote Fiedler again, "the image of man in art – precisely when it is most magnificently portrayed – is the image of a failure" (1960: 7). On this view, readers and audiences identify with or against the protagonist, and approve or condemn the protagonist's fictive choice as if that choice alone produced the sequent actions of the play. That is, *because* Macbeth, Lear, Hamlet, or Coriolanus does such and such, and only because of that, events follow as they do, as if there were no abetting community, circumstances, or context in which the protagonist operates. Seen this way, the protagonist is the sole cause of disaster; the audience can assign fault where it seems to belong and find moral satisfaction in watching the hero fall. This is the audience's or reader's equivalent of scapegoating, the tragic process based in misrecognition (the subject of chapter 4 below). George Steiner notes that by the mid-twentieth century the moral satisfactions derived by Romantic and post-Romantic generations from such testimonials of righteousness no longer spoke with great force, but nothing, in his view, had come to replace them; in the last pages of *The Death of Tragedy*, however, he suggests the very beginnings of a view that unpins itself from a nineteenth-century *zeitgeist*, and as it happens, turns his thoughts towards Brecht and Chinese performance (Steiner 1961: 353–5).

In the mid-twentieth century, Brecht and Artaud offered a way of understanding tragedy that unexpectedly recalls the heart of the Aristotelian position. Perhaps Brecht's association with a radically politicized idea of theater and Artaud's with a visionary intensity diagnosed by his physicians as insanity kept their readers (and themselves) from noticing the classical core in their arguments. The difference between the two modern theorists and Aristotle primarily reflects differences in their respective contemporary theaters and producing cultures, rather than fundamentally different theoretical approaches to the genre of tragedy. Brecht and Artaud share a sense of the possibilities for social change through changes in the production and reception of theater. Brecht was perhaps more of a political optimist than Artaud. But in their views of theater, both Brecht and Artaud understood tragedy in ways remarkably close to Aristotle's and thus to each other's. Brecht opposed Aristotle mainly because he opposed the political priorities of Aristotle's Athenian culture; Artaud does not mention Aristotle at all. But both Brecht and Artaud called for a theater that shook people up and disturbed their complacencies, and Aristotle described one that already did exactly that.

Brecht's passionate inveighing against all "romantic" identification with the hero approached the distance necessary for an Aristotelian view of tragedy: the *verfremdungseffekt* invites us to stand outside the drama looking in, to see the social or political implications framed by the play as a whole, and to avoid the dangerous subjectivity that, for Brecht, occludes the dynamic and dialogic representations of drama. In "The Epic Theatre and its Difficulties" (1927), he argued that the "radical transformation of the theater can't be the result of some artistic whim. It has simply to correspond to the whole radical transformation of the mentality of our time . . . . Instead of sharing an experience the spectator must come to grips with things" (1966: 23). Brecht's great effort in these sentences was to depersonalize theater, to erase the habitual focus on character and actor in favor of the larger view of "things" with which the spectator "must come to grips." His general lesson, as Raymond Williams puts it, is this:

> We have to see not only that suffering is avoidable, but that it is not avoided. And not only that suffering breaks us, but that it need not break us . . . . "The sufferings of this man appal me, because they are unnecessary." . . . Against the fear of a general death, and against the loss of connection, a sense of life is affirmed, learned as closely in suffering as ever in joy, once the connections are made.
>
> (1966: 202–3)

What Brecht called for, as he repeatedly insisted, was new for his time, but it was not altogether new, or perhaps we might say that it was "new again." Next to Williams's claim that Brecht's "new sense of tragedy" affirms life by coordinating joy and sorrow, it is interesting to note Butcher's similar claim for the lessons of Aristotle's *Poetics*: "The poets found out how the transport of human pity and human fear might, under the excitation of art, be dissolved in joy, and the pain escape in the purified tide of human sympathy" (1951: 273). That joyful, life-affirming, celebratory face of tragedy is what makes it festive. Butcher's extended commentary explains how this works; by a process of identification that is exactly the opposite of Brechtian distance, Butcher's Aristotle aims for identical results.

> The true tragic fear becomes an almost impersonal emotion, attaching itself not so much to this or that particular incident, as to the general course of the action which is . . . an image of human destiny . . . .
>
> The spectator who is brought face to face with grander sufferings than his own experiences a sympathetic ecstasy, or lifting out of himself. It is precisely in this transport of feeling, which carries a man beyond his individual self, that the distinctive tragic pleasure resides. Pity and fear are purged of the impure element which clings to them in life. In the glow of tragic excitement these feelings are so transformed that the net result is a noble emotional satisfaction.
>
> (1951: 262, 267)

Artaud's manifesto bears a striking resemblance to the above in that it is also insistently celebratory. Artaud however takes the identity of what is celebrated far beyond the vague and comparatively comfortable "armchair" transport Butcher ascribes to Aristotle's theory:

> Like the plague, the theater is a formidable call to the forces that impel the mind by example to the source of its conflicts . . . .
>
> If the essential theater is like the plague, it is not because it is contagious, but because like the plague it is the revelation, . . . the exteriorization of a depth of latent cruelty by means of which all the perverse possibilities of the mind, whether of an individual or a people, are localized . . . .
>
> We do not see that life as it is and as it has been fashioned for us provides many reasons for exaltation. It appears that by means of the plague, a gigantic abscess, as much moral as social, has been collectively drained; and that like the plague, the theater has been created to drain abscesses collectively . . . .

The theater like the plague is a crisis which is resolved by death or cure . . . . [The] action of theater, like that of plague, is beneficial, for, impelling men to see themselves as they are, it causes the mask to fall, reveals the lie, the slackness, baseness, and hypocrisy of our world; it shakes off the asphyxiating inertia of matter which invades even the clearest testimony of the senses; and in revealing to collectivities of men their dark power, their hidden force, it invites them to take, in the face of destiny, a superior and heroic attitude they would never have assumed without it.

(Artaud1958: 30–32)

The "reasons for exaltation" are what remain after theater has done its cathartic work. However we label them – strategic value systems, the flash of the highest ideals of personal potential – they are sources of communal festivity, of celebration. Artaud was not very far from Aristotle's position in regard to catharsis:

The plague takes images that are dormant, a latent disorder, and suddenly extends them into the most extreme gestures; the theater also takes gestures and pushes them as far as they will go: like the plague it reforges the chain between what is and what is not, between the virtuality of the possible and what already exists in materialized nature. It recovers the notion of symbols and archetypes which act like silent blows, rests, leaps of the heart, summons of the lymph, inflammatory images thrust into our abruptly wakened heads. The theater restores to us all our dormant conflicts and all their powers, and gives these powers names we hail as symbols: and behold! before our eyes is fought a battle of symbols, one charging against another in an impossible mêlée; for there can be theater only from the moment when the impossible really begins and when the poetry which occurs on the stage sustains and superheats the realized symbols.

(Artaud 1958: 27–8)

After the purgation of pity and terror by these "superheated" symbols, what remains, what tragedy clears the way for, is the reaffirmed self-definition of the community. A community is humanity's greatest artifact, the one that all other artifacts commemorate. Artaud's thesis differs from Butcher's commentary mainly in its radical diction. Aristotle, at least Butcher's Aristotle, may have been the first to notice tragedy's constructive, positive charge, but he was not the last.

The focus of tragedy is upon the action of the whole represented community: protagonist, antagonist, servants, soldiers, masters, leaders. These designations refer to the entire dance, movement, and dialogue represented by the dramatic work. The wide-angle lens invites analysis of the structures of society, its constituencies, as the subject of tragedy, not "this man" or "this woman" or even "man," but the human community, human beings *in* community. This is, of course, what Aristotle observed, and he was very careful to say so:

> Tragedy is imitation, not of men, but of action and of life . . . . Dramatic action, therefore, is not with a view to the representation of character: character comes in as subsidiary to the actions . . . . [If] you string together a set of speeches expressive of character, and well finished in point of diction and thought, you will not produce the essential tragic effect nearly so well as with a play which, however deficient in these respects, yet has a plot and artistically constructed incidents . . . . The Plot, then, is the first principle, and, as it were, the soul of a tragedy: Character holds the second place (1450a) . . . . Thus Tragedy is the imitation of an action, and of the agents mainly with a view to the action (1450b).
>
> (Butcher 1951: 27–9)

With characteristic precision, Aristotle identified the kind of action tragedy imitates as the violation of specific social bonds. In Else's translation:

> if by an enemy to an enemy there is nothing pathetic either in the doing or the intention . . . ; nor if by persons who are neither; but when the painful deed is done in the context of close family relationships [cf. Halliwell: "bonded relations"; Telford: "in friendship"; Butcher: "those who are near or dear to one another"], for example when a brother kills or intends to kill a brother, or a son a father, or a mother a son, or a son a mother.
>
> (Else 1967: 1453b18–23).

Aristotle finds the core of tragic action in the violation of kinship and, by extension, of community.

In theater there are "only variations in form . . . and these show

49

no long-term evolution from 'primitive' to 'sophisticated' or 'modern'" (Schechner 1988: 6). Tragedy, then, is perennial and persistent. Kenneth Burke finds the vectors of tragedy so encompassing and so basic that they define what it means to be human (like most of his generation, he constructs humanity as masculine): "man" is "the symbol-using (symbol-making, symbol misusing) animal, inventor of the negative (or moralized by the negative), separated from his natural condition by instruments of his own making, goaded by the spirit of hierarchy (or moved by the sense of order) and rotten with perfection" (Burke 1966: 15).

Burke's "principle of perfection" entails the tendency to conceive a perfect enemy. The "symbol-using/making/misusing animal" embeds this tendency in all representation (Burke 1966: 18). In the logic of what he calls "dramatism," the analysis of language and thought occurs in modes of action rather than in the mode of conveying information, and "drama is the culminative form of action . . . . But if *drama*, then *conflict*. And if *conflict*, then *victimage*. Dramatism is always on the edge of this vexing problem, that comes to a culmination in tragedy, the song of the scapegoat" (1966: 54–5).

For Burke, tragedy is the basic investigation of human action, especially the action of victimage. Unlike Girard (see chapter 4, below), Burke does not try to explain why people are inevitably moved to "conceive a perfect enemy" or why conflict inevitably culminates in victimage, nor does he restrict "dramatism" to theatrical presentations of symbolic action and of language as symbolic action. Working backwards, as it were, from the "archaizing" structures of Freudian nomenclature as "explanations in terms of the *temporally* prior," he concludes that "many aspects of expression that once might have been studied in terms of *rhetorical* resources *natural* to language at *all* stages of history are treated as *survivals* from eras of primitive magic, ritual, and myth" (Burke 1966: 67–8). Burke argues that resonances of ritual within modern cultures are not vestigial or atavistic but perennial expressions of enduring human concerns. They are not survivals of relics from bygone days; instead they address the matter of survival itself, which has never disappeared from the arena of modern anxiety. By reproducing and representing in a secular format the structures, including the ritual structures, of its audience's community, tragedy performs, "in a fiction, in a dream of passion" (*Hamlet* II.ii.552), the fundamental principles of its social and spiritual survival.

3

THE RITUAL
GROUNDWORK

"What is a ceremony?" I asked. "It is a proper way to behave. You do this and that, so the gods do not punish you," said Amah.
                                        Amy Tan, *The Joy Luck Club*

Tragedy is part of a genealogy of related encodings that begins in ritual, myth, and folklore, whose interests are the same and whose vestiges remain visible even in the most complex and sophisticated plays. Since drama is communal production, "the critical intensification of collective life . . . and the possibility it creates for action and initiative" (Bristol 1985: 3), we can expect to find in it the expression of concerns that matter most urgently to the population that produces it. In Shakespearean tragedy, where the protagonists, along with any number of their communities, are destroyed, we find that sociopolitically important rituals have been honored in the breach, that is, they have been perverted or ignored. The community's need for ritual redress is misconstrued or neglected, and, as the Prince says at the end of *Romeo and Juliet*, "All are punished" (V.iii.295).

Ritual is the formal structuring or ordering of the life of any community that seeks to perpetuate itself. The definition of ritual, like that of tragedy, is problematized first of all by variations across different disciplines and disputes among proponents within a given discipline (e.g., anthropology), and further, by a widespread casual application of the term within and outside the academy to refer to any structured or repetitive behavior by either individuals or groups. "Any analytic system that cannot (or does not) discriminate between performances of *Hamlet*, the State Opening of Parliament, and the Mass is wasting our time by trivializing the study of social behavior" (Goody 1977: 28–9). Repetition is an important formal property of ritual, an imitation of "the rhythmic

51

imperatives of the biological and physical universe, thus suggesting a link with the perpetual processes of the cosmos. It thereby implies permanence and legitimacy of what are actually evanescent cultural constructs" (Moore and Myerhoff 1977: 8). But repetition alone does not identify or define ritual. Collective agreement and belief in its efficacy for cultural and physical survival are more significant hallmarks. Regularly repeated conventional behaviors or obsessive–compulsive repetitions in the domain of psychiatry are not rituals. Beyond those distinctions, there is little agreement among sociologists and anthropologists on what ritual is and is not: Durkheimians separate sacred from mundane; others argue that secular ritual is an equally compelling counterpart to religious ritual; still others attempt to distinguish ritual from ceremony and custom from tradition (Moore and Myerhoff 1977: 21–2). Most recent anthropological studies agree, at least, that ritual is social action requiring "the organized cooperation of individuals, directed by a leader or leaders" recognizing a "correct, morally right pattern that should be followed in any particular performance" (LaFontaine 1985: 11–12). It is prescriptive, that is, it *must* be done (but not necessarily by the total community), and its structure is modeled either directly or inversely on that of the community concerned (LaFontaine 1985: 12; T. S. Turner 1977: 61–2). It is indistinguishable from a community's sense of its own complicated identity. As Catherine Bell has recently argued,

> ritual systems do not function to regulate or control the systems of social relations, they *are* the system, and an expedient rather than perfectly ordered one at that. In other words, the more or less practical organization of ritual activities neither acts upon nor reflects the social system; rather, these loosely coordinated activities are constantly differentiating and integrating, establishing and subverting the field of social relations . . . . Insofar as they establish hierarchical social relations, they are also concerned with distinguishing local identities, ordering social differences, and controlling the contention and negotiation involved in the appropriation of symbols.
>
> (1992: 130)

Actions that are communally significant (the core of Aristotle's concept of tragedy) are marked by practices that link the group's past to its present and to its future. In traditional cultures, such practices operated comprehensively in the ordinary life of the community, whereas in modern cultures they operate in distinctly separated areas of life (Douglas 1966: 40). Modern ritual, both ecclesiastic and social, is separated out from daily concerns. The putative "advancements" of industry and technology have enabled us to compartmentalize and manage what we need for survival.[1] In traditional cultures, that management was ensured by ritual, without which survival was considered to be doubtful if not altogether impossible. As a way toward "understanding" Shakespeare, we sometimes try to see his culture as an image, an early pattern, of our own: the term "early modern," which suggests "forward-looking" and "anticipating the modern," has replaced "Renaissance" (the rebirth of interest in the distant past) in many recent discussions of sixteenth- and seventeenth-century culture. Though both rubrics denote epistemic change, it is worth remembering that while it initiated what we now know as industry and technology, Shakespeare's England, both rural and urban, had not yet jettisoned all of its links to its immediate preindustrial past. Pestilence and drought, however abetted by such political and economic (that is, human) interventions as land enclosures and gerrymandered parish boundaries, could still wreak havoc with systems of economic and personal survival on the farms, and drive up prices in the cities. Natural phenomena, as well as human behavior that fell outside the domain of acceptability and management, were the constitutive conditions that called for ritual redress. The continuities of tradition, expressed in ritual practices, reminded people that they lived in a universe larger than individual selves, local events, and personal satisfactions.

On this view, Roger Caillois identifies "two complimentary universes" for religious man: the profane, "in which he can act without anxiety or trepidation, but in which his actions only involve his superficial self" and the sacred, "in which a feeling of deep dependency controls, contains, and directs each of his drives, and to which he is committed unreservedly" (1959: 19). The dialectical opposition between the two is "a genuinely intuitive concept. We can describe it, analyze it into its elements, and theorize about it. But it is no more within the power of abstract language to define its unique quality than to define a sensation" (1959: 20).

Caillois's description of the sacred underpins much of Shakespearean tragedy in the shadows, echoes, and vestiges of ritual that appear, often overtly, in the action of the plays. This is more than a matter of language, although language is a frequent vehicle of expression. The symbolic content of much of social reality is "verbally non-retrievable information . . . . Language and culture are quite different sorts of codes and there is no easy and immediate way of translating from one into the other" (Aijmer 1987: 4). But when language supports and is supported by the specific action of the drama, it is more than metaphor, figurative decoration, or a prod to the intellect. Combined with specifically ritualistic action, the words and actions of Shakespeare's tragic characters reflect the plays' suspension in the dialectic Caillois describes. His point about the ineffable quality of the relation between sacred and profane applies to the powerful affect of the relation between community and hero. In Shakespearean tragedy, the community's commitment to the sacred,[2] its "deep dependency," is threatened by a crisis whose source and embodiment the community assigns to the hero. The community's drive to survive its crisis emerges as an urgent need to kill its hero-scapegoat. Caillois's concept of "two complimentary universes for religious man" applies equally to the Elizabethan audience whose religious concerns were thoroughly infused with secular interests. This interweaving is by no means immediately clear at all points, even to the community that animates it. As Barbara Myerhoff notes,

> All rituals are paradoxical and dangerous enterprises, the traditional and improvised, the sacred and secular. Paradoxical because rituals are conspicuously artificial and theatrical, yet designed to suggest the inevitability and absolute truth of their messages. Dangerous because when we are not convinced by a ritual, we may be aware of ourselves as having made them up, then on to the paralyzing realization that we have made up all our truths; our ceremonies, our most precious conceptions and convictions – all are mere invention.
>
> (1978: 86)

Rituals are containers that shape and reveal the contours of a culture's collective values (Myerhoff 1978: 86). Through precise, regular, repetitive, and predictable formal ritual practice members of a given culture clarify and reiterate those values, most urgently when they seem because of some real or impending crisis to be in question or to have been obscured altogether. Changes in government or impending changes to any level of the sociopolitical structure are the situations that most commonly revive interest in ritual; not coincidentally, these are also the most common situations illustrated in Shakespearean tragedy. The complexities and ambiguities of Elizabethan culture summoned just such clarification during Shakespeare's lifetime. And we can fully expect to find evidence of that summons embedded in the drama of the period, "the abstract and brief chronicles of the time" (*Hamlet* II.ii.524).

Ritual processes are difficult to define because they operate in a domain that defies semantic anchorage. They call for belief, but this may be more a matter of conviction than of cognition. Ambiguity in word or gesture may be

> glossed, even celebrated, then transcended in ritual performances. Through ritual we organize our understandings and dramatize our fundamental conceptions . . . rearranging our fundamental assumptions in the course of rituals themselves. Rituals begin with a cultural problem, stated or unstated, and then work various operations upon it, arriving at . . . reorganizations and reinterpretations of the elements that produce a newly meaningful whole. Achieving the appropriate shift in consciousness is the work of ritual.
>
> (Myerhoff 1982: 128–9)

The origins of ritual behavior are usually unrecoverable; indeed, "in some societies there is no tradition of exegesis or discussion; . . . questions may even be frowned on" (LaFontaine 1985: 12). Understanding complex ritual operations without collapsing important distinctions into meaningless generalizations requires comprehension of what Ronald Grimes has described as two different ritual strategies, "superstructuring" and "deconstructing" ritual performances. The former is a mode of "symbolic amplification," expansive, sometimes inversive, "magnifying and turning a culture's good, virtuous, proper side to public view": this is the mode commonly understood by the term "celebration." The latter is a negative mode of "symbolic stripping" which foregrounds "the under, down, dark, unstructured, or emergent side of culture" (Grimes 1982: 273–4). "Superstructuring" and "deconstruction" in this sense also distinguish comic from tragic drama. Each constitutes a separate "ritual fiction." The object of such a fiction

is not merely to reflect the cultural status quo but to

transform it in a moment of specially concentrated time . . . .
[Rituals and dramas] are not practice for some more real
kind of action, say, pragmatic or economic action, nor are
they sublimations for some remembered or more desirable
action. In a celebratory moment the ritual action is a deed in
which the symbols do not merely point, mean, or recall but
embody fully and concretely all that is necessary for the
moment.

(Grimes 1982: 252)

The specific subject of Grimes's essay is a performance during the
Santa Fe Fiesta, but the principles he outlines apply equally well to
any cultural performance. The "deconstruction" he identifies is
not the nihilism of certain post-modern French theoretical practice;
instead it unpacks the layers of fictional expression to locate
underneath it and reiterate not indeterminacy or meaninglessness
but rather something very real and significant for participating
members of the community: the foundation of values upon which
that community developed. Moreover, as Grimes says, rituals

are not only embedded in social processes, they also process
actors, things, spaces, and times. Furthermore, they are in
process; they develop and decline. So one should not too
quickly summarize the essence of some type of ritual (say,
celebration) without noting . . . the social processes *surrounding* ritual; the work of processing which a ritual *does*; and the
process of change which a ritual *undergoes*.

(1982: 274)

Ritual in performance therefore does not merely remind its
audience/participants of its significance as a purely intellectual or
moral exercise; as a functioning component of the performance it
transforms its agents and its auditors during the course of the
performance in which it occurs, just as it would in a formal,
liturgical setting such as a Mass.

The "under, down, dark, unstructured, or emergent side of
culture" is also the subject of tragedy. As a cultural performance
embodying ritual action, it is not a marker or a prompt for another
kind of action; it is itself a complete action. It tells a story, a "ritual
fiction," for the story's own sake. By mediating fictionalized action
and the "real" or re-cognized world that operates before and after
the performance, ritual performance clarifies and reaffirms the

56

cultural values of the audience/participants. Tragedy "deconstructs," in Grimes's sense, the cultural properties of the audience/participants and brings these up from underneath the historical and mundane layers of experience that conceal them between performances: the mask of performance, as it were, unmasks the cultural substratum. Such disclosure occurs not discursively or analytically, but in a flash. At the conclusions of such performances, "entropy is a fundamental law, and therefore whatever is achieved ritually begins to erode in the very moment of its success" (Grimes 1982: 252).

THE MOCKERY KING OF SNOW: *RICHARD II* AND THE SACRIFICE OF RITUAL

Because of this entropic law, rituals must always be repeated, regularly and systematically. Their efficacy does not last long. Neither does that of theatrical performance, and for the same reason, the flash of specific tragic performance does not ignite revolution and anarchy. From Plato through Gosson (1579) and Stubbes (1583), down to the present time, critics of the drama have been interested in the relation between rebellion and performance, but no clear interpretation emerges. One of the most infamous examples of theater pressed into partisan service – the staging of *Richard II* in February 1601 on the eve of the Essex rebellion – occurred to support a plot already under way. The play did not inspire the rebellion, nor did it engender one on the occasion of its original performance some four to six years earlier.

Noting Elizabeth I's famous remark about the play's performance "40 times in open streets and houses," Stephen Greenblatt asks, "can 'tragedy' be a strictly literary term when the Queen's own life is endangered by the play?" (1982 [ed.]: 4).[3] By decontextualizing Elizabeth's remark, Greenblatt implies that she was responding immediately to the performance of 5 February 1601. But in fact the remark was made much later, in a conversation recorded by the antiquary William Lambard, Keeper of the Records of the Tower. Reviewing the entire set of Tower documents, Elizabeth came to those from the reign of Richard II, and said, "I am Richard II, know ye not that?" Lambard answered tactfully, "Such a wicked imagination was determined and attempted by a most unkind Gent. the most adorned creature that ever your

Majestie made," to which Elizabeth replied, "He that will forget God, will also forget his benefactors; this tragedy was played 40 times in open streets and houses" (Albright 1927: 692; Heffner 1930: 771; Neale 1957: 398). The conversation continued, "until an explanation prompted another reflection: 'In those days force and arms did prevail; but now the wit of the fox is everywhere on foot, so as hardly a faithful or virtuous man may be found'" (Neale 1957: 398). This exchange took place on 4 August 1601, six months after the "dangerous" performance (which proved far more dangerous to Essex than to Elizabeth), and as the queen's further remarks indicate, reflected on the general tenor of politics "in those days" (i.e., in Richard's time) as compared with "now." The threat posed by the performance itself cannot have been perceived, at least by the queen, as very immediate. It was Lambard who made the reference to Essex; there is perhaps a careful distinction to be made between the queen's own perceptions and her awareness of the analogy in the minds of her subjects (Albright 1927: 691).

The ambiguously understood "danger" of Shakespeare's play resides in large part in its "deposition" scene, whose original performative impact remains unknown. There are actually two "deposition" scenes. The first is III.iii.144–77, at Flint Castle before Northumberland as Bolingbroke's emissary. The second is IV.i.162–318, the formal deposition before the Parliament, and is the one usually referred to as "the" deposition scene. Although this second deposition scene was not printed until the fourth quarto of 1608, five years after Elizabeth's death, it may have been *performed* at least once by the Chamberlain's Men, and if the queen's own report was accurate, "40 times," evidently without incident of rebellion. If, like the Essex conspirators, Elizabeth saw a threat to her rule in the play's representations of deposition, this could not have been a widespread association or more than an afterthought; otherwise, presumably, the play would not have been performed *"40 times in open streets and houses"* with apparent impunity. Moreover, it may not have been any particular scenes, but rather the play's whole representation, that prompted Elizabeth's response.

So much has been made of the queen's remark in connection with Shakespeare's play that a corollary situation has been obscured.[4] In 1599, John Hayward's *The First Part of the Life and Reign of King Henry IV* was printed and dedicated to Essex. The dedication was added after the printing had been licensed and was deleted by orders of the Archbishop of Canterbury, but not before some five to six hundred copies had been sold. The book was extremely popular, with another six hundred copies sold after the deletion, and demand continued even after a second printing was suppressed (Albright 1927: 701; Guy 1988: 447–8). Despite the fact that the title pointed to Henry IV, the principal subject matter of this popular book was the reign and deposition of Richard II. Bacon noted in the "Essay Concerning the Earl of Essex" that Elizabeth explicitly found the book "a seditious prelude to put into the people's heads boldness and faction, [and] said she had good opinion that there was treason in it" (quoted in Albright 1927: 700). The charges against Essex at his trial in 1601 included his use of Hayward's book, "no sooner published but the Earl, knowing hundreds of them to be dispersed . . . has confessed that he had the written copy with him to peruse 14 days plotting how he might become another Henry IV" (quoted in Albright 1927: 704). For unknown reasons, but perhaps through the influence of the Lord Chamberlain, or perhaps because the queen's wrath was focused upon Hayward's book (Heffner 1930: 771), Shakespeare's company and their play managed to evade suppression.

The latter-day attribution, adaptation, or interpretation of a Shakespearean performance should not be mistaken for its original, unrecoverable intent (Marcus 1988: 42). The current critical interest in identifying in Shakespeare's plays an array of specific political mirrors ignores the capacity of these mirrors to reflect and refract each other and turn the theater into a funhouse: the critical debate then becomes its own end and its own self-perpetuating subject. There is no evidence that any change to the Elizabethan or Jacobean sociopolitical structure occurred consequent (or even immediately subsequent) to the performance of any of Shakespeare's plays. If they were indeed pressed into subversive service, that subversion, like the Essex plot, failed.

This does not deny a political discourse to Shakespearean tragedy; the shaping of these plays, and in particular their incorporation of selected ritual elements, reveals a dialectic that is unmistakably political. The deposition scenes in *Richard II*, for example, reverse the rites by which the king is invested; their "undoing" in effect deconstructs or anatomizes the process of investiture, arguably for the purpose of "reconstructing" it. It is the interpretation of the dialectic, not its presence within a text or a performance, that is subject to debate. Because the design and application of ritual require communal agreement, the inclusion of ritual elements within a play's action marks that play's concern with how, by whom, and for whom, such agreement is negotiated. When a play such as *Richard II* or *Julius Caesar* performs the breakdown of communal accord, it reveals the conditions necessary for such accord, the consequences of its breakdown, and the potential for a new and perhaps different accord.

Richard II opens with an aborted ritual, the joust between Bolingbroke and Mowbray whose cancellation appears to illustrate Richard's inability to rule: "We were not born to sue but to command; / Which . . . we cannot do to make you friends" (I.i.196–7). The joust is (or would have been) one of several ritual events depicted in the play whose close observation mark the normative relationship of king and state but here, in Richard's crisis of kingship, are aborted or evacuated of meaning. Close examination of those rituals and of the way Richard handles them in his crisis reveals a complex portrait of the king as one who attempts to hold on to certain aspects of a traditional order while violating others. Since that order is itself in the process of change, Richard participates in but does not control the destruction of tradition and, at the same time, of himself. Responsibility for the monarchic disorder that governs this play devolves on other heads besides the king's.

The ritual function of the joust and its sequent events can be understood in terms outlined by Victor Turner. When a "norm-governed social life is interrupted by the breach of a rule controlling one of its salient relationships," a state of crisis results, which splits the community into contending factions. Redress is undertaken by those in authority, usually in the form of ritualized action, either legal, religious, or military. The aim of such action is to defuse the conflict, and then, barring immediate regress to crisis, to reconcile the conflicting parties through the outcome of the ritualized action. Failing that, the alternative solution is a "consensual recognition of irremediable breach" and a "spatial separation of the parties." If neither solution works, the state of crisis prevails "until some radical restructuring . . . sometimes by revolutionary means, is undertaken" (V. Turner 1982: 92).

Richard's management of the joust in the play's sources, radically contracted in Shakespeare's version, shows a complicated dynamic in which the king is an actor in the monarchic crisis, but not its instigator. Both historically and in Shakespeare's representation, Richard's reign was a troubled time in which old orders gave way to new. It is frivolous to attribute the toppling of whole social and political structures to one individual, even to a king, let alone to one who is removed or removes himself from the throne. In the patterned terms Turner uses to describe such crises, the management of ritual in the play reveals a range of social and political meanings in the changes that occur.

The play begins, of course, *in medias res*. The initiating breach was the murder of Thomas of Woodstock, Duke of Gloucester, in which Richard may or may not have been implicated, and for which Bolingbroke accuses Mowbray of treason. Mowbray counters with a similar charge. The ritual of trial by combat was prescribed by tradition in such cases. Shakespeare employed it again in *King Lear* V.iii, when Albany charges Edmund with treason and Edgar arrives to take up Albany's cause. By the time of Richard's reign, the ritual itself had devolved to a theatricalized event, and by Shakespeare's time, in England as well as on the continent, it was more often associated with carnival festivities than with judicial decisions. In Venice, for example, jousts were part of the Sensa festival (celebrating the marriage of the sea) that marked the beginning of the theatrical season (E. Muir 1981: 121 n.) and lent an element of structure to the more topsy-turvy processes of Carnival (E. Muir 1981: 177). The one-to-one combat of the joust originated as a substitute for the dangerously chaotic *mêlée* of the tournament, involving whole armies, that had disturbed the reigns of Henry II and Richard I; the latter attempted to regulate his knights' participation by requiring royal licenses for combats. In time the joust, using blunted weapons and forbidding a fight to the death, replaced the tournament and ultimately became mere ceremony (Bucknell 1979: 148). By the end of the Middle Ages, jousts had become an entertaining part of ceremonial pageantry, "a festival ritual of homage and service to the crown," and had become so controlled and theatricalized that "[in] 1343 the challengers at a tournament in Smithfield came dressed as the Pope and his cardinals. Forty-three years later Richard II looked on to see knights led in by silver chains held by ladies mounted on palfreys" (Strong 1984: 13).

Chaucer's *Knight's Tale*, written during Richard II's reign, gives a detailed account of the preparations for a combat between Palamon and Arcite, which Theseus, whose control is much better than Richard's, cancels swiftly and authoritatively. The Chaucerian version presents in six lines what Shakespeare stretches out over two scenes. Theseus's herald announces:

The lord hath of his heigh discrecioun
Considered that it were destruccion
To gentil blood to fighten in the gyse
Of mortal bataille now in this emprise.
Wherfore, to shapen that they shal nat dye,
He wol his firste purpos modifye.

(2537–42)

The herald then announces in the next nineteen lines the rules and restrictions for the combat, especially stipulating that no lethal weapons be used, and that opponents may only capture each other. The combat is thus transformed into a joust, and Theseus's pacific command receives boisterous popular approval (2561–4). Shakespeare's Richard, pleading the same cause, more than doubles the length of the herald's proclamation, and delivers it himself, closing the distance between king and combatants. His decision, however, does not get the same response as Theseus's.

The account of the cancellation in Froissart's *Chronicle* (translated 1523–5) reveals Richard's predicament in terms omitted by Shakespeare. The king's councillors warn him of popular revolt if the combat proceeds:

> The Londoners and dyvers other noble men and prelates of the realm say howe ye take the ryght waye to distroye your lygnage and the realme of Englande. Whiche thynge they saye they wyll natte suffre. And if the Londoners rise agaynste you, with suche noble men as wyll take their parte, . . . ye shall be of no puyssaunce to resyst they. . . .
>
> (Bullough 1973: III: 424)

Having impressed upon Richard his inability to control his citizens, the councillors remind the king of the people's love for Derby (Bolingbroke) and their hatred for "the erle Marshall" (Mowbray), and point out that when the quarrel first arose, Richard should have settled it and commanded peace. Furthermore, he should have shown Derby some preferential affection in order to maintain the popular good will. Because he did not do that, say the councillors, he is rumored to favor Mowbray. They close by urging him to heed their advice: "sir, ye had never more nede of good counsayle than ye have nowe" (Bullough 1973: III: 424–5).

Froissart's account shows a Richard whose power depends upon popular approval, and who takes the advice of his councillors in order to win that approval. Their advice also included the plan to banish both Mowbray and Bolingbroke. Shakespeare omits the scene of counsel, and has Richard acknowledge it only obliquely in chastizing Gaunt's grief: "Thy son is banish'd upon good advice, / Whereto thy tongue a party-verdict gave. / Why at our justice seem'st thou then to low'r?" (I.iii.233–5). Gaunt replies that he argued as a judge, not as a father: "A partial slander sought I to avoid, / And in the sentence my own life destroy'd" (241–2), taking upon himself what in Froissart's account was Richard's predicament. There are no councillors in the play to tell the king that he should have commanded peace. Richard tries that on his own initiative and it does not work. It is the first form of post-ritual redress noted in Turner's pattern. The banishment is his second choice (in Turner's terms, the "consensual recognition of ir-remediable breach . . . followed by the spatial separation of the parties"); it is prompted in part by his councillors' advice but more by the combatants' refusal to obey, which takes up a substantially greater proportion of the scene than does the brief exchange between Richard and Gaunt. The power of the king is com-promised as much by the combatants' stubbornness as by his own and his advisers' vacillation. The disruption of order is present from the start, and resides both within the king's character and outside it.

The general applicability of the pattern Turner describes indi-cates that structures of authority sometimes do not prevail over recalcitrant subjects. Such failures of authority may indicate a king's unfitness. They may equally well indicate his subjects' viola-tion of their contractual allegiance. Shakespeare's kings never seem to operate in an unreal world of absolute power. When they are shown trying to do that (e.g., Lear, Macbeth, Richard III) they are inevitably stopped. In *Richard II* Shakespeare shows a monarch hewing closely to a normative pattern for the resolution of con-flicts. His effort is overpowered by Bolingbroke's and Mowbray's intractability. Froissart's document presents a clear image of Richard caught in a kind of "Woodstock-gate," and helpless before the threat of popular uprising. Working toward theatrical rather than historical clarity, Shakespeare gives Richard the opportunity to control, and thereby directs our attention to the centrality of the monarch. This is figured both visually and politically in the opening scene as he stands between the two antagonists; the image prefigures his isolation at the center of his circle of supporters in the center of the play (III.ii), when he sits upon the ground and talks of graves. As the first test of his authority in the play, the episode of the combat becomes an emblem of the play's political/ritual crisis.

The situation presented to Richard at the beginning of Shakespeare's play is not only one that performs the failure of kingly authority but one for which the ritual prescribed to close the rupture in the kingdom had long since become theatricalized and ambiguous. Nevertheless, Froissart's account indicates that the combat retained the potential for real danger, not only to the combatants but to the commonwealth as well. There is no suggestion in Shakespeare's play that the combat between Mowbray and Bolingbroke was meant to be merely ceremonial. Historically, by Richard's time it would have been, and it would have been if Richard had declared it so. The difference between theatricality and actual *mêlée* in the fourteenth century depended upon the *ad hoc* rules of the game. Richard's own sense of theatricalism in the play has often been cited as evidence of his unfitness to rule, but as Kernan (1970: 254) and more recently Kastan (1986: 470) have pointed out, the Lancasters, father and son, are no less thespian in mounting their kingly personae. All the characters of the Second Tetralogy live in theatrical times.

The late fourteenth century had long since ceased to honor the original adjudicating function of ritual combat. Strong argues that its growing theatricalism indicates not the form's decline and decadence but rather its response "both to the evolution of the aristocrat as courtier and to the demands of nationalistic chivalries, which focused the loyalty of knights on the ruling dynasty" (1984: 12). The shift was evidently an adaptive strategy, a compromise between the total extinction of old ways and the movement of social change, which often occurs at the cost of stability and peace. If the ritual of combat did not decline and decay, its political function altered radically. Shakespeare's use of it to open his play shows a concern for the progress of a civilization at those moments in its history when the rituals and ceremonies that once signified and guaranteed its orderly functioning and integration had been reduced to outward shows. The dilution by Richard's time of the joust's ritualistic force contextualizes what happens more disastrously, as the play eventually represents, to the sacred permanence of the king's enthronement.

Not all the water in the rough rude sea
Can wash the balm off from an anointed king.
(III.ii.54–5)

Richard counts on his protected status as God's anointed deputy
on earth. But as we have begun to see, when one traditional action
loses its meaning, the significance of and adherence to others are
also problematized. Since rituals are acts of faith, the very act of
questioning is itself dangerous to stability. The play takes up at
other points what happens when traditional understanding of
God's law is suddenly interrogated. The Duchess of Gloucester's
appeal to Gaunt to support her accusation against Richard merits
a whole scene, set between the two parts of Richard's combat
dilemma. Besides inculpating Richard in Woodstock's death, the
scene sets forth the inherent ambiguity in Richard's England regarding kingly immunity when the king is involved in a murder.
The Duchess appeals to the older law of retribution for the murder
of a husband and a brother. Gaunt tells her to go complain to God.
Gaunt's refuge, like Richard's, is in the code of the king's divine
ordination. The Duchess's sympathetic plea, the fact that she can
question the king's immunity, exposes the instability of that code.
Like Richard's command to Mowbray and Bolingbroke, England's
belief in divine ordination by Richard's time lacked the force of
communal agreement. The historical records, including
Holinshed's, show that in the matter of Richard's deposition the
code of divine ordination was in fact ignored: the deposition was
not Richard's own idea – he is consistently a believer in tradition –
but was forced upon him by both Henry and Parliament (Bullough
1973: III: 406). The conditions of social collapse that Girard calls
the "sacrificial crisis" (1977: 49) are set up in the first act of the
play, and all the travesties of formal order that follow are blazes on
the trail toward that end. The detailed formal preparations for the
combat (I.iii.7–45) – the formulaic pronouncements by the
marshall and by Bolingbroke and Mowbray of their names, titles,
and charges against each other, Richard's ceremonial
decoronation before his followers (III.iii.147–53) and again before
Bolingbroke (IV.i.203–15), York's agonized narrations of Henry's
entrée into London followed by the deposed and publicly degraded
Richard (V.ii.23–36) – all punctuate the play with instances of
rituals aborted, inverted, and finally rejected in favor of a new
order, which in turn proved more disordered than Richard's.

The traditional critical response to this series of events is that it was Richard's responsibility, that his was the first rupture in parcelling out the kingdom to profiteers, "Like to a tenement or a pelting farm" (II.i.60), and then appropriating Hereford's estate, "tak[ing] from Time / His charters and his customary rights" (II.i.195–6). But as even those who hold this Richard-centered view have noted, "the old world is breaking up" (Kernan 1970: 247). Shakespeare creates enough sympathy for Richard at several points – most dramatically in the speech beginning "Of comfort no man speak! / Let's talk of graves, of worms, and epitaphs" (III.ii.144–77) at the center of the play – to suggest more ambivalence than blame. In other plays, Shakespeare shows what real disregard for order can unleash. At a similarly transitional moment in *Julius Caesar*, Antony incites the mob to riot and then absolves himself: "Mischief, thou art afoot, / Take thou what course thou wilt" (III.ii.260–1); later, in *Antony and Cleopatra*, he would "Let Rome in Tiber melt, and the wide arch / Of the rang'd empire fall!" (I.i.33–4) rather than give up Cleopatra. In his most intense despair, Lear urges the heavens to "Strike flat the thick rotundity o'th'world, / Crack nature's molds, all germains spill at once, / That make ingrateful man!" (III.ii.7–9). Unlike these later creations, Richard in crisis cleaves to order, the old order of the generation of York and Gaunt, which he honors even as it passes. There is an interesting and subtle irony in this alignment of Richard and Bolingbroke's father: Richard is not absolute villain and Henry is not absolute savior. Even though (or perhaps because) it means his death, Richard ensures the legal passage of control to Bolingbroke before he is finished. Doubtless he has no choice, but his gesture lends formality and legitimacy to the inevitable. Whatever else he misconstrues in his troubled government, he retains to the end a clear sense of purpose in honoring the ritual underpinnings of his culture.

The king realizes his negligence by the middle of the play. He stands far from his London court, with Aumerle, Carlisle, and his soldiers, on the wild Welsh coast. Wales, in this play as in *Henry V*, is home to fierce, primitive, superstitious, mystical, and above all, loyal men like the Welsh captain in II.iv, and Fluellen in the later play. At the margin of England's map, it is the appropriate locus for Richard's transition, and Wales is where he stays until he is brought back to Westminster, "plume-pluck'd," for the formal transfer of power in IV.i. At the Welsh outpost, Richard becomes liminal; such figures are "neither here nor there; . . . betwixt and between the positions assigned and arrayed by law, custom, convention, and ceremonial . . . . Their behavior is normally passive or humble" (V. Turner 1969: 95).

> I weep for joy
> To stand upon my kingdom once again.
> Dear earth, I do salute thee with my hand,
> Though rebels wound thee with their horses' hoofs.
> . . . .
> So weeping, smiling, greet I thee, my earth,
> And do thee favors with my royal hands.
> . . . .
> Mock not my senseless conjuration, lords,
> This earth shall have a feeling . . . .
>
> (III.ii.4–24)

Such reverent animation of the land belongs to a ritual-centered king. The contrast in this regard between Richard and Bolingbroke is most obvious when the latter addresses the land at the moment of his departure into exile: "Then, England's ground, farewell; sweet soil, adieu, / My mother, and my nurse, that bears me yet!" (I.iii.306–7). Bolingbroke relates to the land in terms of himself, not as an externally and independently potent locus for respect as Richard does. With the fatal exception of the leasing-out, the synecdoche of the land was Richard's concern from the start. When he stopped the combat, in language that amplifies Chaucer's model, he did so

> For that our kingdom's earth should not be soil'd
> With that dear blood which it hath fostered;
> And for our eyes do hate the dire aspect
> Of civil wounds plough'd up with neighbours' sword.
>
> (I.iii.125–8)

Yet it will come. The Bishop of Carlisle, keeper of Christian ritual in this play by virtue of his office, warns Bolingbroke's followers:

> The blood of English shall manure the ground
> And future ages groan for this foul act;
> Peace shall go sleep with Turks and infidels,
> And in this seat of peace tumultuous wars
> Shall kin with kin and kind with kind confound.

67

Disorder, horror, fear, and mutiny
Shall here inhabit, and this land be call'd
The field of Golgotha and dead men's skulls.
O, if you raise this house against this house,
It will the woefullest division prove
That ever fell upon this cursed earth.

(IV.i.137–47)

His office may be Christian, but his diction casts the civil war in terms of pre-Christian ritual: kin-killing, civil war, will turn England into its own *pharmakos* whose blood will fertilize the soil, but the dead crop of the "cursed earth" is only skulls. Properly conducted in a culture where such rites still have active meaning, a blood libation would insure fertility, but this England-in-transition has sacrificed its rituals under Richard and will continue to do so in the new (dis)order under Bolingbroke.

In his speech if not in action, Richard often appears as the last true defender of the old faith. From his and the play's opening lines – "Old John of Gaunt, time honoured Lancaster, / . . . according to thy oath and band" (I.i.1–2) – Richard shows himself wrapped for security in tradition and ritual. The ceremonial quality of his language and his reliance on Gaunt's loyalty to the old codes has been well noted (e.g., Berger 1985: 215). Critics have made much of Richard's neglect of inheritance laws, but this neglect is actually brief, confined to Bolingbroke, and committed for political expedience. Richard is certainly not alone in it; at some point in the play, all of the principals neglect the laws of inheritance, most obviously in accepting Richard's deposition and Bolingbroke's accession. York's admonition, "for how art thou a king / But by fair sequence and succession" (II.i.198–9) is ironized by the sequence and succession of the rest of the play: Bolingbroke's "right" to be king, whatever its retributive justice and its parliamentary endorsement, is certainly not granted by the code York endorses in that line. Moreover, the principle of "fair sequence and succession" is problematic for all claimants in this play and in the history behind the play. Richard succeeded his grandfather Edward III, not his father Edward who had died the year before and never inherited the throne; thus Richard's kingship was not by intact dynastic inheritance (Saccio 1977: 19), although York's citation of "fair sequence and succession" suggests that there was no question about Richard's right. Shakespeare notes Bolingbroke's coronation in much the same way as he was later to note Macbeth's: it is simply recorded as a done deed, and attention is given instead to the theatricalism of Richard's public disgrace and Bolingbroke's acclaim (V.ii.23–4). Hall gives little notice to the ceremony, and points out that "who so ever rejoysed at this coronacion, or whosoever delighted at his high promocion" (Bullough 1973: III: 364), certainly Richard's originally designated heir, Edmund Mortimer, Earl of March was not among them. Bolingbroke's real claim rested only on conquest and on parliamentary assent, which was granted immediately upon request, and he became king by election rather than by inheritance or designation (Bullough 1973: III: 364; Oman 1906: IV: 153). Despite the fact that there was some precedent for passing over a designated successor (Arthur of Brittany had been passed over in 1199) as there was, after Edward II, for deposing a king, the cultural significance of substituting election for traditional modes of succession was unmistakably problematic. The rule of primogeniture became ambiguous when Edward III died, and remained so through the generations of the Tudors. Thus everyone who moves to Bolingbroke's side in the course of the play does so not from principled adherence to ancient law but for political exigency; nearly everyone who does not (except for Aumerle, who comes around eventually) is destroyed. The old ways are past, or passing.

Only Richard clings to ritual. His deposition is widely recognized as an inverted coronation ceremony (e.g., Girard 1977: 304). It is usually cited as evidence of Richard's unfitness: he gives up his crown too quickly, too willingly, to his eager cousin. It is, however, also evidence of his care for the proper formalities of his culture's rites. We should focus as much attention as Richard does, and as Shakespeare does, on *how* he gives it up. The first of the two deposition scenes occurs with his homage to the land at Flint Castle in Wales. Richard appears with his supporters atop the castle walls, and receives Northumberland as Bolingbroke's emissary.

> What must the King do now? Must he submit?
> The King shall do it. Must he be depos'd?
> The King shall be contented. Must he lose
> The name of king? A God's name, let it go!
> I'll give my jewels for a set of beads,
> My gorgeous palace for a hermitage,
> My gay apparel for an almsman's gown,

My figur'd goblets for a dish of wood,
My sceptre for a palmer's walking staff,
My subjects for a pair of carved saints,
And my large kingdom for a little grave,
. . . .
What says King Bolingbroke?

                              (III.iii.143–75)

The first four lines of this passage inversely echo the rhetoric of the
"Homilee agaynst Disobedience and wylful Rebellion" (1574): "What
shall subjects do then? Shall they obey valiant, stout, wise, and
good princes, and condemn, disobey, and rebel against children
being their princes, or against indiscreet and evil governors? God
forbid." It may be that Shakespeare's audience heard Richard's
lines ironically in the context of that echo, reminding them that
Richard submits here to nothing less than "Disobedience and
wylful Rebellion." The meticulous catalogue of what Richard will
trade refers to the outward signs of his state, the concrete ways in
which early modern England "knew" its monarch from any other
human being. They are the symbols that most actively occupied
Richard's attention as well: name, jewels, palace, robes, plate,
sceptre, subjects, kingdom. Their exteriority is echoed in the
scene's locus – at an outpost, atop the "rude ribs of that ancient
castle" (III.iii.32), in the open air. Although they are outward
signs, they are not superficial, but as tangible and fragile as the
land itself. They entail all the metonymy that a monarchic symbol-
system imbues in them.

The audience (but not Richard) has just heard Bolingbroke tell
Northumberland the conditions he will offer the king: "Even at his
feet to lay my arms and power, / Provided that my banishment
repeal'd / And lands restor'd again be freely granted"
(III.iii.39–41). Conditional allegiance is no allegiance, and Henry
intends none; his repetition of the name "King Richard" four times
in a speech of thirty-six lines rings with sarcasm (like Richard's
"What says King Bolingbroke?"). More interesting, however, is the
threat that Bolingbroke offers if Richard rejects his conditions. He
will "lay the summer's dust with show'rs of blood / Rain'd from the
wounds of slaughtered Englishmen . . . . The rage be his, whilst on
the earth I rain / My waters – on the earth, and not on him"
(III.iii.43–4, 59–60). Bolingbroke's token respect of the king's
person is meaningless in the face of his anarchy against the king's

other body, the kingdom and its people. Moreover, he immediately retracts even that token respect when Richard, "the blushing discontented sun," appears just after these lines. Caught up in his blood-rain metaphor, Bolingbroke expands it to a cloudburst that will "stain the track / Of his bright passage to the occident" (III.iii.66–7), that is, to the west, where the sun sets. York, in attendance, catches his drift immediately and warns against it: "Yet looks he like a king . . . . Alack, alack, for woe, / That any harm should stain so fair a show" (III.iii.68–71). Richard apparently intuits Bolingbroke's specific threat, as he counter-warns in similar diction: "Yet know, my master, God omnipotent, / Is mustering in his clouds on our behalf" (III.iii.85–6) an appropriate inheritance of pestilence upon succeeding generations. This blood-rain is what Richard offered to prevent at the start of the play, what Carlisle later warned would issue from Bolingbroke's accession, what Bolingbroke himself now actively and irresponsibly threatens, and what in fact plagued his subsequent rule. It is arguably to stave this off as much as to submit to the inevitable that Richard so readily capitulates.

The care with which Richard enumerates his relinquished symbols belongs to all ritual; it is the appropriate preparation for the formal and final rite of the second, "real," deposition scene in IV.i, set at Westminster, in the full court. The procession into the hall is fully ceremonial: "*Enter, as to the Parliament*" (stage direction). As at the beginning of the play, the scene begins with reciprocal charges of treason, this time by Bagot and Aumerle, with Bolingbroke adjudicating. The wheel is coming full circle. Again there is no resolving combat. Bolingbroke says, "These differences shall all rest under gage / 'Till Norfolk be repeal'd" (IV.i.86–7), but Carlisle informs the court that Norfolk is dead. Thus the prescribed restorative rite is again aborted. In this ominous and official setting, Richard's full deposition occurs. The process is the exact reverse of the order of investiture:

> Now mark me how I will undo myself.
> I give this heavy weight from off my head
> And this unwieldy sceptre from my hand,
> The pride of kingly sway from out my heart.
> With mine own tears I wash away my balm,
> With mine own hands I give away my crown,
> With mine own tongue deny my sacred state,

With mine own breath release all duteous oaths.
All pomp and majesty I do forswear;
My manors, rents, revenues I forgo;
My acts, decrees, and statutes I deny.
God pardon all oaths that are broke to me!
God keep all vows unbroke are made to thee!
. . . .
God save King Harry, unking'd Richard says . . . .
                              (IV.i.203–20)

The speech is both pitiable and dangerous. Richard undoes
himself, as well as his kingship. In denying his acts, decrees, and
statutes he erases the record of his existence and occupation of the
throne. This is more than the passage of control; it widens the hole
in the historical record, the breach in the "fair sequence and
succession" of the Plantagenet dynasty that began when Edward III
died. This is nihilism of the most terrifying order, "mark'd with a
blot, damn'd in the book of heaven" (IV.i.236).

Girard reminds us that the traditional monarchic system is
rooted in the function of the king as surrogate sacrificial victim.
"The sacred character of the king – that is, his identity with the
victim – regains its potency as it is obscured from view and even
held up to ridicule. It is in fact then that the king is most
threatened" (1977: 304). Richard himself acknowledges,

Nay, if I turn mine eyes upon myself,
I find myself a traitor with the rest;
For I have given here my soul's consent
T'undeck the pompous body of a king . . . .
                              (IV.i.247–50)

As Girard points out, Richard has become both victimizer and
victim, erasing the distinction between himself and those who do
him violence (1977: 304).

Richard's identification with his enemies is more than histrionic.
From the perspective of ritual it is also accurate. Throughout the
play Shakespeare repeatedly emphasizes the factor of kinship,
especially that of Richard and Bolingbroke. The play insistently
refers not only to the tragedy of state but to that of family as well,
in true Aristotelian fashion. Among the several scenes that illustrate this insistence, two do so with special force.

Just after Richard imaginatively turns his eyes upon himself in the lines quoted above, he calls for a mirror in order to see himself literally. In the mirror he sees "the very book indeed / Where all my sins are writ, and that's myself" (IV.i.274–5). The replication of his face in the mirror enables him, in Girard's terms, "to polarize, to literally draw to himself, all the infectious strains in the community and transform them . . . . The principle of this metamorphosis has its source in the sacrifice of the monarch and . . . pervades his entire existence" (1977: 107). When Richard shatters the glass and says to Bolingbroke, "Mark, silent king . . . / How soon my sorrow hath destroy'd my face," Bolingbroke equivocates, "The shadow of your sorrow hath destroy'd / The shadow of your face" (IV.i.290–3). And well he might; it is urgent for him to distinguish rigorously between the substance and its replicated image. Besides the face reflected in the glass, so easily "crack'd in an hundred shivers," the other double of Richard is Bolingbroke himself. Shakespeare unmistakably presents this relationship to us earlier in the same scene, just before the formal deposition:

> . . . Here, cousin, seize the crown.
> Here, cousin.
> On this side my hand, and on that side thine.
> . . . .
> That bucket down, and full of tears am I,
> Drinking my griefs, whilst you mount up on high.
> (IV.i.181–9)

The tableau presents the two men frozen in the liminal moment, equal and opposite.[5] On stage this moment represents what Girard calls the "sacrificial crisis," built on "fierce mimetic rivalries" that oscillate constantly until distinction between the two is blurred, undifferentiated. Noting the prevalence of enemy twins and mirror effects in traditional ritual and mythology, Girard concludes that such symmetries of conflict must represent a genuine threat to cultural identity: the "world of reciprocal violence is one of constant mirror effects in which the antagonists become each other's doubles and lose their individual identities" (1978: 164, 186). The threat of indistinction is removed by redifferentiating the twins, establishing stable binary patterns in place of the "fearful symmetry."

Shakespeare ensures that we will see the binding symmetrical patterns of rival brothers at the beginning and end of the play. When Mowbray charges Bolingbroke at the start, "and let him be no kinsman to my liege," Richard answers that he would be impartial "Were he my brother, nay, my kingdom's heir, / As he is but my father's brother's son" (I.i.59, 116–17), although he later confides to Aumerle that he suspects Bolingbroke feels a little less than kin: "He is our cousin, cousin; but 'tis doubt, / When time shall call him home from banishment, / Whether our kinsman come to see his friends" (I.iv.20–2). Meanwhile Bolingbroke vows to avenge the Duke of Gloucester, whose "blood, like sacrificing Abel's, cries / . . . To me for justice" (I.i.104–6). By the end of the play, in a structural symmetry, Bolingbroke is associated not with Abel but, via Exton's surrogacy, "With Cain [to] go wander thorough shades of night" (V.vi.43).

Neither the historical sources nor the recognized dramatic antecedents for this play (the anonymous *Woodstock* and Marlowe's *Edward II*) suggest any association of Richard and Bolingbroke with Cain and Abel; it was apparently Shakespeare's own idea to bind this play in the framework of the First Murder. On first glance this frame might appear to be merely decorative, a foil against which Richard's fall and Bolingroke's ascent stand out clearly. But after that first glance, it immediately seems more than that. Gloucester is likened to Abel (I.i.104) with Mowbray standing in for Cain, and Bolingbroke casting himself as God the avenger; why then at the end does Bolingbroke link his surrogate murderer Exton (and thus himself) with Cain? And why introduce the biblical analogy at all, let alone as the bracketing format of the play, at I.i and V.vi? At the end, the analogous positions are reversed in a complicated twisting of narrative strands that began early in the play: Richard (as Abel) is killed, and Bolingbroke, whose Cain-like banishment began in I.iii, at the end imposes upon himself the penance of pilgrimage to expiate the double sin of regicide and fratricide.

Because they are, *seriatim*, kings, the crimes attributed to Richard and Bolingbroke respectively must be displaced. Richard's involvement in Woodstock's murder is the unresolved charge displaced onto Mowbray at the start of the play; Bolingbroke's "contract" on Richard is displaced onto Exton and revealed only by report and implication in the very brief conversation between Exton and "a servant": "'Have I no friend will rid me of this living fear?' / . . . he spake it twice, / And urg'd it twice together, did he not?" (V.iv.2–5). Because Richard and Bolingbroke are each other's doubles, the surrogated murder puts

Bolingbroke in the position not of avenger but of fratricide. There is no doubt of his identification with Exton/Cain, for in the next lines he pledges to "make a voyage to the Holy Land, / To wash the blood off from my guilty hand" (V.vi.49–50). Like the other restitutive rituals represented in the play, Bolingbroke's expiation too was aborted by the continuing civil strife, as dramatized in the rest of the Second Tetralogy.

Cain's punishment, exile from Eden, is accompanied by the divine protection of God's mark; thus, in the 1560 Geneva Bible: "Douteles whosoeuer slayeth Kain, he shalbe punished seuen folde. And the Lord set a marke vpon Kain, lest anie man finding him shulde kil him" (*Genesis* 4:15).[6] The mark is both stain and anointment; the marked one is both shunned and protected, villain and consecrated victim, in other words, the tragic protagonist. In Shakespeare's play, Cain is incorporated in both Richard and Bolingbroke, serving as a link that binds them together.

The mirrored relationship of Richard and Bolingbroke is set forth once more, this time by verbal recitation. The Duchess of York reminds her husband to "tell the rest / When weeping made you break the story off, / Of our two cousins coming into London" (V.ii.1–3). Besides the immediate pairing of "our two cousins" as kin and equals, the narrative relates the double royal *entrée* as the last formal ceremony in the play. Since there cannot be two kings, the description images appropriately York's – and England's – crisis in witnessing and recording it, and completes the redifferentiation of the royal pair.

> Then, as I said, the Duke, great Bolingbroke,
> Mounted upon a hot and fiery steed
> Which his aspiring rider seem'd to know,
> With slow but stately pace kept on his course,
> Whilst all tongues cried, "God save thee, Bolingbroke!"
>
> (V.ii.7–11)

In grotesque contrast, there is the mirrored reverse:

> As in a theatre the eyes of men,
> . . . .
> Did scowl on gentle Richard. No man cried, "God save him!"
> No joyful tongue gave him his welcome home,
> But dust was thrown upon his sacred head –
>
> (V.ii.23–30)

No doubt the sight of a monarch so degraded and abused by the citizenry was too painful to be enacted, and so it is theatrically displaced as narrative. According to a Tudor law derived from a 1352 statute from Edward III's reign, it was also treason even to imagine it (Kastan 1986: 473). The verbal re-creation crystallizes York's own crisis of partisanship so that weeping chokes him off. But York did see it; his narrative underscores the painful paradox of what cannot be and nonetheless is. In the exchange between the Duke and his wife, the audience hears it twice, in York's line and in the Duchess's recall of "that sad stop, my lord, / Where rude misgovern'd hands from windows' tops / Threw dust and rubbish on King Richard's head" (V.ii.4–6), and knows that it was said a third time, when the Duke broke off. The imagined/actualized scene also constitutes a third deposition, the public witness and approval of Richard's disgrace. The unthinkable has come to pass, "But heaven hath a hand in these events" (V.ii.37). The issue has already been foretold, and now is told again: "To Bolingbroke are we sworn subjects now, / Whose state and honour I for aye allow" (V.ii.39–40). It is easy to hear this as the "eye for eye" of retribution; indeed in the next lines we learn that Aumerle has been stripped of his title by Henry for supporting Richard, though allowed to remain Earl of Rutland, recreating in part Bolingbroke's position in the early scenes of the play.

In his degraded state, Richard's passage through liminality is momentarily frozen; he is stuck in a nameless, faceless, uncreated condition, neither what he was nor what he will be:

> I have no name, no title –
> No, not that name was given me at the font –
> But 'tis usurp'd. Alack the heavy day,
> That I have worn so many winters out
> And know not now what name to call myself!
> O, that I were a mockery king of snow,
> Standing before the sun of Bolingbroke,
> To melt myself away in water drops!
> (IV.i.255–62)

He has assumed, in Girard's terms,

> the role of the unworthy king, the antisovereign. The king then unloads on this inverted image of himself all his negative attributes. We now have the true pharmakos: the king's

double, but in reverse. He is similar to those mock kings who are crowned at carnival time . . . . But once the carnival is over the anti-king is expelled from the community or put to death, and his disappearance puts an end to all the disorder that his person served to symbolize for the community and also to purge for it.

(1977: 109n.)

The redifferentiation of paired contestants is necessary for both individual and national identity and is accomplished through the ritual process. The relationship between Bolingbroke and Richard, and the double identification of both, at different moments, with both Cain and Abel, is more than a matter of imagistic or symbolic cross-matching. In so far as the stewardship of the "blessed plot" of Gaunt's famous speech (II.i.40–68) is a material manifestation of God's blessing, the differentiation of paired contenders is reiterated throughout the tetralogy, reflected in only slightly altered forms in the pairings, in *1* and *2 Henry IV*, of Hal and Falstaff (or as versions of the father, of Henry and Falstaff), and Hal and Hotspur, and in *Henry V*, of England and France.

Ricardo Quinones locates the origin of civilization with the biblical brothers: "Cain, who aspires to possession, to rights, to identity, is the founder of the first city. Abel then becomes the figure of the right-thinking man who knows he is a stranger and a sojourner among earthly things" (1991: 26–7). Both Richard and Bolingbroke so aspire, and both Richard and Bolingbroke become at alternate moments the stranger and sojourner: Bolingbroke when he is banished and returns in *Richard II*, and again as he waits to die in the "Jerusalem Room" in *2 Henry IV*, and Richard politically excommunicated as "landlord of England" at the start of his play and marginalized at Flint Castle towards the end. In the next generation, Hal reiterates this duality in the Gadshill and Boar's Head episodes, and in a different way, at Agincourt.

The "monstrous Cain" is at once a criminal and a permanent outcast, marked to prevent any possibility of reassimilation. As Quinones argues, the threat that such outcasts pose to material societies is the possibility that they may return to avenge their deprivations; that threat is interpreted not only as against the specific agent of their exclusion but as against civilization itself (1991: 41–3). In the extant dramatic versions of the Cain-and-Abel narrative, the medieval cycle plays, Cain's act of fratricide is given a specifically materialist base; that is, the differentiation of the brother-rivals for God's blessing occurs in the context of their respective "professions," Abel's as shepherd and Cain's as farmer. Specifically, in the Towneley *Mactatio Abel* (Stevens and Cawley 1994), Cain evinces a certain stinginess in regard to the number of sheaves of grain to be offered, and his grudging sacrifice produces only a choking smoke in contrast with Abel's clean voluntary burning. The Chester Cain (Lumiansky and Mills 1974), is even more fully dramatized and presents a more complicated discourse. There he hopes to get away with offering his second-best cuttings, saving the best for himself: Cain's polluting sin was not only his unwilling sacrifice but his conversion, or perversion, of sacred ritual to economic or material concerns. Cain not only refuses God any grain fit for human consumption: "This corne standinge, as mote I thee, / was eaten with beastes, men may see. / God, thou gettest noe other of mee" (533–5), but offers fruitless stalks only: "This earles corne grewe nexte the waye; / of these offer I will todaye. / For cleane corne, by my faye, / of mee gettest thou nought" (541–4). His whole intention is only "too looke if hee / will sende mee any more" (519–20). His offering does not catch fire at all; it is rejected totally. Cain is thoroughly shamed: more than the grain, he himself is an abomination. His punishment is prophesied down to the seventh generation (659–60), which situates the Chester play at the foundation of the genre of dynastic drama and thus of the Shakespearean tetralogies.

The political and economic impact of the Cain-and-Abel narrative resonates in Shakespeare's play, where the crisis of the monarchy stands in close parallel to the contest for land and/or divine favor, which may ultimately be the same thing, the one manifesting the other in material terms. This is clearly illustrated in the Gardeners' scene in III.iv, and in the resonating language and imagery of aborted or inverted crop production throughout the play: in Carlisle's terms, "the blood of English shall manure the ground" and yield "the field of Golgotha and dead men's skulls" (IV.i.137, 144). Both narratives are concerned with kinship and its sacred ritual status, but if one asks why that relationship is sanctified, the materialist answer is because of land use. That issue, we will recall, was the principal charge laid against Richard in Gaunt's deathbed speech: Richard "leas'd out" the "blessed plot," the "other Eden, demi-paradise," and became "landlord of England . . . not king." The commodification of land through enclosures had been an accelerating factor in a growing social and economic crisis from Richard's time through Shakespeare's. There is an interesting symmetry between the banishment of Cain and his loss of the post-Edenic garden, and Richard's undoing and his commodification of the "blessed plot." Such evidence of materialist realism serves, as Robert Weimann pointed out, to anchor awareness of "an aesthetic and historical problem beyond the traditional context" as well as within it, and to record "a new mimetic form of self-expression and self-portrayal" (1978: 63). The way in which a late Elizabethan audience responded to a cycle play such as *Cain and Abel* probably differed from the way a medieval audience did, just as twentieth-century responses to Shakespeare's plays (and to medieval drama) must differ from those of the original audience. In the case of *Richard II* and the Cain-and-Abel plays, the awareness Weimann identifies resonates with multiple referents: the ground of Eden is in Shakespeare identical with England (Berninghausen 1987: 4). Sibling rivalry for God's blessing, the urgency of redifferentiation, fratricide, and the establishment of a new dynasty: these are among the emphases Shakespeare found in the drama of Cain and Abel that linked the crisis of the Tudor monarchy with the history of the world, rendering it at once unavoidable, contemporary, and cyclical.

The idea that the Second Tetralogy, and *Richard II* in particular, tells the story of the passage of England from the Middle Ages into "history" has been widely recognized (Berninghausen 1987; Kernan 1975: 273; cf. Frye 1967: 14). But critics differ in the interpretation of that idea. The general interpretation suggests that the loss of Eden equates with the loss of a medieval "world view," that the historical and political passage we witness in the Second Tetralogy is a fall tantamount to Adam and Eve's, and then again to Cain's. But this view requires a nostalgia that may not have been universal in Tudor England, especially when we consider that the Tudor reign depended heavily upon the deposition of Richard in the first place. As Kernan writes,

> In that Edenic world which Gaunt describes and Richard destroys, every man knew who he was. His religion, his family, his position in society, his assigned place in processions large and small, his coat of arms and his traditional duties told him who he was, what he should do and even gave him the formal language in which to express this socially assigned self. But

79

once, *under the pressures of political necessity and personal desires,* the old system is destroyed, the old identities go with it. *Man then finds himself* in the situation which Richard acts out in IV.i, the deposition scene.

(1975: 273; emphasis added)

In the story of Cain Shakespeare found the movement of historical change "under the pressures of political necessity and personal desires." Cain's banishment extends the map of the world beyond Eden, and further, beyond that East-of-Eden legitimized for Adam and Eve after the expulsion from the garden. In the 1560 Geneva Bible, Cain is the "vagabonde and rennegate" whose punishment clearly differentiates center (Eden), margin (East-of-Eden), and outside (the Land of Nod, where Cain lived out his banishment). In this instance too we find material that is replicated in *Richard II.* Before the murder, Cain and Abel inhabit ground that is already outside of Paradise, from which their parents had been expelled (Frye 1967: 14). But it is still legitimate ground, in so far as their residence there is divinely authorized. It is, in other words, the "margin" between Eden and elsewhere, and is identified as "East-of." Such marginal loci, like marginal statuses, are liminal, ambiguous, and therefore both vulnerable and dangerous (Douglas 1966: 145). This marginalization of Cain and Abel, the immediate context of the fratricide, is replicated in Shakespeare's III.ii and III.iii, in Wales, just before the first deposition. There, abject Richard embeds the humble figure of Abel, with the mocking Henry Bolingbroke in the role of arrogant, rebellious Cain. At this liminal outpost, in this liminal moment, the roles of both men in relation to each other and to the crown and kingdom are ambiguous, ambivalent, neither what they were nor what they will be. They are *becoming* what the historical record will say they were, but Shakespeare stops the action of that passage and centers attention on Richard's self-deposition and his inscription of his own story among the "sad stories of the death of kings" (III.ii.156). In both *Richard II* and *Cain and Abel,* we have more than a version of an historical/biblical record; we have a dramatic interrogation of the reasons for and the process by which it happened, and this interrogation yields a complicated thesis. In the story of Cain we find the explanation of political necessity, for when Cain rose up against his brother, partisanship and dynasty were invented. Gaunt's famous identification of England as "other Eden" would be meaningless if his audience could not distinguish "other *than* Eden," to differentiate "demi-Paradise" from the fallen world. By echoing the cycle play's resonance, Shakespeare directs his audience's attention to both its own proximal past – the generation that saw cycle plays performed – and its very distant past. The contest for husbandry of the "blessed plot" did not begin with Richard II and Henry Bolingbroke but with Cain.

Just as tradition and custom serve political ends, so do retentions of specific traditions and customs a generation or more after they have apparently departed the scene of contemporary life. Foucault's definition of "subjugated knowledges," mentioned earlier, serves well to describe the Elizabethan fate of the cycle plays and all such occluded traditions and customs. Subjugated knowledges are

> a whole set of knowledges that have been disqualified as inadequate . . . or insufficiently elaborated: naive knowledges, located low down on the hierarchy. . . . [A] particular, local, regional knowledge . . . which owes its force only to the harshness with which it is opposed by everything surrounding it . . . [and] allowed to fall into disuse whenever they are not effectively and explicitly maintained in themselves.
>
> (Foucault 1980: 82)

The mechanism of suppression first trivializes and then erases both the knowledge and the language that sustains it. Subjugated knowledges "entertain the claims to attention of local, discontinuous, disqualified, illegitimate knowledges against the claims of a unitary body of theory which would filter, hierarchise and order them in the name of some true knowledge" (Foucault 1980: 83). The relation of this strong language to the demise of the cycle plays may not be immediately evident, especially in view of the relatively privileged and protected status of cycle plays authorized by town, guild, and to some extent ecclesiastic warrant, compared with the marginalized loci and status of Elizabethan public playhouses (Mullaney 1988: 26–59). But Foucault's definition of "subjugated knowledges" applies easily to the demise of the cycle plays in general as a social and theatrical institution, and in fact illuminates Shakespeare's imbrication of the cycle play material in *Richard II*. Localized by both townships and guild management, cycle plays constitute exactly that "particular, local, regional knowledge . . . allowed to fall into disuse whenever they are not effectively and explicitly maintained in themselves." It is useful to recall that although they operated for a time under the aegis of the Catholic Church, they were not strictly the productions of that Church, and therefore when Catholicism and its festivals were suppressed in England, the cycle plays did not immediately suffer the same radical fate. Drama that endures through long passages of time functions kaleidoscopically: turned one way or another, it yields one or another view, or one or another perspective of any particular view, and perhaps reveals more about the focusing powers of the observer than about the observed. What did Shakespeare hear in the *Cain and Abel* play that still spoke loudly to his Elizabethan audience? If, as some critics believe, *Richard II* is "about the end of medieval history" (Berninghausen 1987: 5), then echoes from a specific medieval play about the first murder and the first dynastic differentiation, the first play of politics, serve as a carefully chosen mnemonic of how such a horrific event as fratricide could happen in "demi-paradise." It could happen precisely because it replicates the first such event in the first paradise. The basic outline of the story could of course be identified in the biblical tale, but not the concerns and dimensions of Cain and Abel as *homo economicus*, each negotiating for his patch of the garden and favorite-son status. For that fleshed-out model Shakespeare had the dramatic antecedent of the cycle play, which fills in the outlines of the biblical tale in economic terms. The issue of material concerns is evident elsewhere in the Second Tetralogy: in all of the tavern and Gadshill scenes in *1* and *2 Henry IV*, and in the opening dialogue between the Bishops of Ely and Canterbury in *Henry V*, where the contested matter of lands promised for the church is the reason why the bishops urge Henry to engage the war against France that takes up the rest of the play. The Cain-and-Abel play is the first play, and one already known to many in Shakespeare's audience, that interrogates the issue of land use and retention of goods. Shakespeare's selection and placement of the mnemonic as the frame of his play anchored the transition from medieval history to Elizabethan early-modernity.

Tracing the roots of *Richard II* back to the Cain-and-Abel cycle play offers a view of several kinds of succession, both dynastic and dramaturgical, as the process of political and material selection. Shakespeare's interpolation of the cycle play material was deliberate and pointed: it reminded his audience that what they were seeing in *Richard II* was something they had seen in another form in a previous generation's drama. The public theaters and the plays they housed were the functional archives of what Linda Woodbridge calls "shadow genres,"[7] her term for what Bakhtin describes, in language reminiscent of Foucault's, in discussing the development of the novel:

> Contemporaneity, flowing and transitory, "low," present –
> this "life without beginning or end" was a subject of re-
> presentation only in the low genres. Most important, it was
> the basic subject matter in the broadest and richest of realms,
> the common people's creative culture . . . . The "absolute
> past" of gods, demigods and heroes is here . . . "contemp-
> orized": it is brought low, represented on a plane equal with
> contemporary life, in an everyday environment, in the low
> language of contemporaneity.
>
> (Bakhtin 1981: 20–1)

The *Cain and Abel* cycle play stands in precisely this relation to Shakespeare's *Richard II*. As a popular genre, the cycle play mediates the canonical biblical text and the *de casibus* material of Holinshed, Hall, Froissart, and *The Mirror for Magistrates*; it constitutes a "shadow genre," a parallel text which stands in relation to the canon in much the same way as a *Haftorah* encodes a portion of the *Torah*, as a covert echo of a subjugated knowledge. Despite, or perhaps because of, its discontinuation by 1595, the cycle play's echoes in *Richard II* establish a Bakhtinian *heteroglossia* (Bakhtin 1981:428) of related discourses – theatrical, biblical, historical, and contemporary. Such a view "reveals the same kind of continuity in drama that was characteristic of early modern culture as a whole. Rather than sacred culture suddenly giving way to secular, what we find is a gradual transformation of ideology that accompanies the transformation of social and political relations" (Cox 1989: 31). The ritual foundation of *Richard II* anchors its act of fratricide in a long and authorized tradition rooted in the economic motivations of political action. In this mirror of English "history," both biblical and dynastic, the Tudor age checked its own appearance.

Folded in with the "shadow genre" of the cycle play is another discourse "subjugated" during Elizabeth's reign. Richard's self-carnivalization as "a mockery king of snow" condenses an extended narrative in Holinshed which begins: "Thus was king Richard deprived of all kinglie honour and princelie dignitie, by reason he was so given to follow evill counsell, and used such inconvenient waies and meanes, through insolent misgovernance, and youthfull outrage, though otherwise a right noble and woorthie prince" and ends: "[Yet] hee was a prince the most unthankfullie used of his subjects, of any one of whom ye shall lightlie read" (Bullough 1973: III: 408–9). His sins are enumerated by Holinshed as prodigality and lasciviousness, in which he was not alone: "speciallie in the king, but most cheefelie in the prelacie" (Bullough 1973: III: 409). These are hardly high crimes and capital treasons; Holinshed's Richard was more a Lord of Misrule than a criminal. His implication in Woodstock's death is barely noticed in Holinshed, and however much is made of it by Shakespeare, it is not mentioned again after Act I.

The seriousness of identifying an anointed monarch as Misrule would not have been lost upon Shakespeare's audience. For clearly political reasons, Misrule performances were discontinued in the courts of Mary and Elizabeth after periods of great popularity under Edward VI and occasionally under Henry VIII (Barber 1959: 26; Laroque 1991: 68). Although Elizabeth promoted and supported various seasonal festivities in and out of court, Misrule was not one of them. Even a temporary release of control is fatal to the monarch in unstable times. Elizabeth knew that; Richard learned it in a shower of dust and rubbish.

The carnivalization of Richard, first by himself and then by his trash-throwing subjects, prepares him, as Girard notes, for the role of *pharmakos*, for it is only as his own double, not as his kingly self, that he can take on the sacrificial function of the scapegoat. Richard wants to see Henry, not himself, as the *roi soleil.* But Henry has already identified himself inversely with rain, not sun, in the lines quoted earlier from III.iii. It is Richard who is linked with the defeated sun (II.iv.21). Richard thinks himself inadequate to the role of sun; he is the sun's son (or, if "sun" signifies an anointed king, the sun's grandson): "Down, down I come, like glist'ring Phaeton" (III.iii.178); in that image is his own admission of his failed potential. The mockery king of snow is the inverse and alter-ego of the sun-king; in those terms, as sun turns to snow, Richard undoes himself. But snow is also the frozen, rigid form of rain, Henry's symbol, and rain melts and washes away snow. Sun and rain are potentially both destructive and restorative elements. The ambivalent meanings of these meteorological images prevent facile conclusions about Shakespeare's view of Richard's sins and Henry's heroism.

Commenting on Richard's humiliation, Bristol writes:

> These images of royal abjection and victimization do not
> have the purely redressive and exemplary features of an
> actual ritual. The violent uncrowning of the royal martyr or
> royal villain is invariably accompanied by a more generalized,
> pervasive social violence or civil war . . . . The relationship
> between victimized king and victimized kingdom is complex
> and elusive.
>
> (1985: 197–8)

For Richard's deposition and Henry's accession to have those
redressive features, the ambiguity of Richard's alternately conservative and destructive behavior would have to be resolved as
preeminently negative, and the matching ambiguity of Henry's
restructuring of the monarchy would have to appear as positive.
But the play does not allow such an easy and comfortable resolution; the sugar-coating of the "Tudor Myth" did not entirely mask
the bitter taste of Richard's deposition and the continual
outbreaks of rebellion during Henry IV's reign. The restorative
function of uncrowning followed by new crowning is absent from
the play because the redressive capabilities of such rituals had long
since been lost to medieval and Renaissance England, leaving only
the outward forms of ritual actions. Rituals evacuated of meaning
cannot work, and historically they did not work; the restoration of
England's political stability took longer than the unquiet reign of
Henry IV. Against the backdrop of an England whose rituals had
turned from religious to secular to spectacular, and from purgative
to political to *pro forma*, *Richard II* performs the "movement from
ceremony and ritual to history" (Kernan 1970: 247) of the rest of
the Henriad. By attending to the changes during Richard's reign
in the way ritual was variously honored, aborted, subverted, debased, and ignored, *Richard II* dramatizes the inescapable cost of
secularizing a ritual-centered political ecology. The price of
"history" is a loss of the ritual integrity that stabilizes its movement
and protects its original social, political, and religious structures.

THOU BLEEDING PIECE OF EARTH:
THE RITUAL GROUND OF *JULIUS CAESAR*

The process through which a particular ritual emerges as a reposi-
tory of core values is in part explained by Claude Lévi-Strauss's

principle of *bricolage*. In contrast to the ordering and regulating processes of ritual, its originary structural elements can seem to have been assembled at random, as a *bricoleur* or "jack-of-all-trades" assembles the tools and media that may "come in handy." The *bricoleur*'s

> universe of instruments is closed and the rules of his game are always to make do with "whatever is at hand," that is to say with a set of tools and materials which is always finite and is also heterogeneous because what it contains . . . is the contingent result of all the occasions there have been to renew or enrich the stock or to maintain it with the remains of previous constructions or destructions. [It] is to be defined only by its potential use or . . . because the elements are collected or retained on the principle that "they may always come in handy." Such elements are specialized up to a point, sufficiently for the "bricoleur" not to need the equipment and knowledge of all trades and professions, but not enough for each of them to have only one definite and determinate use. They each represent a set of actual and possible relations
> . . . .

> (Lévi-Strauss 1966: 17–18)

Bricolage is Lévi-Strauss's model for the construction of mythic thought and its expression in ritual action. A large variety of constitutive combinations is possible, and these are expressed as needed in signs linking images and concepts. Over time, the signs are reified and codified into a recognizable and repeatable rite. Mythical thought is itself a *bricoleur*: it "builds up structures by fitting together events, or rather the remains of events . . . . [It] is imprisoned in the events and experiences which it never tires of ordering and re-ordering in its search to find them a meaning. But it also . . . protest[s] against the idea that anything can be meaningless" (Lévi-Strauss 1966: 22).

The seeming randomness of *bricolage*, in contrast to the systematic accretions of scientific operations, is one of the issues in Lévi-Strauss's work which Derrida attacks with some passion in "Structure, Sign, and Play in the Discourse of the Human Sciences" (1978: 282–92), on the grounds that it implies uncritically "all reference to a *center*, to a *subject*, to a privileged *reference*, to an origin, or to an absolute *archia*" (1978: 286). In fact, although it seems so, *bricolage* is not random selection; selection occurs because an event or element bears a meaning or use that initially contributes to, and then becomes constitutive of, the whole, as Lévi-Strauss makes clear in the passage quoted above (1966: 17–18). It does not assign "an origin" or "an absolute *archia*," firstly because there is often a plurality of origins, subjects, etc., and secondly because these are often unrecoverable by ethnology. The obscurity of originary meanings and uses, Geertz's "thick description" (1973: 7–10), makes the tasks of anthropologists difficult and problematizes their complex findings. Accumulation or *bricolage* is the process of culture, which Geertz calls an "acted document"; reading it is "like trying to read . . . a manuscript – foreign, faded, full of ellipses, incoherencies, suspicious emendations, and tendentious commentaries, but written not in conventionalized graphs of sound but in transient examples of shaped behavior" (1973: 10).

Bricolage's "protest against the idea that anything can be meaningless" is the core function of mythical thinking; meaninglessness, ambiguity, arbitrariness, and marginality are dangerous to cultural stability. Ritual action is a community's way of containing events within the boundaries of understandable and thus manageable meanings. This capacity for creating and managing meaning is the reason why Lévi-Strauss calls mythical thought "an intellectual form of 'bricolage'" (1966: 21). Events that appear meaningless or whose meanings cannot be assigned, understood, or agreed upon pose an enormous threat to a community's or an individual's survival. And when survival's at the stake, human beings get into devastating conflict.

Whereas Derrida's rejection of identifiable origin and "absolute *archia*" cautions against any implication that ritual operates independently of particular dominant political interests, that it has a life of its own, anthropologists such as Geertz, Lévi-Strauss, and Durkheim (1963: 1972) grapple with admittedly broad but important generalizations about cultural processes. It is easy enough, perhaps too easy, to reject such generalizing theses because a particular instantiate structure entails a visible politics which the general thesis fails to accommodate. It is important to recognize that both subjects and controlling hierarchies are themselves part of a diachronically flexible framework not only of "culture" (in whatever sense a particular theorist means the term) but of the theorist's or analyst's viewpoint as well.

Although it certainly reflects power relations, communal ritual itself does not "control" individuals or society; generally it is not, where consensually practiced, imposed as a tool for control in the sense of domination. (I am, for the moment, specifically excepting colonialist, imperialist, or inquisitional coercions, which are among the ritualistic concerns of *Titus Andronicus* discussed in chapter 4, and reconsidered in the concluding chapter.) As Catherine Bell has recently argued, ritual often constitutes a site where power relations are contested because it expresses "an ordering of power as an assumption of the way things really are . . . . Hence, the relationship of ritualization and social control may be better approached in terms of how ritual activities constitute a specific embodiment and exercise of power" (1992: 170). Such an approach, she adds, investigates not "how ritual 'controls' but how it 'defines' social norms and presents them for internalization" (1992: 175). Ritual practice is itself a social institution, created, sustained, and deployed – sometimes even manipulated – by larger social institutions. This is not always a bad thing, depending upon which institution one subscribes to and where one stands in relation to it. The questions that ought to be put, in negotiating Geertz's or Lévi-Strauss's useful categories with Derrida's objections, are these: whose interests does a particular ritual action serve at a specific moment in "real life" or in a dramatic representation? What interpretation is given of that action? By and for whom is it given? Who accepts that interpretation? Within the parameters of what I am calling consensual practice, as in the case of *Julius Caesar*, there is both a Lévi-Straussian *bricolage* and a Derridean "play" (1978: 278–9) in the representation of ritual.

Julius Caesar begins at the Feast of the Lupercal, the Roman celebration on 13–15 February which later became St Valentine's day and often coincides in the Christian calendar with Mardi Gras and the Carnival season, and which, in Shakespeare's play, quickly passes into history's most famous *ides* of March. An earlier generation of critics explained the conflation of the festival and Caesar's assassination primarily as a "dramatic economy," a structural device for the exposition of the main characters and the juxtaposition of the rather "sporty" aspects of the holiday to the more serious political business of the conspiracy, murder, and civil war to follow (Dorsch 1955: xvi; J. D. Wilson 1968: xvii–xviii; Bonjour 1958: 16–17; Stirling 1951: 767–8). But perhaps because of the shift in anthropological theory since the late 1960s away from "concern with consensus at the expense of conflict" (P. Burke

1978: 203), more recent studies (Laroque 1991: 206–7; Liebler 1981; R. Wilson 1987: 36–9) consider the play's opening on the Lupercal as a very different kind of "dramatic economy." It is the strategically applied marker for a ritual whose purpose and practice, like the joust in *Richard II*, had devolved by the time of the play's historical setting to an ambiguously construed Derridean "event" (1978: 278). The first act's Lupercalian setting is an effective context for a play shot through with socially and politically disastrous misconstructions and misrecognitions, beginning with the opening scene's confusions about exactly what – or who – is being celebrated. It situates Brutus's idea of the assassination as a "sacrifice," the ultimate failure of the design, and the cataclysmic political and religious changes in Rome in 44 B.C.E.

Of all the festivals referred to in Shakespearean drama, the Lupercal is given remarkably detailed attention, which in itself raises questions about what Shakespeare knew about it and why he thought it so important. The ethnocentric critical claim of an earlier generation – that Shakespeare was "producing a *mimesis* of the veritable history of the most important people (humanly speaking) who ever lived, the concern of every educated man in Europe" (Spencer 1957: 28),[8] and that therefore all things Roman were interesting because they were Roman – now seems insufficient.

The fullest discussion of the Lupercalia extant during Shakespeare's lifetime was Ovid's *Fasti*, printed in a 1574 Latin octavo by T. Vautroullier, and unavailable in English until the 1640 translation by John Gower as *Ovids festivalls, or Romane Calendar*. The references to the Lupercal in North's translation of Plutarch's *Lives* of Caesar and Antony (there are none in that of Brutus) are brief and playful: in the *Life of Caesar* we learn only that it was "the feast of sheap heards or heard men," that the race was run by "divers noble mens sonnes . . . striking *in sport* them they meete in their way with leather thonges . . . to make them geve place" (Plutarch 1967: V: 62, emphasis added) and that being touched by these thongs was believed to cure barrenness and ease childbirth. Similarly, in the *Life of Antony* we read again of the "*sport* of the runners," who, "running naked up and downe the city . . . *for pleasure* do strike them they meete in their way" (1967: VI: 13, emphasis added). The *Life of Romulus*, however, the first Roman *Life* in the collection, provides a substantive and serious account of the festival, its history and implications, and its actual as well as its symbolic relation to the last days of Julius Caesar. In the *Romulus*

Plutarch explains that the Lupercalia were the oldest and most sacred rites of purgation and fertility in the ancient Roman calendar, originating before history, and celebrated on the "unfortunate days of the month of February, which are called the purging days" (1967: I: 98–100). Their association with the figure of Romulus situates them within the foundation myth of Roman civilization. Much of Plutarch's later narrative of Caesar's death echoes that of Romulus (1967: I: 102–10); in the linkage of the two biographical narratives as well as in fact, the culture that so powerfully captured Shakespeare's imagination effectively began with the one and ended with the other. In the long and imprecise period of time between the two lives, the reduction of the festival's observance to "sport" locates a cultural "play" whose lurching trajectory inscribes the tragedy of republican Rome.

Because its origins are pre-historical, the Lupercal is rooted in an unrecoverable mythical golden age, a reference of nostalgia and anxiety by the end of the first century B.C.E. When Ovid, at around the turn of the milennium, and Plutarch, toward the end of the first century C.E., write about the Lupercal, they are describing what is already a product of *bricolage*. Their narratives, laced with disclaimers of disputed reports and received lore, constitute more instances of *bricolage*, and reconstruct a cultural "memory" of foundation, of a centered stability sprung from and thus incorporating instability. Lévi-Strauss's principle comfortably accommodates contradictory and unstable narratives, without attempting to reconcile the contradictions. Derrida's remarks about the apparent indeterminacy of *bricolage* underlie his concept of "contradictorily coherent" structures (1978: 279) within whose aegis the center is both present and absent. In *Julius Caesar* the center is the object of continual contestation. Whereas the Lupercal as an institution is explicable as a product of *bricolage*, its contested status in 44 B.C.E. submits to the Derridean principle, which is useful in explaining how culture stands on such "slippery ground" (where Antony, in a wonderful pun, locates both his credibility and his feet on a stage soaked in Caesar's blood at III.i.191). Derrida writes,

> The concept of centered structure is in fact the concept of a play [i.e., flexion] based on a fundamental ground, a play constituted on the basis of a fundamental immobility and a reassuring certitude, which is itself beyond the reach of play.

And on the basis of this certitude anxiety can be mastered, for anxiety is invariably the result of a certain mode of being implicated in the game, of being caught by the game, of being as it were at stake in the game from the outset.

(1978: 279)

The lost origins of the Lupercalia matter only in so far as they constitute an imaginary memory of purpose, for "repetitions, substitutions, transformations, and permutations are always *taken* from a history of meaning . . . whose origin may always be reawakened or whose end may always be anticipated in the form of presence . . . which is beyond play" (Derrida 1978: 279). The Lupercal entails this immanence for all its participants in Shakespeare's drama; conflict arises from the outset because the identity of that immanence is itself subject to "play," in the full range of the word's meanings.

There is "play" in the several interpretations of what is being celebrated when the tribunes confront the carpenter and cobbler in Shakespeare's opening scene. The laborers think they are celebrating a civic festival commemorating a military action, Caesar's victory "over Pompey's blood." For the tribunes, the celebration of Caesar's victory reveals a popular fickleness; Marullus reminds the workers that not long ago they had similarly congratulated Pompey (I.i.32–47). Such flexible loyalty, combined with the conversion of the Lupercal to a secular event whose observation has become ambiguous (I.i.64–9), constitutes a sacrilege: "Run to your houses, fall upon your knees, / Pray to the gods to intermit the plague / That needs must light on this ingratitude" (I.i.53–5). Obviously from the start of the play, the festival's "meaning" has already begun to slip from consensus. This Shakespeare would have read in Plutarch's descriptions in the *Lives* of Caesar and Antony noted above, with its brief and sportive references to the Lupercal, and echoed in Brutus's assertion that he is "not gamesome" and lacks "some part / Of that quick spirit that is in Antony" (I.ii.28–9). In a Derridean "series of substitutions of center for center" (1978: 279), the ancient, sacral, mythic center symbolized by the Lupercalia, the root definition of Roman civilization, has collapsed into a redefinition of Rome "founded" by Julius Caesar, whose appropriation is, in turn, challenged by the tribunes and the conspirators. This ceremonial ambiguity also would have a powerful contemporary resonance for Shakespeare's audience, recalling perhaps the abolition by the Crown in 1536 of between forty and fifty local and national *festa ferianda*, or holy days requiring church attendance and abstention from servile work, a Reformation maneuver that met with particular resistance from agricultural and other workers, and particular support from landowners and employers (Duffy 1992: 42–3). In light of these sixteenth-century alterations, the contested nature of the Lupercalia emerges as part of a deeper contestation of the economic matrix of the political balances at stake in Rome and the roles of the *plebs* (their autonomy vs. their submission) in sustaining class divisions.

Brutus's design for the conspirators as "sacrificers, but not butchers," and "purgers, not murderers" occurs in the context of these cultural redefinitions: he would reverse the opening scene's transformation of a religious event to a secular one. But more than that, he articulates this objectively political act in manifestly religious terms. Indeed, for Brutus, the language of politics is simultaneously the language of religious ritual. The play's opening upon the Lupercal prepares a way for us to see Brutus's ritualistic coloring of the assassination as something other than naive or evil. It is not a design he has simply made up, but rather one which the transitional atmosphere that hangs over Rome allows him to construct as credible.

Even more than Richard II, Brutus is basically a conservative. He fights to keep Rome a republic, whereas Caesar seeks to reinvent it as a monarchy. This battle over cultural redefinition constitutes a crisis which finds its model in the moment of first definition, the Romulean foundation commemorated in the Lupercal. Plutarch's narratives of the lives of Caesar and Romulus make several suggestions towards this linkage; Shakespeare makes at least one of his own, in an incident in the play that appears only in the *Romulus*. Among the "horrid sights" that forewarn of Caesar's death, Calphurnia describes a vision of "clouds / . . . Which drizzled blood upon the Capitol" (II.ii.19–21). There is no such image in the *Lives* of Caesar, Antony, or Brutus, but there is one in the *Romulus*. Plutarch reports a retaliatory ambush by Romulus against neighboring Fidena, after which "there rose suche a great plague in Rome, that men died sodainely, and were not sicke: the earth brought forth no fruite: bruite beasts delivered no increase of their kynde: there rayned also droppes of bloude in Rome, as they saye" (1967: I: 102). A few pages later, Plutarch describes the meteorological events that accompanied the death of Romulus:

sodainely the weather chaunged, and overcast so terribly, as it is not to be tolde nor credited. For first, the sunne was darckned as if it had bene very night: this darcknes was not in a calme or still, but there fell horrible thunders, boysterous windes, and flashing lightnings on every side, which made the people ronne away . . . but the Senatours kept still close together.

(1967: I: 107)

There is a striking similarity between these descriptions and that which ends the *Life of Caesar*:

Againe, of signes in the element, the great comet which seven nightes together was seene very bright after Caesars death, the eight night after was never seene more. Also the brightnes of the sunne was darckned, the which all that yeare through rose very pale, and shined not out, whereby it gave but small heate: therefore the ayer being very clowdy and darke, by the weaknes of the heate that could not come foorth, did cause the earth to bring foorth but raw and unrype frute, which rotted before it could rype.

(1967: V: 70-1)

These are doomsday images of sterility (which Shakespeare had earlier suggested in *A Midsummer Night's Dream*, in Titania's allegations against Oberon [II.i.88–114]) that threaten the welfare of any agrarian state, against which purgation and fertility rituals such as the Lupercalia were invented. They suggest too the plague against which Marullus warned, and the sense of dis-ease evoked in the play: Calphurnia's sterility; Brutus's unaccustomed estrangement ("Vexed I am / Of late with passions of some difference" [I.ii.39–40]), and his plea of ill health to deflect Portia's questions. The most significant instance of disease in the play is, of course, the catalogue of Caesar's infirmities, and especially his "falling sickness," which Cassius immediately analogizes to the community's political illness:

CASCA.   He fell down in the market-place, and foam'd at mouth, and was speechless.

BRUTUS.   'Tis very like, he hath the falling sickness.

CASSIUS. No, Caesar hath it not; but you, and I, And honest Casca, we have the falling sickness.

CASCA. I know not what you mean by that, but I am sure
Caesar fell down.

(I.ii.252–8)

Plutarch barely mentions Caesar's epilepsy (1967: V: 17);
Shakespeare certainly seems to have exploited this brief notice. It
is interesting to note that in *The Romane Questions* (available in
English by 1603, in Philemon Holland's translation, too late for
Julius Caesar), Plutarch specifically associates the "falling sickness"
with the goats (and sometimes dogs) that, as the *Romulus* indicates
(1967: I: 98–100), were usually sacrificed at the Lupercalia.
Plutarch writes at Question 111:

> there seemeth not to be a beast in the world so much given
> to the falling sicknesse, as [the Goat] is; nor infecteth so
> soone those that either eat of the flesh or once touch it, when
> it is surprised with this evill. The cause whereof some say to
> be the streightnesse of those conduits and passages by which
> the spirits go and come, which oftentimes happen to be
> intercepted and stopped. And this they conjecture by the
> small and slender voice that this beast hath; & the better to
> confirme the same, we do see ordinarily, that men likewise
> who be subject to this malady, grow in the end to have such
> a voice as in some sort resembleth the bleating of goats.

(1892: 161–2)

Shakespeare's dubious Latin literacy and the date of Holland's
translation make it uncertain whether Shakespeare knew this as-
sociation of goats with the "falling sickness" and its contagion, and
then linked Caesar's "sacrifice" with that of the Lupercalian goat.
This is a particularly regrettable critical uncertainty, because *The
Romane Questions* offers a mine of intriguing connections with
Shakespeare's play. Question 63, for example, investigates the
Roman "Rex sacrorum," or "king of sacrifices":

> the Romans having cleane chased and expelled their kings,
> established in their stead another under officer whom they
> called King, unto whom they granted oversight and charge of
> sacrifices onely, but permitted him not to exercise or execute
> any office of State, nor to intermedle in publick affaires; to
> the end it should be knowen to the world, that they would
> not suffer any person to raigne at *Rome*, but onely over the

ceremonies of sacrifices, nor endure the verie name of
Roialtie, but in respect of the gods. And to this purpose upon
the verie common place neere unto *Comitium*; they use to
have a solemn sacrifice for the good estate of the citie; which
so soone as ever this king hath performed, he taketh his legs
and runnes out of the place, as fast as ever he can.

(1892: 97)

Ovid incidentally notes that two days after the Lupercal was the
Feast of Quirinus, the name Romulus was given upon his posthu-
mous deification; the Feast of Quirinus, he says, is also called the
Feast of Fools (*Ovid* 1931: II: 513).

Shakespeare suggests these metatheatrical connections
between Caesar and Romulus in the remainder of Casca's report:

> CASCA.   . . . If the tag-rag people did not clap and hiss him,
> according as he pleased and displeased them, as
> they used to do the players in the theater, I am no
> true man.
> BRUTUS. What said he when he came unto himself?
> CASCA.   Marry, before he fell down, when he perceiv'd the
> common herd was glad he refus'd the crown, he
> pluck'd me ope his doublet, and offer'd them his
> throat to cut . . . . And so he fell.

(I.ii.258–68)

Caesar's gesture toward himself as sacrificial goat is repeated later
on in Brutus's address to the crowd after the assassination: "as I
slew my best lover for the good of Rome, I have the same dagger
for myself, when it shall please my country to need my death"
(III.ii.45–7). Both Caesar and Brutus understand the popular
appeal of a displayed willingness to serve as *pharmakos*, though
Caesar understands better than Brutus the pure theatricality of
such a gesture, and knows also how to work the crowd to "clap and
hiss him, according as he pleased and displeased them, as they
used to do the players in the theater." His sacrificial gesture may
be insincere, but it is nonetheless crucially important as a gesture.

These connections support the view of some recent critics (R.
Wilson 1987; Laroque 1991: 206) that Shakespeare fashions Caesar
as a Carnival-king, the *rex stultorum* whose festival day of "monarchy" ends in deposition and sacrifice. But these ancient
connections also problematize such views, because the deposition

and sacrifice of the *pharmakos/rex stultorum* was supposed to purify the community, cleanse it of disease and restore its health. That is what (ideally) happens in the case of actual ritual practice, but not in tragedy, and not in Shakespearean tragedy. In *Richard II*, as we have seen, the expiation that would have completed the king's "sacrifice" was aborted; in *Julius Caesar*, Rome's "plague" has, in the conspirators' view, progressed too far to be stopped. As Cassius says, everyone "hath the falling sickness." People walk the streets at night in this play, instead of sleeping peacefully, even though, as Cicero advises, "this disturbed sky / Is not to walk in" (I.iii.39–40). Insomnia, morbidity, and a general feeling of disease prevails. Casca plays dumb; he "puts on this tardy form" (I.ii.299) to match the requirements of the time; and Ligarius arrives at Brutus's house cloaked in his shroud, anxious for Brutus's "piece of work that will make sick men whole" (II.i.327). After the assassination, "Men, wives, and children stare, cry out, and run, / As it were doomsday" (III.i.97–8).

One of the last acts of Romulus's life was the institution of the very system Brutus seeks to preserve. When he inherited control of the city of Alba, in order to "winne the favour of the people there," Romulus

> turned the Kingdome to a Comon weale, and every yere dyd chuse a new magistrate to minister justice to the Sabynes. This president taught the noble men of Rome to seeke and desire to have a free estate, where no subject should be at the commaundement of a king alone, and where every man should commaund and obey as should be his course.
>
> (Plutarch 1967: I: 106)

Under this system, the patricians had no real power, just honorific titles, and were called upon only *pro forma* in governmental matters. Romulus offended the Senators by acting without their consultation, and now Plutarch's narrative really begins to sound familiar:

> Whereupon the Senatours were suspected afterwards that they killed him, when with in fewe dayes after it was sayed, he vanished away so straungely, that no man ever knewe what became of him . . . . Howbeit, Romulus vanished away sodainely, there was neither seene pece of his garments, nor yet was there found any parte of his body. Therefore some have

96

thought that the whole Senatours fell upon him together in the temple of Vulcan, and how after they had cut him in peces, every one carried away a pece of him, folded close in the skyrte of his robe.

(1967: I: 106)

In the end, Romulus's death is accompanied by the same sort of meteorological disturbance that we read of at the end of the *Life of Caesar*. The similarity may not have been coincidental, since all accounts of Romulus's death written after 44 B.C.E. were modeled on Caesar's murder (Ogilvie 1965: 85). The *Romulus* supplies details missing from the *Life of Caesar*: confused and credulous plebeians running about in a state of panic, a controlled Senatorial conspiracy, and Romulus's posthumous deification by the Senate, to appease the plebs. And this is where, with Shakespeare's play, we came in.

The cataclysm with which the *Romulus* ends is a prototype of the one that threatens throughout the first two acts of *Julius Caesar*, erupts in the third, and engulfs Rome in "domestic fury and fierce civil strife" – as Antony promised Caesar's corpse – until the play's end. The "division 'tween our souls" that nearly destroys the friendship of Cassius and Brutus, the disjunction of remorse from power that Brutus fears in Caesar, the insurrection in the state of man that Brutus finds in himself: the play abounds in images of fission within and between individuals as well as in the *polis*. But the "ambivalent," "ambiguous," and "divided" (Schanzer 1963: 23; Rabkin 1967: 114, 119–20; Champion 1976: 113; de Gerenday 1974: 25, 32), or more recently "paradoxical" readings (R. Wilson 1987: 41) that critics have found in this play belong not only to the behavior of characters or to critical responses. In Caesar's last days, ambiguity was the plague that threatened Rome's cultural identity. Shakespeare's play concentrates a fairly accurate sense of the conditions represented in Plutarch's narratives.

Such confusion situates the play's discourse in the contest for power, not only in terms of who shall rule but also in terms of what is being ruled. It was this confusion that enabled power-hungry men like Caesar and Antony to alter the very nature of the state from republic to empire and redirect the course of its history. Richard Wilson argues plausibly that "the Shakespearean text anticipates the counter-revolution of the Cromwellian Commonwealth and faithfully enacts the coercive strategy of those subtle London masters who 'stir up servants at [*sic*] an act of rage' the better to control them," but not, as he says, "for the restoration of the status quo" (1987: 41). The "status quo" is precisely not what Caesar and Antony seek to preserve; that project belongs, unsuccessfully, to Brutus the idealist,[9] who wants to hold fast to a Rome that, from the beginning of the play, is already evaporating. His design for the assassination – that it look like a religious sacrifice – seen in the context of the play's Lupercalian opening, shows how far gone and past recovery the old Rome is.

Historically, in 44 B.C.E., subversion of the meaning and significance of "all true rites and lawful ceremonies" (III.i.241) was abetted specifically by Caesar's design. It was at that year's Lupercal that Caesar changed the nature of the festival's observance by adding a new team of celebrants bearing his own name (the *Luperci Iulii*) to the traditional two (the *Luperci Fabiani* and *Quintiliani*), and appointed Antony as its leader. This gave Antony the "right" to offer him the laurel crown "on the Lupercal" (III.ii.95), thereby making the holiday a political one in Caesar's honor. As the Lupercal had once been Romulus's festival, so now it becomes Caesar's, and equates him with the posthumously deified Romulus (Plutarch 1967: I: 108). Thus Caesar pretended to both a contraventional Roman "monarchy" and an equally contraventional *living* human "divinity"; Cassius's complaint that "this man / Is now become a god" (I.ii.115–16) is entirely justified.

The contestational ambiguity that clouds and subverts the ritual practices of this Rome-in-transition grounds all of the play's "ambiguities," and makes Cicero's apothegm, "men may construe things after their fashion, / Clean from the purpose of the things themselves" (I.iii.34–5), emblematic for the whole play. These misconstructions align with the specific misconstruction of ritual and tradition with which the play opens. Misconstruction and misrecognition are inevitable when the "true rites and lawful ceremonies" that reify cultural identity and assure its continuation are suddenly changed or erased. Marullus's altercation with the laborers at the start of the play is only the first instance of this pervasive ambivalence. He represents a remnant of the Old Roman conservatism, and his argument with the workers reminds them of both traditional ritual observance and old Roman values such as loyalty, constancy, and gratitude. In this he prefigures Brutus, and like Brutus he fails because Rome has lost touch with the real sacramental import of the ritual. He does not acknowledge the

holiday's transformation from religious to secular and therefore
"misconstrues" it. The same conditions allow for the contradictory
interpretations of Calphurnia's dream and for the mob's shifting
approval first of Brutus's, then of Antony's presentations of the
murder. Portia fatally misreads reports of the battle, and Cassius
mistakes shouts of victory from Brutus's camp for those of Antony's,
leaving Titinius to wail: "Alas, thou hast misconstrued everything!"
(V.iii.84). Cicero's warning and Titinius's lament bracket the play
in a framework of misrecognition that encloses Brutus, the
"noblest Roman of them all" (V.v.68), who acted "only in a general
honest thought / And common good" (V.v.71–2), and all of the
play's Resistance Movement against the changes of Caesarism.

Such confusions signal the split world of Rome, where the
month between the Feast of the Lupercal and the *ides* of March
comprises the last days and nights of the Republic. The
accustomed ground of social, political, and religious practice is
cracking open, or so the omens indicate: Casca asks, "Who ever
knew the heavens menace so?" and Cassius answers, "Those that
have known the earth so full of faults" (I.iii.44–5). Within the
fissure can be seen the structure of the civilization that underlies
the imminently toppling order. It is not only Caesar's death that
the play encompasses, or the deaths of the principal conspirators,
or that of the poor poet who had the wrong name, or even those
of the hundreds of nameless Romans who burned with the city.
Besides all these, we witness the end of a political as well as a
religious order: Caesar's coronation would have signified the end
of the Republic, and his death fails to preserve it. It is important to
remember that all the prodigies and portents, all the insomnia,
estrangement, and confusion, all the signs of disease occur before
Caesar is killed, even before the full conspiracy is mounted. They
are not responses to Caesar's death but rather to conditions set in
the last month of his life. The disturbance noted in the opening
scenes of the play is the gathering movement of catastrophe, of the
"plague" Marullus warned of, that grows from the events of this last
month. The prayer to "intermit the plague" to which Marullus
exhorts the carpenter and cobbler should be a prayer for cleansing
and purification. The need would have been met by traditional
observance of the Lupercalia, but in 44 B.C.E. such traditions were
vitiated and little respected beyond their empty ceremonial forms.

Without proper observance of the appropriate purgative ritual,
some other ceremony, or the semblance of one, appears in its

place. The imagery of blood sacrifice, so abundant in this play, is more evidence of the perversion of traditional rites. Virtually all of this is Shakespeare's invention: although Plutarch describes Caesar's assassination vividly, his image is "as a wilde beaste taken of hunters" (1967: V: 68), which of course gives Antony his image of Caesar as "a deer, strooken by many princes" (III.i.209).[10] In fact, none of the images in the play suggesting blood sacrifice or ritual of any kind (aside from the references to the Lupercal race) derives from any of the three main *Lives*. Calphurnia's dream of Caesar's statue, "Which, like a fountain with an hundred spouts, / Did run pure blood; and many lusty Romans / Came smiling and did bathe their hands in it" (II.ii.77–9), and Decius's flattering interpretation that it "Signifies that from you great Rome shall suck / Reviving blood, and that great men shall press / For tinctures, stains, relics, and cognizance" (II.ii.87–9) are both Shakespeare's ideas; Plutarch simply reports the dream as an image of Caesar slain and the statue toppled (1967: V: 65). Brutus's design to "carve" Caesar as "a dish fit for the gods," to be "call'd purgers, not murderers" (II.i.173–80), to "be sacrificers, but not butchers" (II.i.166), and his enactment of Calphurnia's dream: "Stoop, Romans, stoop, / And let us bathe our hands in Caesar's blood / Up to the elbows" (III.i.105–7) – all of these rhetorical images are Shakespeare's embroidery over the plain presentation in Plutarch.

Without any recognizably direct warrant from the three *Lives* for these gory images, critics have read them as Shakespearean shock tactics meant to present "the noble Brutus suddenly turned into a savage" (Kirschbaum 1949: 523–4; also Welsh 1975: 500), and have thought that Shakespeare invented the bloody hand-washing as he seemed to have invented the expanded imagery of Calphurnia's dream. But the cutting up of the *pharmakos*, whose blood is then smeared upon the flesh of the priestly celebrants, is one of the central rites of the Lupercalia. This is described at length in the *Romulus*:

> For goates . . . are killed, then they bring two young boyes, noble mens sonnes, whose foreheads they touch with the knife bebloudied with the bloude of the goates that are sacrificed. By and by they drye their foreheads with wolle dipped in milke. Then the yong boyes must laugh immediately after they have dried their foreheads. That done

they cut the goates skinnes, and make thongs of them, which
they take in their hands, and ronne with them all about the
cittie.

(Plutarch 1967: I: 99)[11]

This passage locates Shakespeare's otherwise inexplicable bloody
images as consistent with and traditional to the fertility aspect of
the Lupercalia and contextualizes Brutus's insistence on the semblance of a ritual as the pattern for Caesar's assassination.

It is important to remember that it is Antony, not Brutus, who is
the new-made official Lupercus, and that while he opposes Brutus
both covertly and openly until the end of the play, he actually
endorses the idea that Caesar's death is a sacrifice. It is Antony who
privately addresses Caesar's body as "thou bleeding piece of earth"
(III.i.254), and publicly markets Caesar's body as a sacred object:

Let but the commons hear this testament,
Which (pardon me) I do not mean to read,
And they would go and kiss dead Caesar's wounds
And dip their napkins in his sacred blood;
Yea, beg a hair of him for memory,
And dying, mention it within their wills,
Bequeathing it as a rich legacy
Unto their issue.

(III.ii.130–7)

These lines recall John Heywood's interlude, *The Four PP* (printed
1544), whose Pardoner's pack is filled with "the great-toe of the
Trinity," the "blessed jaw-bone of All-Hallows," and "the buttock-bone
of Pentecost" (Heywood 1970: 497–521), and other phony relics, and
anticipate Shakespeare's own Autolycus: "They throng who should
buy first, as if my trinkets had been hallow'd and brought a benedic-
tion to the buyer" (*Winter's Tale* IV.iv.600–2). But in *Julius Caesar*, this
mercantilism is not used for parody: it is a very serious maneuver by
Antony to "sell" Caesar's sacrificial function. Whereas Brutus ritual-
izes Caesar's body, Antony literally commodifies it as a collection of
relics which he then peddles to the crowd. Caesar's sanctification is
bought by giving "To every several man, seventy-five drachmas"
(III.ii.242). This gesture effectively dismantles the collective
"commons" and fractures it into an aggregation of individuals ("every
several man"); the body itself becomes a property whose numberless
individual hairs can be passed on "as a rich legacy."

As leader of the Julian Luperci, Antony represents the sacramental system invented by Caesar. The difference between the old system and the new is precisely the difference between Republic – a franchise of equals within ranks – and Empire, which recognizes the primacy of an individual. This is the core of Cassius's complaint against Caesar:

> When could they say (till now) that talk'd of Rome
> That her wide walks encompass'd but one man?
> Now is it Rome indeed, and room enough,
> When there is in it but one only man!
>
> (I.ii.154–7)

The new order, whose shrine is Caesar's individual but divisible corpse, is a duplicitous, mercenary, opportunistic one whose ritual practice is inscribed within an emergent market economy; "this man is now become a god" by purchasing the rights/rites.

Whereas Brutus invites the conspirators to bathe their arms in Caesar's blood, in a private in-gathering gesture of solidarity, Antony parcels out the body, along with seventy-five drachmas and Caesar's "walks, / His private arbours, and new-planted orchards / On this side Tiber" (III.ii.247–9) like a feudal lord distributing largesse to the general populace. This gesture is simultaneously one of commodification and domestication: Caesar is redesigned as a god of the people, priced accordingly. Caesar's body is thus at once mystified and demystified, elevated and deposed: "O mighty Caesar! dost thou lie so low? / Are all thy conquests, glories, triumphs, spoils, / Shrunk to this little measure? Fare thee well!" (III.i.148–50). This emergent economy of the body inscribes perfectly the ritual crisis enacted in this play; Antony's post-mortem of Caesar's mantled corpse (III.ii.174–97) includes the famous line, "This was the most unkindest cut of all" (183), which Plutarch explicitly identifies as a cut to Caesar's "privities" (1967: V: 68). Portia's inexplicable "voluntary wound / Here, in the thigh" (II.i.300–1) has also been identified in criticism (though not by Plutarch) as genital, or as the displacement of a genital wound (Paster 1989: 294). The speculation is an interesting one in the context of the Lupercalia, which involves cutting up the sacrificial goat as, in part, a fertility rite, and thus attaches to Calphurnia's and Caesar's childless status. Incision is a form of inscription: both Caesar's and Portia's wounds locate symbolic references to sterility and impotence, the conditions the Lupercalia were designed to relieve. Both likewise constitute futile gestures, misdirected (per)versions of Lupercalian rites. At this stage of Roman history, the body of the Republic, antithesized in Caesar and incorporated in Portia as the daughter of its preeminent spokesman Cato, is dying; by the end of the play it is dead and buried. Fertility and potency only *appear* to be issues at stake at the start of the play; it is actually too late to be concerned about reproductive capabilities, symbolic or biological. That is the point of the narrative of ritual misrecognition with which the play begins.

Critics have noticed, if perhaps overemphasized, the implicit cannibalism of this body imagery, its connection to the Carnival riots at Romans in the French province of Dauphiné in 1580, and Antony's transformation of the murder to a triumph of Misrule (R. Wilson 1987: 40): "Mischief, thou art afoot, / Take thou what course thou wilt" (III.ii.259–60). This is more than mischief. Antony is willing to see Rome burn for his revenge and to trade the lives of relatives and friends with the other Triumvirs in the deadly post-cataclysmic quiet of Act IV. Wilson is right, however, in pointing to the events of 1580. Antony's manipulation of the populace is not unlike the beginnings of the eruption at Romans, which, interestingly, was also preceded by crop failures, reported sightings of comets and other portents. The Romans riots started at the Carnival season in 1579 and again in 1580 (Le Roy Ladurie 1979: 93–4, 175) on 3 February (the same date in both years), at the Feast of St Blaise, the patron saint of carders, drapers, and plowmen. St Blaise was "a sort of textile, agrarian deity, also representing fertility and music. He was supposed to have been tortured to death by being torn to pieces" with carders' tools and threshing flails (Le Roy Ladurie 1979: 99, 176). Like the Lupercal, his festival (lasting from three to ten days, which would extend it to the Lupercal's date) also began with a foot-race for which the prize was in this case a sheep, which was sometimes subsequently killed in a sickle-throwing contest (Le Roy Ladurie 1979: 177).

In 1580, however, a faction of patricians decided to sponsor an alternative race whose prize was not the commoners' sheep but the bourgeoisie's partridge, and the winner was "crowned" not as the traditional St Blaise's Sheep King but as a newly established Partridge King. The race, says Le Roy Ladurie, was fixed (1979: 184–7). A traditional celebration by textile and farm workers, under the banner of their shared patron saint, was suddenly and quickly – within ten days – contested by one bourgeois faction, who were answered by a proliferation of popular factions, or what Le Roy Ladurie calls "wildcat Carnival celebrations in working-class neighborhoods" (1979: 201). Two "kingdoms" of sheep (for the workers) and partridge (for the patricians) quickly split into eight, adding neighborhood-kingdoms of hare, capon, and briefly donkey and bear to the workers' sector and rooster and eagle to the patricians'. As Le Roy Ladurie says, "A town of 7,000 with eight kings . . . . There was bound to be trouble" (1979: 214).

In both Rome and Romans, what appear to be instances of Misrule spontaneously run amok are actually instances of traditional festive practice abruptly factionalized, maneuvered first into a political contest and then into a massacre. The central and crucially important points of similarity between the two are these: a popular, anti-despotic group uses a festival occasion to protest against an incipient threat to its stability; the threatening patrician faction then seizes control of the festival and its signification, out-maneuvering and overpowering the protestors. The contest for control of a festival celebration as a nexus of symbol systems erupts as a real blood-bath.

The real events of 1580 and both pro- and anti-Caesar factions in the play demonstrate that radical political moves can be made under cover of festivity and ritual (as distinct from the controlled performance of a licensed play). In England, too, certain uprisings coincided with ecclesiastical calendar events disputed during the Tudor reigns: the Cornish rebellion of 1549 that started at the Whit Sunday and Whit Monday assemblies, and Ket's rebellion in Norfolk, in the same year, following the celebration at Wymondham of the "presumably illegal" feast of St Thomas the Martyr (Cressy 1989: 6). Thus the question that troubles investigations of *Julius Caesar* is not whether a murder can be made to look like a ritual sacrifice. The question is rather to what power the "sacrifice" will be made, and in whose interests. Just as Caesar's blood was offered in libation upon the Capitol, the political center made into an altar, so the blood of the Republic, its people and its ceremonies, will be spilled all over Rome. Antony's curse "upon the limbs of men,"

> Blood and destruction shall be so in use
> And dreadful objects so familiar
> That mothers shall but smile when they behold

104

Their infants quartered with the hands of war,
All pity chok'd with custom of fell deeds . . . .
(III.i.265–9)

sounds remarkably like Bolingbroke's threat to "lay the summer's
dust with showers of blood / Rain'd from the wounds of
slaughter'd Englishmen" (III.iii.43–4) at the center of *Richard II*.
In both instances, the implied ceremony of purgation and renewal
is deliberately perverted to one of holocaust, which is no ceremony
at all but a perversion of ceremony – for ceremony is designed to
be orderly and constructive toward some idea of fruition.

From its first reference to the ambiguously understood holiday
to the last lines of the play, *Julius Caesar* is grounded in this context
of ceremonies and rituals (Velz 1968a: 156–7): some observed,
some ignored, some twisted to suit particular interests. The social
rituals traced within the play occur within the larger context of the
Lupercalia as a perennially observed religious ritual. And it is
within this larger context that the conservative Brutus operates.
His desire to make Caesar's murder seem ritualistic is not the same
thing as an attempt to make it an *actual* ritual, nor does he say
anywhere outside the confidential circle of conspirators that it is
one. His orations to the people (III.ii.12–47) do not refer to ritual
(although, as we have seen, Antony's do); they only appeal to the
commons' sense of republicanism. The image that Brutus seeks to
create is not, therefore, impossible; it is not even unlikely. It is
entirely consistent with what he believes (and Antony proves) to be
an acceptable avenue to public approbation. What, then, went
wrong?

Brutus's "errors," including his reluctance to kill Antony and his
permission for Antony to speak (and speak last) at Caesar's
funeral, have been noted by nearly every critic since Plutarch
himself pointed them out (1967: VI: 200). As I have already suggested, several of the play's characters understand the world
imperfectly. Brutus is not wrong, however, to see Caesar's arro-
gance as a threat to the Republic; Caesar's language and actions in
the play just before the assassination show that Brutus's fears are
well founded: besides Casca's reports (I.ii.235–87), which could
have been unreliably inflected by the conspirator, there is, immediately before the stabbing, Caesar's directly represented
behavior towards those who should have been treated as his equals

105

in a republic: "I could be well mov'd, if I were as you"; "Hence! Wilt thou lift up Olympus!"; "Doth not Brutus bootless kneel?" (III.i.58–75). Even Plutarch asserts that "the chiefest cause that made [Caesar] mortally hated, was the covetous desire he had to be called king: which first gave the people just cause, and next his secret enemies, honest colour to beare him ill will" (1967: V: 60). Nor is Brutus wrong in trying to use a familiar ritualistic paradigm to support his co-conspirators in their sense of justice. Brutus's *hamartia* is his inability to preserve the Republic, to predict the outcome of the history in which he himself participates.

"History" is rarely clear to those for whom it is still the present; perhaps only soothsayers and manipulators like Antony can foresee the future.[12] Brutus does understand the history of the age preceding his own. Cassius reminds him of the Rome that was:

> O, you and I have heard our fathers say
> There was a Brutus once that would have brook'd
> Th'eternal devil to keep his state in Rome
> As easily as a king.
>
> (I.ii.158–61)

And Brutus later reminds himself: "My ancestors did from the streets of Rome / The Tarquin drive when he was call'd a king" (II.i.53–4). He is persuaded best by arguments that refer to the past, to tradition, and especially to family traditions. Brutus's sense of history enables him to identify the "tide in the affairs of men" (IV.iii.218) that governs their successes in the world. The problem is that "we must take the current when it serves / Or lose our ventures" (IV.iii.223–4). Unfortunately Brutus misses *his* current (in both senses of tide and immediate moment): his *hamartia* is literally a "missing of the mark."

The tide of political history is defined in this play as repetitive, if not altogether cyclical. Caesar triumphed over Pompey and died under his image, at the foot of Pompey's statue; Brutus in turn dies with the image of Caesar in his mind's eye: "Caesar, now be still" (V.v.50). Antony's eulogy over Caesar as the "noblest man / That ever lived in the tide of times" (III.i.256–7) echoes in his final praise of Brutus as "the noblest Roman of them all" (V.v.68). When Cassius reminds Brutus that "there was a Brutus once," the present Brutus remembers that he too has a cycle to repeat. It would appear that this Rome sees itself as recyclable, but not renewable. Cassius's cryptic prophecy that in "many ages hence / Shall this our lofty scene be acted over" (III.i.111–12) lends a particularly mimetic emphasis to the recurrent politics of history.

Ultimately the tide in the affairs of men has its own energy, stronger than and indifferent to individual human concerns. Once initiated, events are answered with consequent events. "The evil that men do lives after them" (III.ii.75) not only in Antony's sense of reputation but also in the historical sense of repercussion: an act of tyranny calls for one of liberation; assassination in turn is answered by revenge, and so on.[13] The tide whose current Brutus misses becomes a flood of anarchy, of the "mutiny" Antony calls into being (III.ii.211). The play offers other metaphors for this action: the "dogs of war" will be unleashed (III.i.273), and mischief, once afoot, will take its own course (III.ii.259–60). Antony understands this perfectly; Brutus never tells us whether he does.

Brutus is old-fashioned, out of time as it progresses over and around him. He does not seem to realize that he cannot stop the flow of events. His action is as heroic as it is futile. In the play's final analysis, he is "the noblest Roman of them all"; more specifically, he is the noblest Roman of the Rome that was, and is finished (Burckhardt 1968: 9).[14] The Triumvirate presents a sickening image of Octavius, Antony, and Lepidus coldly trading names and lives of relatives and friends marked for annihilation. And whereas Brutus's committee of conspirators, in the parallel scene in II.i, honestly and honorably excludes men like Cicero whom they cannot count on to support a united effort, the Triumvirate itself is a sham perpetrated by Antony and followed by Octavius. They will use Lepidus to "ease ourselves of divers sland'rous loads" and then "turn him off / (Like to the empty ass) to shake his ears / And graze in commons" (IV.i.20–7). These three are the leaders of the Rome that is left smoldering after the commons, ignited by Antony's precise rhetoric, fire the city and slaughter the unfortunate poet with the wrong name. The Rome that Brutus wants to preserve is perverted into a self-devouring creature (the "humanity" that Albany predicts in *King Lear* "must perforce prey on itself, / Like monsters of the deep" [IV.ii.49–50]), and the intended purgative and regenerative ritual becomes the mere anarchy of bacchanalian frenzy. Ironically for Brutus, Caesar's blood could never have nourished a *polis* far too desiccated by opportunistic corruption to profit by such remedy; it is simply absorbed into the earth.

We have access to past civilizations and cultures primarily through two kinds of records: historical ones of singular events and traditional or repeated ones, such as rituals. In reading Plutarch, Shakespeare found both kinds of records. But Shakespeare's interest was surely not that of the historian or the ethnologist. Whatever prompted him to incorporate and apply the Lupercalian images from the *Romulus*, it must have been for the sake of theatrical interest, not scholarship. He had to know that the patterns and concerns of his play matched those of his audience, who undoubtedly did not share our modern delight in footnotes and esoterica.

Shakespeare's audience's general interest in Roman history and its major figures is a critical commonplace (Spencer 1957; Charney 1961; Cantor 1976). A very strong concern for historicity might move a playwright toward so complete a mimesis that he includes in his play even ritual practices already dying out in the culture his play presents. But neither *Julius Caesar* nor any other play suggests that Shakespeare had any such compulsion to observe *minutiae* of that sort, nor, we may suppose, did most of his audience. Yet these elements are consciously and effectively woven into this play, and clearly as an artistic representation rather than an academic didacticism. Why would Shakespeare have been interested in the rituals of a decaying Roman religion, and further, how could he have counted on his audience's interest in these issues?

However sophisticated and secular it may have been, the life of a Londoner in Shakespeare's time was in many respects ordered by rituals both civic and ecclesiastic. Shakespeare's plays often reflect the importance of that combined ordering as law and religion, the two coordinates of human governance. For example, in *The Merchant of Venice* (quite distant from *Julius Caesar* in genre and style, but only about three years earlier in composition), these coordinates intersect at several points, most strikingly in a perverse image of practiced abuses when Bassanio chooses the right casket:

> In law, what plea so tainted and corrupt
> But being season'd with a gracious voice,
> Obscures the show of evil? In religion,
> What damned error but some sober brow
> Will bless it and approve it with a text
> Hiding the grossness with fair ornament?
> (III.ii.75–80)

These lines concentrate for us the full context in which the play's action occurs, the major bonds by which Venetian society regulated its ordered and self-perpetuating system. The interrelation of these bonds is in a sense the nexus of Shakespeare's world, powerfully evident in the civic and ecclesiastic festivals of London as well as in the much older and lasting seasonal celebrations of his native Warwickshire. Such concerns were part of every Elizabethan's life: they were not only historically but perennially significant. The primacy of this combination of concerns is obvious in Hooker's *Laws of Ecclesiastical Polity*, whose Preface and first four books had appeared by 1593. According to its modern editors, it was received "more as an articulate statement of what England had already accepted than as a polemic against powerful religious alternatives. Within twenty years of its writing, Hooker's work was already being read as a monument" (A. S. McGrade, in Hooker 1975: 12).

Certain features of the festivals celebrated by both urban and rural Elizabethans suggest that *Julius Caesar*'s incorporation of Lupercalian elements would have struck familiar chords for its audience. The play's concerns with right rule and order, and their passage, are essentially the same as those of popular and civic festivals generally. Shakespeare's familiarity with the rural practices of various festivals in Warwickshire sensitized him to the analogous rites he read about in Plutarch. These English rites ensured his audience's comprehension of those elements in the play as necessary guarantors, whether pagan or Christian, ecclesiastic or secular, rural or civic, of order, succession, and fruition in the realm.

The custom most remarkably similar to certain aspects of the Lupercalia is called in England "Beating the Bounds" (in Scotland, "Riding the Marches"). It was practiced this way in Warwickshire:

Walking the parish boundaries . . . was an essential part of parish administration before maps and literacy were commonplace . . . . At the boundary marks (a tree, a stone, a pond) the parson paused to give thanks for the fruits of the earth and to read the gospel . . . . The company, carrying peeled willow wands, then turned to the boys and, more or less severely according to the period, beat and bumped them or pushed them in a nearby stream, all excellent reminders of boundaries.

(Baker 1974: 158; also R. Palmer 1976: 164–7)

The resemblance of these practices to the Lupercalian race around the city of Rome and the thong-lashing is worth noting; like the Lupercalia, their origins, the accumulated layers of *bricolage*, belong to an unrecoverable past. The timing of these customs in England varied by village: at Stratford, for instance, they occurred in the spring, but elsewhere in Warwickshire, at Warwick, Ilmington, and Birmingham, the custom was specifically a Michaelmas tradition.[15] Michaelmas was the festival that most evenly blended civic and religious occasions. Ecclesiastically, it celebrated angelic protection over human affairs. In the secular domain it was the traditional time for signing contracts, trying lawsuits, harvesting crops, and electing the Lord Mayor of London and the town Bailiffs in the shires (Hassell 1979: 156–66; Palmer and Lloyd 1972: 74–5, 153–7). Thus it distinctively commemorates the dual order of divine and civil law, the passage of political power, and the rites associated with the harvest which guarantee the next year's crops – all themes with which *Julius Caesar* is concerned. And although Stratford did not "beat the bounds" at Michaelmas, the town was otherwise engaged in what is called the "most famous" of its Michaelmas traditions, the Stratford Hiring or "Mop" Fair, which served as a marketplace or labor-exchange for hiring farmhands and housemaids (hence, the "mop" or sign of the profession). The Stratford Mop was almost always accompanied by Morris dancing and a variation on the Hobby-horse dance called "Grinning," a contest for the "frightfullest grinner" through a horse-collar (R. Palmer 1976: 124).

Although significant attention has been given to the Roman Saturnalia as analogous to these seasonal folk practices in England, the equally close relation of the Lupercalia has not been recognized. Certain elements of these festivals are Lupercalian rather than Saturnalian. Besides the mildly violent boundary-running, there is for instance the whipping of the spectators by the Fool during the Morris dance, which inverts the Saturnalian scapegoat sacrifice and more closely resembles the flagellation of the Lupercal race. The Hobby-horse too is related to the fertility aspects of the Lupercalia, whenever, as in Cornwall, it chases and traps the village girls under its hood. To be so caught was considered a sign of luck, and especially of fecundity. On occasion, the "Horse" would "smear its captives' faces with tar or soot as part of the initiation process" (Palmer and Lloyd 1972: 25). This last act recalls the equally unexplained blood-smearing initiation of the

Lupercalia, reflected in the blood-bath scenes, including Antony's hand-shake, in *Julius Caesar.*

Although they might seem both dramatically and historically distant, set off in a world more than one and a half millennia away, the rites and signs of the Lupercal would have seemed familiar to Shakespeare's audience. They need not have known that these were specifically Roman rites; they need only have understood what the rites symbolized in their own terms, what urges, necessities, fears, or assurances they stood for. Such recognition is by no means the exclusive business of the educated classes; echoes of domestic practices – and their dissolution – can produce connections in the mind of any viewer. The Lupercalian elements in *Julius Caesar* not only authenticate the representation of historical and political Rome but also resonate with the semblance of native English rites; the audience thus receives the play on, as it were, a two-tiered stage.

4

COMMUNITAS,
HIERARCHY,
LIMINALITY, VICTIMAGE

Ritual mediates, focuses, contains, but does not erase the perennial human tendency to conflict. Writing about the native populations of the northwest American coast, Stanley Walens concludes:

> [They] saw their world as one where myriad forces were at work, all influencing food, and humans' ability to obtain food. Every animal, every human, every clan, had its own needs, its own demands, its own hunger [all needing] to be balanced against one another, to be directed for the greatest mutual benefit. It was through ritual that this balance was obtained, that the competitive forces which could have brought about the destruction of the universe were tamed. It was a delicate balance; the slightest misweighing could send the world back into the chaos of selfishness and conflict from which Raven had delivered mankind. The judicious balancing of one's needs against one's obligations was a difficult and complex task.
>
> (1982: 182)

In every known culture, physical survival is the primary interest served by ritual practice, explained by the development of mythical thought, and procured by the "judicious balancing of one's needs against one's obligations" (a serviceable definition of civilization, although, as we have seen, its interpretation may be contested). Investigators identify the threat to that survival in various ways: Douglas (1966) calls it filth; Walens calls it "the chaos of selfishness and conflict"; Grimes (1982) focuses on violence, as does Girard (1977), who explicitly defines violence as "victimage." And Aristotle asserts that kin-killing is the specific "action having magnitude" that is the subject of tragedy.

112

It is important to remember that these destructive forces always inhere in the structures they threaten; that is, communities contain within themselves their pollutants, their dangers, their "negative" impulses. The assignment of threat and consequent victimage to an outsider or marginal figure is a mechanism constructed by societies to avoid the suicidal nihilism that is labeled in several of Shakespeare's tragedies as "monstrous" or "unnatural." This nihilism is most often presented in images of *omophagia*, as in Albany's emblematic vision of humanity preying on itself (*King Lear* IV.ii.49–50), or as in *Coriolanus* where Rome "like an unnatural dam / Should now eat up her own!" (III.i.291–2) and Volumnia threatens to "sup upon" herself and "starve with feeding" (IV.ii.50–1). In so far as communities are organisms cloned from their constitutive memberships, they replicate their constituencies' organic structures. The biological model of Menenius's "Fable of the Belly" applies here: just as organisms contain both the potential to self-destruct and certain autoimmune mechanisms to combat that potential and maintain a homeostatic balance, so too do human communities. That balance is not to be confused with unalterable stasis. "Balance," not stagnation, is the desideratum. Properly maintained, ritual is the work of the community's autoimmune system, the inherent check against infection (internal or external) and annihilation.

In the examples from *Lear* and *Coriolanus* just noted, the nihilism of "monstrous" self-destruction is delivered as a simile or a metaphor, that is, as a rhetorical figure. Actual *omophagia* occurs only twice in Shakespearean tragedy: in *Titus Andronicus*, when Tamora unwittingly eats the pie containing the remains of her sons, and in *Macbeth*, in the report of Duncan's horses eating each other (II.iv.18), where the event is narrated in the list of omens attached to Duncan's murder. It is as "unnatural" for horses as for humans. Such extreme inversions can only be rendered imaginatively or symbolically. They are what Geertz calls the "counteractive patterns" of "a culture's own negation" (1966: 65) and Babcock calls "symbolic inversion" (1978: 14), terms displacing the now generally rejected notion of such reversals or negations as forms of *ventilsitten*, "letting off steam." This latter formulation is the old "safety valve" argument that seasonal inversion and rites of reversal, because "permitted" by dominant structures of authority, actually strengthen and preserve the status quo and occur "*only* within an established and unchallenged social order" (Babcock

1978: 22–3). Inverse ritual behavior is not confined to seasonal rituals; it is a central component of the liminal period of all rites of passage, as part of the necessary distinction from normative, orthodox behavior, and thus part of the process of change and development, with all the risks to stability that such change entails (Babcock 1978; Bateson 1958; Geertz 1966; 1973; Smith 1987; V. Turner 1967; 1969; 1974).

Only the most Orwellian imagination would argue that unorthodox and unauthorized activity is always to be read as subversive and therefore always to be suppressed. The critical challenge is to avoid a reductively symptomatic reading of the ritual practices of traditional cultures. The project is slippery; it is difficult for modern Western critics to read accurately systems of belief in which we cannot participate even imaginatively (cf. Greenblatt 1982). The idea that ritual always validates a specific instantiation of political hierarchy occurs within the conceptual frame of a supreme hierarchical occupancy temporarily disempowered by inverse ritual. But such an approach begs the question. Within traditional societies where the structure of social relations prevails over particular occupancies of power, there is no question of subversion in the exercise of ritual behavior. Instead, higher and lower exist, and alternate, in a sustained rhythm of power exchange. Babcock makes the important point that inversion rituals "remind us of the arbitrary condition of imposing an order on our environment and experience, even while they enable us to see certain features of that order more clearly simply because they have turned inside out" (1978: 29). MacAloon describes the southern African Swazi ceremony of Incwala, in which the king is sequestered from his community in a sacred enclosure (which thereby marginalizes him), and attended by priests who treat him with powerful medicines. At the full moon, he reappears among his subjects, stripped of all the outward attributes of kingship, costumed as a monster wearing a cover of sharp grass blades which cut him as he dances wildly, enraged and in pain. Discrete groups of his people surround him during this phase; through dance, chant, and gesture, they alternately express pity for him, taunt and vilify him, and then extol his strength and triumph. He emerges from the rite again a fully anointed king, reunited with his people. MacAloon observes that "The oscillations between expressions of rebellion and solidarity within the rite [are] part and parcel of one another" (1982: 256). There is no question of overthrowing the king, even during his debasement. In accordance with long-standing belief and tradition, his passage from one status to another and back again is tacitly agreed to by the whole community, all of whose members have distinct roles to play in the rite. The performance of this passage across boundaries functions as the mechanism which reinforces cultural definition as a complex range of oscillating positions, not a static fixture of high and low.

To focus on the debasement as an axiomatically subversive or rebellious overthrow of royalty is to see the Swazi through a Eurocentric politics of self-consciousness and class antagonism, and to read the rite as many have read *Richard II*'s deposition scenes. Among traditional communities like the Swazi, such internal shifts in sociopolitical status are not only temporary but also necessary for the maintenance of group identity, and, far from constituting a threat to community, are seen instead as salutary and constructive in the life of the community. The king is seen as a "human" subject whose "humanity" is both naturalized and universalized. As Victor Turner wrote of similar rites of passage among the Ndembu,

> This is not simply . . . a matter of giving a general stamp of legitimacy to a society's structural positions. It is rather a matter of giving recognition to an essential and generic human bond, without which there could be *no* society . . . . [The] high could not be high unless the low existed, and he who is high must experience what it is like to be low.
>
> (1969: 97)

It is an irony of "progress," the legacy of historical accretion, that modern Western cultures treat difference *within* a group as a kind of hyperdifferentiation whereby the debasement of an authority figure is seen as a serious threat to the stability of the community itself. But as Bristol astutely observes, even in Elizabethan England, "Communal well-being depends on observing the rhythm of alternation . . . . Social conflict is a salutary force, which . . . contributes to the tradition of mutual and reciprocal responsibility for sustaining collective subsistence" (1985: 78, 87). Among the Swazi, Ndembu, and similarly traditional cultures, unless something truly extraordinary and unforeseen were to occur during the period of debasement, thereby aborting the rite, not only are the community's and the king's well-being *not* endangered by his temporary lowliness, they are on the contrary assured by it. This assurance is guaranteed by the whole community's agreement in both the processes and the significance of the rite, which has been structured to achieve this explicit purpose (LaFontaine 1985: 14).

Rituals, even (or especially) rituals of debasement and restitution, are normally not revolutionary but rather conservative activities.[1] The periodic reiteration and affirmation of a society's knowledge of itself is seen to ensure its survival and to continually clarify the values on which survival is based, whether the rite is practiced perennially (e.g., seasonal rites) or occasionally (e.g., the investiture of a ruler). Communal belief in the validity and efficacy of the rite is the *sine qua non* of ritual practice. Its opposite or inverse, the combined breakdown of communal referent and ritual efficacy, is one of the subtexts of Shakespearean tragedy.

Ritual action is not always sacred ritual; that is, it need not have specifically religious validity. It is a form of mimesis that belongs to all members of a community, not only to a priestly or ruling constituency, and is not only reserved for authorized occasions. Such action entails the mnemonic of something sacred, something upon which survival depends, whether spiritual, physical, or communal. While it is sometimes given to a priestly elite to manage its formal expression, it always remains the possession of the mass population. At the beginning of the twentieth century, Benjamin Kurtz identified this possession as a sense of "the marvellous," which "multiplies under religious and faithful sanction. With the rise of a critical philosophy it is subjected to searching analysis, but no philosophy or science of a few can check its advance, for it lives perennially in the hearts and in the superstitions of the . . . masses" (1910: 3). Kurtz belonged to an early generation of anthropologists that included Frazer, Tylor, and others whose work was driven by an idea that the religious beliefs of non-Western societies were "survivals from the past, from which Western nations have advanced further" and that "rituals play a more important part in the life of these peoples than in our own" (LaFontaine 1985: 19). The transparent Eurocentrism and correlative "temporocentrism" in the views of these early anthropologists are based on an evolutionary sense of "progress" from magic to religion to science. Through this lens, what is modern and Western is by definition better, advanced, and morally "right," and the study of traditional cultures is a study of fossils that shows us how far we have "progressed" in our social evolution.

While the "sense of the marvellous" found wide acceptance

during and since the time of Kurtz and Frazer, it was also contested vigorously by two of their contemporaries, van Gennep ([1909]; 1960) and Durkheim ([1912]; 1965), who have supplanted Frazer and Kurtz in canonical modern anthropology. As LaFontaine notes, "hindsight allows us to see that when *The Golden Bough* was published it was already out of date" (1985: 21). Durkheim gave priority to social groupings and divisions within systems of religious beliefs; the emerging moral precepts of a group's social life, generated and reiterated both collectively and individually, were then codified and validated by the authority of religious systematization. For Durkheim, ritual action represented groups and social relations within groups. Van Gennep shared Durkheim's valuation of the social function of ritual, but his focus was narrowed to the study of one particular kind of ritual, the individual rite of passage.

Unlike Frazer and Durkheim, van Gennep did his own fieldwork, studied specific rites for their component symbolic acts, and from his observations derived his concept of liminality, which he also described as marginality. For van Gennep, the term "rite of passage" covers a variety of practices attached to numerous kinds of personal transitions: boundary-crossings, changes in social status, seasonal and other kinds of temporal change. Territorial borders and social distinctions are by nature fragile; their edges must be marked and those markings observed by members of a culture to protect both its physical integrity and conceptual identity. Such boundaries, whether of individual social status (child/adult, single/married, living/dead) or territorial or even seasonal designations, are socially defined. They are also for the most part imprecise, ambiguous, and therefore require custodial vigilance. Marking boundaries and phases of social life by ritual protects both individuals and communities from the danger of indefinition. Whatever is undefined is vulnerable; its identity is at stake because identity *is* a matter of definition and boundary. Definition is the fundamental issue for any community that seeks to exist as a community. Hence the importance of liminality, the transitional time or condition in which one, or a group, or a territory, or the season, is not what it was and not what it will become, but something in between, something marginal, vague, and flexible.

Van Gennep described three phases common to the structures of all rites of passage: separation, transition, and incorporation.

During first phase the initiand is removed, often physically, from the familiar environment and its trappings; in transition, or liminality, the old identity is dissolved and a new one created; and finally, the subject is reintegrated with the community in a new or renewed role. Victor Turner appropriated van Gennep's work, secularized the issue of liminality, extended its application to non-religious activities, and expanded his discussion to "ritualistic" action as distinct from ritual *per se.* Turner worked among the Ndembu of northWestern Zambia in central Africa during the 1960s, although he later turned his attention to Asian cultures and to Shakespeare. His models of "communitas" and "structure," together with his interpretation and dissemination of van Gennep's identification of liminality, constitute one of the most important recent interventions in anthropological and performance theory.

Turner observed two coexisting, alternating ontological models in human communities: "structure" is a "differentiated, and often hierarchical system of politico-legal-economic positions"; "communitas" emerges during liminality as "an unstructured or rudimentarily structured and relatively undifferentiated *comitatus* . . . of equal individuals who submit together to the general authority of the ritual elders" (1969: 96). The usefulness of such a distinction to a study of tragedy becomes evident in the following:

> The distinction between structure and communitas is not simply the familiar one between "secular" and "sacred," or that, for example, between politics and religion . . . .
>
> [For] individuals and groups, social life is a type of dialectical process that involves successive experience of high and low, communitas and structure, homogeneity and differentiation, equality and inequality. The passage from lower to higher status is through a limbo of statuslessness. In such a process, the opposites, as it were, constitute one another and are mutually indispensable.
>
> (1969: 96–7)

Turner's models of structure and communitas are the mathematical coefficients of civilization; they satisfy a recognized human demand for comprehension and order.[2] Societies create such order through agreements or contracts about borders and loyalties, familial bonds, structures of rule. If we break these, we break everything. We often do, and this is what tragedy performs. Beneath the surface of these constructs is an endless energy that threatens at various moments to boil up over the orderly containers we have shaped. The tension that results in the eruption of this energy, to the point where it challenges definitional constraints, is the essential action of tragedy (Michel 1970: 12–18). It tests the strength of definitions by examining closely what is taken for granted as insuring order: laws, ranks, codes of behavior, bonds of kinship and kingship, even provisions for survival (food, shelter, clothing) that become the encoded trappings of civilized culture.

Initially adhering closely to van Gennep's distinctions, Turner later elaborated them to encompass, as he said, "all types of rites as having the processual form of 'passage'" (1982: 24). Whereas van Gennep focused on rites of passage in the life of an individual or a cohort of individuals (an age-group, for instance, within a community), Turner thought the application of the term "rite of passage" to communal rites for an entire society was implicit in van Gennep's formulation (1982: 24). His extension seems entirely persuasive. Although the focus may be on the individual or the cohort during the rite itself, the rite exists for the sake of the community which, in turn, by sanctioning the rite, participates in more than just an observer's role. This is both implicit and explicit in the final phase, when the subject is reincorporated into the group. To the extent that some rites have widely applicable sociopolitical functions (e.g., ceremonies of kingship, transitions in government, or rites associated with seasonal holidays from work), they concern the community as much as, if not more than, the individual initiands. Because theater represents communally significant events, the processes represented in theatrical performance must be morphologically recognizable to the audience in order for the theatrical event to do its representational cathartic work. Every dramatic *agon* is inherently liminal, representing the process of a contest, transition, or transformation somewhere in the course of the play's action. Thus Shakespearean tragedy is significantly illuminated by exploring its dual constitutive liminalities, the protagonist's and the community's.

Transitional or liminal phases are for Turner the crucial ones. They occasionally represent clear, direct, and intensified inversions of normal reality, as for example in carnivalized events, but more characteristically offer symbols of ambiguity and paradox, both socially and politically dangerous. We see this, for example, in the first scene of *Hamlet* (a play which could arguably be read as a discourse of liminality), when, aside from the as-yet-unexplained appearance of the ghost, Marcellus anxiously questions the other changes he has observed in daily life: the nightly watch, the accelerated market in domestic and imported munitions, the endless employment in shipyards that "Does not divide the Sunday from the week" and makes "the night joint-laborer with the day" (I.i.70–8). This is a marked instance of Turner's example of a shift "from a period of peace as against one of war, from plague to community health" (1982: 24) as a communal "separation" phase.

Such anomalies, as Horatio says, bode strange eruptions to the state. Liminality is always ambiguous, always blurs and merges distinctions between normal oppositions such as night and day, Sunday and the work-week, life and death; thus it always produces anxiety. Liminality, ambiguity, anomaly, indeterminacy are all antithetic to the human desire for systems and structures. Transformational operations in themselves are dangerous because, being dynamic and fluid, they can neither be controlled nor defined, nor even formulated clearly. Therefore, when such descriptions or formulations are attempted, they tend to be given in terms of paradox, ambiguity, or negative or inverted forms of some recognizable status or normative category of experience. Danger is situated in the implied negation of a normative specific status, boundary, or relationship (T. S. Turner 1977: 58). Douglas's definition of dirt as "matter out of place," the contravention of an orderly system (1966: 35) makes a similar point. What members of a society label "dirt," "disorder," or "pollution" reflects precisely by inversion their concepts of cleanliness, order, and purity. In removing dirt, as in clarifying ambiguity, we are "positively re-ordering our environment, making it conform to an idea" (Douglas 1966: 2).

Resolving liminality, completing the process through to incorporation, is crucial to reaffirming the structures and systems that define a culture. When that process is aborted, as in tragedy when the protagonist dies, the community's state of crisis threatens to remain unresolved, which is an intolerable situation. In such cases, the community *declares* completion by defining the anomaly as clarified. Douglas cites as an example, derived from E. E. Evans-Pritchard's study of the Nuer, their method of dealing with congenital deformity:

> [When] a monstrous birth occurs, the defining lines between humans and animals may be threatened. If a monstrous birth

can be labelled an event of a peculiar kind the categories can be restored. So the Nuer treat monstrous births as baby hippopotamuses, accidentally born to humans and, with this labelling, the appropriate action is clear. They gently lay them in the river where they belong.

(1966: 39)

Cultural categories, says Douglas, "are public matters. They cannot so easily be subject to revision. Yet they cannot neglect the challenge of aberrant forms. Any given system of classification must give rise to anomalies, and any given culture must confront events which seem to defy its assumptions" (1966: 38–9). Human anomalies are by definition ambiguous or liminal. They share in the community's humanness, yet they challenge it by being noticeably different. An aberrant shape, like that of Shakespeare's Richard III, is enough to create marginality, liminality, and all the danger that such difference constitutes. Had Richard been born to the Nuer tribe, he would have been reunited with his fellow hippopotamuses, or river-horses. In Shakespeare's play, when Richard calls for a horse, two affects occur: pragmatically, the horse raises him off the ground, restoring his distinction from common soldiers; at the same time, mounted on a horse, he embodies the satyr-like morphology appropriate to a monstrous human.[3] In other tragedies, Shakespeare makes the anomalous monstrosity of his protagonists less physically obvious, more culturally subtle. In this context, the Macbeths constitute an extreme case: their monstrosity is internalized but nonetheless identified at the play's conclusion. The "dead butcher and his fiendlike queen" (V.ix.35) are the "rarer monsters . . . / Painted upon a pole" (V.viii.25–6). Claudius is "a satyr" compared to Hamlet Senior's "Hyperion" (I.ii.140). Difference too clearly outlined, as Aristotle insisted, precludes pity. At its most effective and most affective, tragic aberration is abetted by the shadings of liminality, and that liminality belongs to both the community and the protagonist.

Aberration most commonly appears in Shakespearean tragedy as political. This is so because the political structures of Shakespeare's England were preeminently hierarchical and represented ideologically as static, fixed, inviolable; like the proverbial tree that must bend or break, they were thus highly susceptible to breach. Political structures in any human society are, as Douglas argues, "held precariously."

So we find their legitimate pretensions backed by beliefs in extraordinary powers emanating from their persons, from the insignia of their office or from words they can utter. Similarly the ideal order of society is guarded by dangers which threaten transgressors . . . . They are a strong language of mutual exhortation. At this level the laws of nature are dragged in to sanction the moral code: this kind of disease is caused by adultery, that by incest; this meteorological disaster is the effect of political disloyalty, that the effect of impiety. The whole universe is harnessed to men's attempts to force one another into good citizenship.

(1966: 3)

Good citizenship normalizes social and political behavior by its definition, and that, too, is held in precarious balance. The complexities of heroic behavior in Shakespeare's tragedies illustrate just how precarious the balance is. The Roman tragedies offer particularly good examples: the values of personal sacrifice to state and patriarchy, evidenced in the willing loss of twenty-one sons, make Titus Andronicus an engaging and sympathetic figure at the start of his play. But the next sacrifice he makes to the same set of cultural values, when he kills his son Mutius, marks him as a monster. Conversely, Tamora's protective passion towards her sons, because they contravene the good of Rome, is negatively valued. And Aaron, the most marginalized of *Titus Andronicus*'s characters, displays the very model of paternal care toward his son, yet he is condemned to permanent liminality, planted in the earth, neither alive nor dead, neither buried nor walking, at the end of the play. As we shall see in the next section, it is difficult to determine in *Titus Andronicus* just what constitutes good citizenship. *Julius Caesar* interrogates a similar ambiguity: the titular hero is destroyed in mid-play for reasons, as Brutus so powerfully argues, that problematize the very nature of Roman citizenship in a state that changes in the course of the play from republic to triumvirate to the beginnings of empire. Throughout his play Coriolanus is consistently the Roman he was trained to be and is celebrated by Rome for being, until the rules are contested.

Liminality in the form of ambiguity is a conditional premise of Shakespearean tragedy. It inheres in the community from the start of each play, and is crystallized in, but not limited to, the tragic protagonists. They are designed for that purpose; that is their function, inextricably entailed in their construction as *pharmakoi*. They are sufficiently *of* the community to represent it, and sufficiently marginalized to do the work of victimage or sacrifice. Because they die, they cannot themselves complete the cultural process from separation through liminality to reincorporation; but the body for which they stand, the community, can and does complete the process, and each of the tragedies ends with someone saying so, declaring (though perhaps inaccurately) communal completion and restoration.

Ritual and ceremonial actions are discrete, controlled, and controllable responses to transitional, ambiguous, conflictual, or chaotic situations that threaten a given structure of relations either explicitly or implicitly (T. S. Turner 1977: 60). They are, above all, mechanisms for control, for manipulating or restoring a communal *perception* of order, clarity, and safety. Tragic protagonists are engaged less in personal rites of passage than in localizing their community's process from initial crisis to reconstruction. The operation of this function is the mechanism of victimage.

In his "Definition of Man," noted earlier in chapter 2, Kenneth Burke asserted that "the principle of drama is implicit in the idea of action, and the principle of victimage is implicit in the idea of drama"; by "drama" he clearly means the specific genre of tragedy (1966: 18, 81). Girard's elaborate analysis of victimage moves Burke's premise to a provocative, indeed highly problematic, principle. For Girard the starting point of all cultural orders is the differentiation of human thought expressed as violence. This violence is specifically a collective murder engendered by the differentiation (separation, alienation) of one individual from within the group, who becomes the victim. Girard's thesis was prompted in part by Freud's *Totem and Taboo,* and rests on the hypothesis of a spontaneous, real, "unanimous victimage" that "would terminate a truly disruptive mimetic crisis by reuniting the entire community against a single, powerless antagonist" (1978: xii). Girard assigns a "mimetic" quality to this crisis on the grounds that imitation is inherent in and characteristic of all higher vertebrates: it is imitation (rivalry) that prompts one individual to oppose another; it is likewise imitation (reciprocity) that prompts the latter to react violently, and that incites the group to follow suit.

Girard's hypothesis is disturbing, not least for its circularity, and because it challenges cherished assumptions about the human capacity for rational judgment in the face of violent action. But those are, after all, assumptions; the Western cultural (i.e., historical and literary) record of riot and *mêlée* tends to support Girard's argument (Davis 1975: "The Reasons of Misrule"; Freud 1950: "The Return of Totemism in Childhood," and 1955: "The Group and the Primal Horde"; also Armstrong and Tennenhouse 1989). Violence, says Girard, "has its reasons . . . and can marshall some rather convincing ones when the need arises" (1977: 2). An exemplary explanation comes from a later essay, "Violence and Representation in the Mythical Text": "If a community is deprived of political and legal means to deal with internal division and agitations, there will be an irreversible tendency to pin the responsibility for whatever ails it on some individual . . . close at hand," that is, to identify a scapegoat. The "conflictual aspects in the narrative elements [of many foundation myths] suggest violent disorder rather than a mere absence of order, primordial or otherwise. We often have a confused struggle between indistinguishable antagonists" (Girard 1978: 185). Since two bodies cannot occupy the same space or fulfill the same social function at the same time, these "indistinguishable antagonists" must be distinguished. This is accomplished when one of them is *ex*tinguished, either by killing or by differentiation of character, which, for Girard, represents the "differentiation of human thought" necessary for the birth of cultural order. Differentiation, i.e., separation, alienation, is served by scapegoating, for which a given myth provides the narrative context. Scapegoating requires motive; thus the victim is invested with "a truly fantastic and superhuman power to harm the community" (1978: 187).

For Girard, myth (narrative) and ritual (performance) are the mimetic re-enactments of an originary act of seemingly spontaneous and arbitrary murder, rationalized as a necessary act of differentiation. In this he counters Durkheim's argument for the anteriority or primacy of the social group or system over its individual constituents. Durkheim also sees differentiation as the source of sacrificial violence, but as the virtually accidental product of "effervescence" during a ceremonial or ritual gathering. Durkheim and Girard occupy opposite positions in a "chicken/egg" dialectic. For Durkheim, ritual is the original ground of violence that is subsequently encoded as "sacrificial"; for Girard, a specific act of violence is the original ground of what is subsequently encoded in ritual. Girard argues that the "founding event" of Western cultures is a spontaneous collective murder, of which ritual is the re-enactment. It is thus a "real event, not a ceremony that constitutes the earliest social groups. And these groups are formed through their unanimous sharing of a single illusion, that of the mythical transformation of the victim . . . . The specific determination of the victim is . . . 'arbitrary,' but the murder itself is not" (Livingston 1988: 122–3).

Derrida advances a similar argument in "Plato's Pharmacy." He begins by quoting an account of the "rite of the *pharmakos*" from Tzetzes's *Thousand Histories* (not further identified): during a period of calamity, "the most unsightly" person in the community is "led forth as though to a sacrifice," fed with cheese, figs, and barley cake, then struck down "with leeks and wild figs and other wild plants," and finally burned, his ashes scattered "into the sea and to the winds, for a purification . . . of the suffering city" (Derrida 1981: 133). Derrida's commentary makes it clear that "the city" in this description acts like, and is to be understood as, a living organism, a "body" in the literal, physical, sense, and not just as a personified abstraction:

> The city's body *proper* thus reconstitutes its unity, closes around the security of its inner courts . . . by violently excluding from its territory the representative of an external threat or aggression . . . . Yet the representative of the outside is nonetheless *constituted*, regularly granted its place by the community, chosen, kept, fed, etc., in the very heart of the inside.
>
> (1981: 133)

The city with which Derrida is specifically concerned is Athens, which apparently kept a supply of "useless and degraded beings," "parasites," for sacrificial emergencies (1981: 133). It would appear that the world of Athens and its recorded ritual practices is very far indeed from the world of Shakespearean (or, for that matter, Athenian) tragedy where the "representatives" of threat, aggression, otherness, evil, are anything but "useless and degraded beings" kept in stock for pharmacological purposes. And yet, in a sense equally valid, these tragic protagonists, these representatives *constituted* in the Derridean sense for the purpose of sacrifice, are likewise "granted [a] place by the community, chosen, kept, fed, etc., in the very heart of the inside." One of the transformations that dramatic tragedy applies, then, to the Greek model of "real" ritual sacrifice, is the selection not of a degraded and useless "parasite" for the purification of the city but of a prince, a patrician, a king – and it will be noticed that this is true for Greek and Roman tragedy as much as for Shakespearean.

What then is being represented in this alteration from lowly to noble victim? In part, the answer is given in Victor Turner's explanation of liminality, quoted above: "the high could not be high unless the low existed, and he who is high must experience what it is like to be low" (1969: 97). In such cases, lowliness is artificial, temporary, theatrically impersonated. In the West African tribal practices that are the focus of Turner's early work – the Ashanti and Tallensi of Ghana, the Ndembu of Zambia – low status is part of the passage through liminality to reincorporation in the community. It is part of the process of purification which the king or chief undergoes on behalf of his community, or the youth undergoes on the way to adulthood. The intention in these cases is that the initiand survive.

Because it is representation, tragedy (whether Shakespearean or Greek) effects a communal process that is more like those of West African tribal practices than the ancient Athenian rites that Derrida describes. Through impersonation, what is represented is a fictional sacrifice of "personae" of noble status, who are in the course of the play radically degraded, on behalf first of the community represented within the play's fiction (Thebes, Rome, Denmark, Venice, Verona, Scotland, Britain), and next of the community watching the play, Shakespeare's London audience or Sophocles's, Aeschylus's, or Euripides's Greeks. Nobody really dies; the actors rise from the stage floor, take their bows, and go home. It is ideally the audience that is transformed in the course of the play; what has been represented has been represented on its behalf.

But I have only partly answered my own question: what exactly is being represented? Not primarily the degradations and deaths of protagonists, but the interrogation, the anatomy, of the values from which they are constructed and for which they are selected not out of a reserve of slaves but precisely because they embody or impersonate the societal constructs under examination. It has long been a matter of critical surprise that many Elizabethan and Jacobean dramatists, especially Shakespeare, managed to avoid censure (or worse) to the extent that they did, given the frequency with which monarchs in their tragedies wreak havoc upon their own communities. The dramatic process by which they so eluded

126

Masters of the Revels and Privy Councils has something to do with the ritualistic aspects of tragedy itself, and is identical with the process by which the ritual subject's victimization (degradation, destruction) occurs.

The transformation of the sacrificial victim occurs through the mechanism of misrecognition, which operates on several levels in several ways. The victim is, first of all, differentiated by either execration or valorization, and sometimes both, depending upon the "reasons" that violence finds for itself as expressed in the explanatory myth or the performative ritual. The victim thus acquires alterity, is understood as "different from" the group in some significant way, or is spatially removed from the community's center to or beyond its periphery. The first kind of misrecognition, then, is of the victim as "not one of us," exogenous, special, and therefore deliberately chosen. A second kind of misrecognition is of the mechanism itself, which depends for its efficacy on the performers' belief in its "truth." Recognizing the random selection of the victim betrays the performance and ensures the collapse of the ritual, the myth, or the social system for whose sake the myth and the ritual exist (Atlan 1988: 195). A third kind of misrecognition is entailed in the institutionalization of the ritual action; although humanly generated, it is believed to be divinely or supernaturally ordained and required for the perpetuation of the community. The danger that underlies all ritual performance is "the possibility that we will encounter ourselves making up our conceptions of the world, society, our very selves. We may slip in that fatal perspective of recognizing culture as our construct, arbitrary, conventional, invented by mortals" (Moore and Myerhoff 1977: 18). And finally, there is for modernity a fourth type: the misrecognition of misrecognition, or the price of demystification. Modernity

> is the knowledge that men owe the laws of the polis to none but themselves. Can the law remain the law if there is no longer, between it and man, that distance once generated by the sacred? Putting the law above men, even though men make their own laws and *know it*, is a problem Rousseau compared to squaring the circle.
>
> (Dupuy 1988: 95)

This is the challenge *King Lear*'s Edmund puts to the institution of legitimacy; it echoes as well from the opposite corner of the arena of differentiation when Richard II questions his attendants: "I live with bread like you, feel want, taste grief, / Need friends. Subjected thus, / How can you say to me I am a king?" (III.ii.175–7).

Misrecognition, in this sense, is the refusal to see that the emperor is naked, that the Wizard of Oz is really a short, middle-aged, bald fellow behind a screen. That refusal comes not from the observers' inadequacy but from their acknowledgement of the law, their agreement to see robes and crowns where there are none. Such agreements are the polarized bases of cultural structures. Ritual heroes encompass all the binary oppositions of their cultures: rags and crowns, power and powerlessness, anarchy and hierarchy. "Feared and admired, isolated and 'incorporated'; at the center of his heroic/sacrificial agon, he is one with the evil he acts to purge . . . . [The] world of reciprocal violence is one of constant mirror effects in which the antagonists become each other's doubles and lose their individual identities" (Girard 1978: 164, 186).

Girard's theory depends upon a principle of initial equation or indistinction between potential antagonists, similar to Turner's notion of "communitas," anterior to any idea of doubles or mirror effects. Difference or opposition is, on this view, an acquired rather than an inherent trait, a processual action explicit in the form of the word "differentiation," that is, *making* different. Such a process occurs because it is felt to be a necessary hedge against chaos. The significant difference in the views of Freud, Durkheim, and Girard, ultimately, is their respective priorities. For Freud, "from the first there were two kinds of psychologies, that of the individual members of the group and that of the father, chief, or leader" (1955: 123).[4] For Durkheim, the primary social organization was a unitary solidarity: "It is because men were organised that they have been able to organise things . . . and, through their union, form an organic role, the tribe. The unity of the first logical systems reproduces the unity of the society" (1972: 259; also Durkheim and Mauss 1963: 82–3). Girard makes differentiation the starting point for all social structures (a view which, curiously, aligns him more closely with Freud than with Durkheim, but without Freud's insistence on the erotic–parental rivalry).

Ultimately, all three of these theorists construct closed interpretive systems that are perforce both reductive and self-sustaining, though each offers an interpretive apparatus that is useful and can be applied to a reading of Shakespearean tragedy without requiring total subscription or a pledge of allegiance. In literary as in historical and anthropological studies, more often than not, actual instances puncture the circles of totalizing hermeneutics. As Jonathan Z. Smith has noticed, "having given priority to the dual, Durkheim and Mauss have difficulties dealing with classification systems that are more complex," and more important, they "fail to perceive the issue of ideology: that the tribe as observed need not correspond to their own systematic statements about themselves" (1987: 40). In an eminently rational approach, Smith undercuts all such dualistic systems by calling attention to an embedded conflict between the "socially real" and the "socially ideal":

> There is a specious symmetry to language of the dual – the implication of equality, balance, and reciprocity . . . . *Up* and *down*, *front* and *back*, *right* and *left* are almost never dualities of equivalence; they are hierarchically ranked in relations of superordination and subordination with radically different valences. If our bias is to see equality in such arrangements, the *tendenz* of the social documents from which we extract our notion of the dual is clearly toward hierarchy . . . . Alongside the tension between equality and hierarchy must be placed that between polarity and continuity. Both egalitarian and hierarchical dualisms conceal a far less highly profiled "reality." What appears, ideologically speaking, as dual is a radical reduction of an extended plenum of graduated positions.
>
> (1987: 41–2)

Smith's important cautionary logic raises further questions about the relation between "social documents" that demonstrate hierarchy and the real history of the groups those documents purport to record. Informed readers and audiences always have choices to make: there is as much "radical reduction" in blindly insisting on specific ideological interventions in reading as there is in blindly ignoring such interventions. Performance itself can be a "radical reduction" of a particular ideology. Among the multiple referents of Foucault's famous challenge to Beckett in "What Is an Author?" (1977) – "What matter who's speaking?"– are the author, the represented characterological positions, the numberless contemporary and later audiences and readers who distill the received performance, and even, as R. Wilson (1987) and Mullaney (1988) have argued, the physical space in which a play is performed, all interpreting, all perhaps with very different ideological inflections. Theorists cannot and should not do the readers' or spectators' work for them.

Like Durkheim and Mauss (Smith 1987:40), Girard also "fail[s] to perceive the issue of ideology," and naturalizes victimage in the context of a social, political, or economic crisis that rhythmically and periodically resurfaces in society alternately with periods of stability. As social theory, Girard's totalizing view is problematic, but as an explanation of the selected and crafted structure of tragedy it is very helpful. The heightened and intensified discourse of the genre is the representation of a particular crisis whose resolution occurs through the mechanism of victimage. Girard's explanation of victimage foregrounds the necessary function of the victim and thus obviates attributions of "fault." His argument is in this view compatible not only with the Aristotelian view of *hamartia* but also with the structural observations of Victor Turner and his school. Turner's interests center in the relation between hierarchy and community in a way that accommodates Smith's objections by substituting "community" (more accurately, "communitas") for "equality," allowing for all of the graduated and continuous distinctions Smith recommends. Taken together, Turner and Girard offer a framework within which the ritual components of Shakespearean tragedy can be brought forward and examined to disclose the operations of the genre for the culture that produced and was reproduced by it.

Linda Woodbridge has recently suggested that Shakespeare's sonnets "undo ritual" by "focusing on individual life . . . , reflect[ing] impersonative thinking" (1994: 252). Similarly, tragedy tends to "undo ritual" by foregrounding a figure so recognizably human as to invite critical analysis, sometimes even *psycho*analysis. At the same time tragedy resists specific "personation" (as early modern dramatists called it), not only because its (im)personations are fictive, but also because its closure implies the potential recycling of misconduct by some other agency than the (dead) protagonist. Tragic closure is thus immanently unstable. It resists itself; like Brutus, it is "with [itself] at war." Implying conclusion, it also implies opening; suggesting resolution, it hints at renewed conflict. Macherey explains that this structural contradiction is

> generated from the incompatibility of several meanings, the strongest bond by which it is attached to reality, in a tense

and ever-renewed confrontation . . . . If the work does not produce or contain the principle of its own closure, it is nevertheless definitively enclosed within its own limits . . . . The work is finite because it is incomplete.

(1978: 80)

Tragic closure is elliptical rather than circular; because something in the fictive situation has changed, closure occurs in a context different from the one in which it began. The fictive community is still threatened, but it is threatened anew. Energies still boil below the surface of the fragile structure; tragedy itself is a momentary and self-subverting tableau.

SCATTERED CORN: RITUAL VIOLATION AND THE DEATH OF ROME IN *TITUS ANDRONICUS*

[We] never really confront a text immediately, in all its freshness as a thing-in-itself. Rather, texts come before us as the always-already-read; we apprehend them through sedimented layers of previous interpretations, or . . . through the sedimented reading habits and categories developed by those inherited interpretive traditions.

Fredric Jameson, Preface, *The Political Unconscious*

"Tragedy conjures the extinction of the human race" (Woodbridge 1994: 179). The ominous loading of the stage at the ends of Shakespearean tragedies encourages the view that tragedy is about death: the death of the body, of the spirit, of the polity. In that sense, *Titus Andronicus* (which rivals *Hamlet* in its final on-stage body count) should be judged one of Shakespeare's most successful tragedies, a *tour de force*, the quintessence of the genre itself. But many critics have argued that it was the least successful of Shakespeare's tragedies (Bevington 1980: 956; Rackin 1978: 10; J. D. Wilson 1948: li–lvi). A notable exception is Maurice Charney's observation that, along with other revenge tragedies of its generation, *Titus Andronicus* "helped to explore the possibilities of tragedy," and "shows the way that leads to greater plays . . . . The greatness of Shakespearean tragedy is already manifest" (1990: 9–10).

It was, however, Terence Spencer who reminded us of a generation ago of the context in which an Elizabethan audience would have received *Titus*. Citing Antonio Guevara's *Decada*, translated by Edward Hellowes as *A Chronicle, conteyning the lives of tenne Emperours of Rome* (1577), as an "established" source for the play, he notes

that among the "lives" an Elizabethan reader would have found
therein,

> appears a blood-curdling life of a certain Emperor Bassianus
> .... [It] is one of almost unparalleled cruelty .... I will not
> say that it is a positive relief to pass from the life of Bassianus
> by Guevara to Shakespeare's *Titus Andronicus* (and there to
> find, by the way, that Bassianus is the better of the two
> brothers) .... *Titus Andronicus* is Senecan ... a not untypical
> piece of Roman history, or would seem to be so to anyone
> who came fresh from reading Guevara. Not the most high
> and palmy state of Rome, certainly. But an authentic Rome,
> and a Rome from which the usual political lessons could be
> drawn.
>
> (Spencer 1957: 32)

The fact that *Titus Andronicus* follows classical models should not
be ignored or explained away; neither should the idea that it
offered its original audience "the usual political lessons" for which
they turned to Roman history in the first place, although Spencer
does not say what those were. More recent critics (Miola 1981;
Charney 1990) have historicized the play from this hybrid
Elizabethan–Roman point of view. This is not easy to do; as Miola
says, "any approach which seeks to fit the various incarnations of
Shakespeare's Rome to a single political or theological Procru-
stean bed does violence to the heterogeneity of the city's origins
and character" (1981: 95).

The horrors that the play represents, however shocking they
may be to the kinder, gentler culture that we think we are, would
probably not have shocked an audience regularly entertained by
what Steven Mullaney calls the "dramaturgy of the margins," by
which "the horizon of the community was made visible, the limits
of definition, containment, and control made manifest," and which
included "hospitals and brothels, . . . madhouses, scaffolds of
execution, prisons, and lazar-houses" (1988: 31), not to mention
various animal and human atrocities going on virtually next door
to the Theater in bear-baiting and cock-fighting dens, and similarly
heterodox, disorderly, or "incontinent" cultural entertainments.
As John Velz notes, walls are the most important edifices in
Shakespeare's Rome, which is "above all *urbs* in its etymological
sense, the enclave of civilization ringed round with a protective
wall, outside of which the dark forces of barbarism lurk" (1978: 11).

Evidently one did not have to venture very far outside those walls to find lurking barbarism.

A "margin" is not only linear, defining a city's limits, but also spatial, a topology inhabited and informed by a social behavior and a political status. A space that delimits ambiguity and flux, that defines and contains by describing a boundary, a margin is itself a locus for alteration. In the terms by which a *polis* defines itself, "margin" represents the verge, the limits, by which one is citizen or alien, endogenous or exogenous, "one of us" or "one of them." Once again Mary Douglas's observation applies: "all margins are dangerous. If they are pulled this way or that the shape of fundamental experience is altered. Any structure of ideas is vulnerable at its margins" (1966: 121). In *Titus Andronicus*, as in *Othello* and *The Merchant of Venice*, one may live, or be brought to live, within a city's walls, and still be marginalized. That, surely, is one of the play's "usual political lessons."

Titus Andronicus is in many respects a marginal play. As Shakespeare's first tragedy, it was the *terminus a quo*, the initial boundary for the rest of his work in the genre. But most important is the play's concern with marginality and its threat to political identity. Rome in this play is a city of ambiguity, whose cultural identity is challenged from the outset by the incorporation of aliens within its boundaries, by confusion and dissension about its rules of conduct and their consistent applications, and by the hybridization of its central leadership.

Previous attempts to identify the play's sources have yielded a patchwork of less than satisfactory nominations, aside from the usual round-up of Ovidian, Senecan, and Virgilian – that is, literary – analogues. With every suggestion, scholars have noted how little may be said with certainty about Shakespeare's acquisition of the plot concerning the Goths and Aaron, as well as any story about any actual Andronici (Bullough 1973: VI: 3–82; Maxwell 1961: xxvii–xxxii; Charney 1990: 7; D. J. Palmer 1972: 323). The closest parallel texts are a prose story and a ballad printed in an eighteenth-century chap-book owned by the Folger Library, but as Bullough says, these are as likely to have followed Shakespeare's play as to have preceded it. The uncertainty of the date of the play itself (Hill 1957) makes it difficult to determine what Shakespeare knew and how he could have known it. What history of fifth-century Rome was available to him? All of Shakespeare's usually accepted classical sources significantly antedate the famous Gothic

"Sack of Rome." Tacitus's *Histories* and *Annals* (translated into English in 1591 and 1598, respectively), and Pliny's *Natural History* (translated into English in 1566) merely mention among various Germanic tribes the *Gothones* (Tacitus) or *Gutones* (Pliny); in any case both historians wrote during the first century C.E., long before these "Goths" became any sort of threat to Roman borders or territories. Moreover, in Shakespeare's play, it is the Romans who are victorious, and nothing in the play indicates who started the war, or who invaded whose territories.

It may be said with some safety, then, that Shakespeare's "Goths" are not the ones who overthrew Rome in the fifth century, and indeed may not be any particular historical Goths at all. "Goth" may be a generic term for barbarian, especially barbarians of Eastern origin and fierce and bloody reputation: in "A Valediction: Of the Book," Donne employs the image of "ravenous / Goths and Vandals" to signal the end of civilization and especially of literacy and learning. In *As You Like It*, Touchstone compares his displacement in Arden with that of "honest Ovid . . . among the Goths" (III.iii.9), alluding to Ovid's description of his banishment among the Getae (formerly identified with "Goths") in the *Pontic Epistles*. Lear, in banishing Cordelia, compares her to "The barbarous Scythian, / Or he that makes his generation messes / To gorge his appetite" (I.i.116–18), incorporating a reminder of the reputation of invaders from the East for intrafamilial cannibalism that is, of course, reflected in Tamora's unwitting consumption of her children.[5]

The term "Goth" functions in Shakespeare's play as part of a differential economy as the "other" of Roman civilization. In fact, long before any *Gothic* invasions, Rome was nearly destroyed from within by the same Bassianus Spencer mentions. This Bassianus was a Libyan on his father's side (the emperor Septimius Severus) and a Syrian on his mother's (Julia Domna), and converted his court to the manners and customs of Syrian theocracy. His reign and those immediately following constituted a long and bloody period of religious and political instability in Rome. For these events Shakespeare did indeed have a specific source, previously unidentified by the play's editors and critics. That source, which is also the source of Guevara's *Decada* and thus of Hellowes's *Chronicle*, is Herodian of Antioch's *History of the Roman Empire*. Herodian tells of a Rome governed for sixty years by an Afroasiatic dynasty, its religion converted to a Syrian theocracy spearheaded by a politically clever and ambitious *materfamilias* and her two sons, one of whom had the other killed and proceeded to rule as one of the more vicious tyrants in Roman history. There are only two extant contemporary records of this period of internal destruction, this undoing by a marginalized and demonized force ruling from within Roman borders. The Greek Dio Cassius's *Roman History* was not translated into English until the twentieth century. Herodian's *History* was translated into English by Nicholas Smyth and printed by William Coplande *circa* 1550 as *The history of Herodian*,[6] a chronicle, modeled on Plutarch's *Lives*, of the late empire from Marcus Aurelius (161–80) to Gordian III (238–44), including the reign of Bassianus and his successors. Here is the lesson Tudor England would have learned from Herodian.

The historical Rome that later failed to stave off the Gothic invasion had long since already destroyed itself from within. Herodian's claim to the authority of an eye-witness may well be believed, since the Afroasiatic dynasty covers a period of only some sixty years (180–238): "And when by the space of lx. yeres, the Citie of Rome had sustained more gouernours then for the time sufficed, it came to passe, that many straunge thinges and worthy admiracion chanced" (Herodian 1550: sig. B.iv).

The story that interested Shakespeare began under Bassianus's father, Septimius Severus, a Libyan who had gained control of Rome without significant opposition during an interregnum in 193 when Rome had no central leadership. His main rival for control of Rome was one Niger, a former consul and governor of Syria. Niger's belated (and futile) campaign to defeat Severus deployed troops of Moroccan javelin-throwers, famous (says Herodian) for bravery, brutality, and savagery, and in Herodian's account Shakespeare might have found inspiration for his Moor.[7] Severus's most famous exploit was the attempted subjection of Britain, to which Herodian devotes detailed attention. He died in the middle of this prolonged effort, and was succeeded by Bassianus (also known as Caracalla, and as Antoninus, an honorific attached to all Roman emperors from Septimius Severus to his grandson Severus Alexander). Bassianus was preferred to the throne by his Syrian mother, Julia Domna, herself a formidable and assiduous politician, mostly on behalf of her sons but with almost equal dedication to her own licentious and ambitious leanings. Several years before he died, Septimius Severus married Bassianus to the daughter of his Libyan compatriot, one Plautianus.

The marriage was far from happy. To avenge his daughter's neglect, Plautianus hired a tribune out of the praetorian guard to kill both Bassianus and Severus, but the plot failed when the tribune betrayed his employer. The tribune's name was Saturninus, and he too was Syrian by birth (sig. M.iii, fol. xlii-xliii).

The historical Bassianus's brother was actually named Geta; perhaps the name Saturninus sounded more "Roman" for the brother of Shakespeare's Bassianus. It is entirely possible, as well, that "Geta" suggested "Goth" to Shakespeare; in fact, early histories of the Goths refer generally to the scattered tribes of Goths as Getae or Geticae.

In Herodian several missing links come together. The matter of religious controversy and Julia Domna's manipulations behind palace doors suggest two of the structural elements of the plot concerning Tamora. If Saturninus is indeed a name-replacement for Geta, Shakespeare simply reversed the personalities of the brothers, for the historical Bassianus killed his brother, annexed his lands, and ruled most tyrannically. In explaining himself to his people, Bassianus cited historical precedents for "kynred"-killers, naming, among others, "Romulus hym selfe, the buylder of this Citye," and Domitian's murder of his brother Titus (there is no connection between Shakespeare's Titus and Domitian's victim, but the name may have stuck in Shakespeare's mind). In the end, having killed too many of his own people – "he began to destroye euery man from the verie bedde syde, as the prouerbe sayth" (sig. N.iii, fol. xlv) – Bassianus was slain by the surviving brother, Martialis, of yet another of his victims. The manner of his death is worth noting: in Mesopotamia, returning from worship at the Temple of Diana, he stopped, as Herodian narrates,

> to do the requisites of nature. Then Martialis, (which awaited euery conuenie~t howre) seyng the Emperour alone, & all other farre of, made haste towardes him asthough he were called for some businesse, & running vpon him unwares, as he was vntrussing his pointes, stabbed him in w~ a dagger, which he of purpose, secretly bare in hys sleaue.

> (fol. lv.)

The reign of Bassianus lasted altogether six years, and ended, ironically, in an act of defecatioñ.

The utility of Herodian's narrative to a study of *Titus Andronicus* is not only as a previously unrecognized source for Shakespeare, the only one that links the names of Bassianus and Saturninus. Its special value is in its presentation, certainly available to Shakespeare, of a peculiar period in Roman history when Elizabethan England's favorite cultural antecedent was itself hybridized and feminized. Rome's "Syrian phase" began in 186, when a legion commander married the daughter of a Syrian priest of Elagabalus. In 193, when the Libyan Septimius Severus became emperor, Rome had a Syrian empress, Julia Domna, "the key figure in Rome's Syrian dynasty . . . . A shrewd, highly capable woman [who] assumed imperial responsibility with her husband" (Echols 1961: 4). When Bassianus (Caracalla) became emperor in 211, Rome had a Syrian–Libyan emperor, and when Elagabalus became emperor in 218, Rome had a Syrian emperor. The Syrian domination of Rome continued through the reign of Alexander Severus, a pacifist whose weak military command ultimately led to the return of "European" leadership under Maximinus (235–8), who was born in Thrace.

Thus, in Herodian we find not only some of those names that have baffled *Titus*'s editors, but perhaps more importantly, a slice of Roman history which saw Rome dominated from within by "barbarians,"[8] its values compromised and perhaps by Elizabethan standards bastardized and miscegenized,[9] its pollution led and orchestrated by a politically ambitious and calculating matriarch who gave him his model for Tamora, and a dynasty of African rulers. *Titus Andronicus* may be Shakespeare's attempt to accommodate that long and problematic episode in the history of a Rome which England preferred not to recognize. The Roman history that Tudor England read about in Herodian was not the masculine, European Roman history of Marcus Brutus, Julius Caesar, and Marc Antony; it was not the Rome upon which England in part rested its own cultural genealogy. It was a Rome dominated by feminine influence,[10] subverting everything that was understood by the ideology of *romanitas*.

The relation of the cultural displacements in the play, as suggested by Herodian's *History*, to ritualistic action is significantly illuminated by other ancient sources known to Shakespeare. There are certain aspects of Seneca's *Thyestes* that are undervalued in most criticism of *Titus Andronicus*. The *Thyestes* was already an old Elizabethan story when Shakespeare was born. Jasper Heywood's 1560 English translation was more than twenty years old when Thomas Newton published it in *Seneca His Tenne Tragedies*

(1581). More familiar to the Elizabethans than the Aeschylean version preferred today, it told the base legend, the ur-myth, on which classical familial tragedies are modeled. Zeus's son Tantalus kills *his* son Pelops (in Seneca, constructed sentimentally as a baby "running to kiss his father" [1966: TLN 145]) and feeds him to the gods assembled at a formal banquet, with catastrophically inverted results for the entire community: "The consequence of this repast was hunger, / Hunger and thirst for all eternity" (1966: TLN 149–50). Similarly, in the Ovidian source for Lavinia's rape and mutilation, Procne retaliates against her rapist-husband Tereus on her sister Philomel's behalf by killing their son Itys and feeding his baked body to his father. Neither Ovid nor Seneca gives any reason for this originary, causeless infanticide, which in Seneca is reversed when Zeus restores Pelops. Pelops's two sons, Thyestes and Atreus, compete for their father's throne. Thyestes seduces his brother's wife; Atreus retaliates by killing and feeding Thyestes's sons to their father – all except Aegisthus (born of Thyestes's incest with his sister Pelopia), who grows up to seduce Clytemnestra, wife of Atreus's son Agamemnon, who had meanwhile sacrificed his daughter Iphigenia in order (he said) to summon the winds and save his navy. Clytemnestra kills Agamemnon, ostensibly in revenge for Iphigenia's death, and Orestes retaliates by killing his mother Clytemnestra while Electra, the remaining sister, urges him on, pours libations, and curses everyone in her whole sad family.[11]

This dizzying synopsis illustrates a mythic base of infanticide and incest, laundered in the Aeschylean *Eumenides* to suggest an evolution towards "modern" and "humane" systems of justice. Seneca, however, was more interested in the foundational significance of *sparagmos* and *omophagia* than in institutionalized forms of civil retribution. Foundational stories define a culture to itself, setting standards and parameters by which it distinguishes itself from others. Originary violence, as Girard argues, is a given in foundation myths; it is nonetheless interesting to notice *against whom* and *in whose behalf* that violence occurs. The story of the House of Atreus deals entirely with intrafamilial or endogenous relations; kin-killing and incest are at the heart of both Aeschylean and Senecan versions of the story. The larger political narrative is just barely remembered in the face of these horrors: the Argive victory over Troy; the endless hunger in the aftermath of a banquet at the very beginning, and of course the fact that the "kin" in these stories are royalty (and earlier, deity), and therefore responsible for the welfare of whole polities.

It is worth noting how closely Shakespeare hews to his Senecan antecedent. The Gothic family looks much like the Thyestean side of Seneca's story: although Tamora does not kill her own children, she does, like Thyestes, eat them; the miscegenation of Tamora and Aaron can be seen as an inversion (a radical exogamy) of the incest (a radical endogamy) that produced Aegisthus. Recalling the Atreidan side of the story, Titus kills both a son and a daughter, as Tantalus killed his son and Agamemnon killed his daughter,[12] and plays the role of Atreus in feeding Tamora's sons to her.

The Thyestean pie put before Tamora, however, is more than a Senecan or Ovidian exercise by a novice playwright; it is appropriate justice. From the beginning of his career, Shakespeare understood the resonances of ritualistic action in performance. The baking and serving of Chiron and Demetrius is a fitting response to Lavinia's rape and mutilation. Tamora is literally made to swallow the agents of the grotesque violations she has engineered. A formal banquet is perverted into a mythologically antecedent act of *omophagia*, which in the mythic base devolves to a cycle of revenge with no resurrective or regenerative possibilities. In *Titus*, *omophagia* repays outwardly directed crimes of mutilation and murder with an inwardly directed pollution. The punctilious design of Titus's revenge reflects the power of inversion as redress.[13]

Jan Kott's investigation of ancient rites involving *sparagmos* and *omophagia* as the cultural context of Euripides's *Bacchae* locates maternal *omophagia* as a structural inversion of incest, and also of giving birth and feeding. It is "*genesis* annihilated, moved back to its origins," negating both time and succession. "This simultaneous fili-, regi-, and dei-cide is the ultimate completion of the cycle. Cosmos has become chaos again so that everything can begin anew .... Fertility is mortally wounded in order that it may be renewed" (Kott 1973: 200). Kott's focus on maternal *omophagia* brings us closer to Tamora's punishment in *Titus Andronicus* than does any segment of the Atreus legend, in which all the child-eaters are male. "In such myths and *sparagmos* rites, women are the priestesses. They tear bodies to pieces and partake of the raw flesh. The sacrificial victim is always male: a child of the male sex, or a young man, or a ram, he-goat, or bull" (1973: 199).

Shakespeare aborts the ritual intention of *sparagmos* and *omophagia*; *Titus* is set not in the world of the Eleusinian rites but in late

Imperial Rome as performed for Elizabethan England. In the violent and violational world of Shakespeare's play, cosmos becomes chaos but nothing can begin anew. This is evident from the specific nature of the Gothic family's crimes against the Andronici, which are themselves retaliation for the play's initial *sparagmos*, the "lopping" of Alarbus's "limbs." As Miola notes, "Instead of beginning the Roman Empire, the rape of Lavinia signals the end of whatever civilization Rome possesses and the triumph of lawless savagery" (1981: 88–9). Her mutilation signals the end of civilization in yet another way: the loss of hands and tongue deprive her of both writing and speech, which Ben Jonson called "the only benefit man has to expresse his excellencie of mind above other creatures. It is the Instrument of Society" (1965: 347). Their deprivation, then, signals the removal of the speechless from the social construct and renders her, by definition, inhuman.

The implication for the larger order of Rome in the play is disastrous: not only is Lavinia dehumanized, but as the only Andronica (and one of only three females in the play, all dead or imminently so by the end), her death, like her silencing and her rape, undermine Marcus's weak charge to the "sad-fac'd *men*, people and *sons* of Rome" (my emphasis) to "knit again / This scatter'd corn into one mutual sheaf" (V.iii.67–71). The phallocentric image of the sheaf, the seminal one of scattered corn, and the address to men and sons are curious. On the one hand, Tamora's feminization of the Roman emperorship figures as the primary source of Rome's destruction,[14] not only as a masculine civilization but as a civilization of any kind. On the other hand, without women, Rome's hopes for renewal reside in an impossible parthenogenesis. The reconstruction of the body politic is highly doubtful after so much dismemberment: the bodies of Lavinia and Titus (and Martius and Quintus Andronicus, and Alarbus) are not the only ones dismantled in the play. The dismemberment of Rome as a polity is declared at the play's outset when Titus is invited by his brother on behalf of "the people of Rome" to accept the emperorship, "and help to set a head on headless Rome" (I.i.186). Shakespeare's pun is clearly intended; Titus's refusal inculpates him in his city's *sparagmos*.

A completed ritual would require both *sparagmos* and *omophagia*, dismemberment *and* ingestion or reintegration in a new body. Shakespeare fragments the ritual process by assigning the agency of *sparagmos* both to Chiron and Demetrius and to Titus, and that of *omophagia* to Tamora. Alarbus's and Titus's respective "lopp'd" limbs and Martius's and Quintus's severed heads all separately and collectively represent fragments of a body of ritual *practice* that in another time and place would have signalled the start of a healing rite. This play's deployment of *disjecta membra* demonstrates the nihilistic impact of ritual gone awry. Consequently, the promised end, the scattered corn knit into one mutual sheaf, is set up as an impossibility. There is no renewal, none is possible, for a Rome so torn apart and so far from the proper management of its foundational ritual practices.

In *Titus Andronicus* Shakespeare does not simply replicate the *Thyestes* or interpellate several foundational stories; he inverts them, foregrounding the political implications for Rome. Beginning with the election of Titus as emperor and his rejection of the honor, this aborted ceremony is immediately conflated with the entry of the Andronicus funeral procession, which takes us immediately to the sacrifice *ad manes fratrum* of Alarbus (D. J. Palmer 1972: 327). The play is arranged as a central story of *sparagmos* (Alarbus, Lavinia, Titus, Martius and Quintus) bracketed by infanticide (Mutius in Act I and Lavinia in Act V) and *omophagia* (Act V). This structuring foregrounds the confusion or interpenetration of political and religious ritual, which makes it much more than a Senecan imitation. It is a dissection of cultural formation and its definition, an interrogation of the inextricable relation between the political and ritual in culture. Ritual becomes not the effective redress for which it is designed but the actual site of contestation (for which there is no redress) and a reminder of the consequences to the polity of ritual violation or neglect.

The play's numerous and various examples of *sparagmos* enact a dissection or anatomy of culture that discloses its fault-lines. The intersections of axes along which culture is produced are also its vulnerable points; what can be joined can also be sundered. Shakespeare's meticulous attention to these junctures might seem remarkable in such an early play. But the discourse of the body that contextualizes this attention was a long-standing and well-known commonplace by the late sixteenth century. The observation that the body is especially vulnerable at its joints and orifices belongs to Sir John Cheke, who noted in *The Hurt of Sedicion Howe Grevous it is to a Commune-wealth* (1549; STC 5109) that, like the natural body, the body politic "cannot bee without much grief of inflammacon, where any least part is out of joynt, or not duely set in his owne natural place" (quoted in M. James 1983: 8n.). The Rome that interested Shakespeare in *Titus Andronicus* was for sixty years a sutured patchwork of European and Afroasiatic population, politics, and religion.

What happens to such a sutured civilization? What specific junctures make it vulnerable? In *Titus*, culture is literally articulated in terms of body parts (D. J. Palmer 1972; Tricomi 1974; Paster 1989; Kendall 1989), which are further arranged into male and female categories. These anatomical assignments are expanded into gendered social roles, which are then undermined by constant inversion and re-inversion in this play. The consistency with which Shakespeare attaches such imagery to Roman history is worth noting; we find it again in *Coriolanus* in Menenius's Fable of the Belly. Remarkably, Shakespeare's first tragedy looks ahead to his final one when, in *Titus*, Aemilius looks "backward" by invoking the "historical" Coriolanus as a model for Lucius's revolt against Rome (IV.iv.68).

A culture defines itself in part by distinguishing self from other, "them" from "us," citizen from alien, and does so along both national and racial lines of demarcation. Out of such defining divisions, or rather to secure them, ideology is formed, and ritual's primary function, after guaranteeing physical survival, is to guarantee the survival of the cultural definition, that is, its ideology. But the Rome of *Titus Andronicus* has no unifying ideology. Titus believes that it does, as we see by his actions in the first moments of the play; but his faith is immediately contested by his sons and further problematized by the union of Tamora, the Asiatic Goth, and the Roman Saturninus.

The combined ritual function of *sparagmos* and *omophagia* belongs to that of the scapegoat or *pharmakos*. Again the matter of cultural distinctions, "them" and "us," is crucial. As Girard has explained, in order for a scapegoat rite to be effective, the *pharmakos* must resemble the rest of the community enough to represent it, and at the same time must be sufficiently alienated, misrecognized as *other*, to be killed with impunity (1977: 13). The opening scene of *Titus Andronicus* positions the political and ritual requirements of the victorious Romans against those of the defeated Goths, thereby interrogating the definitions that distinguish self from other, "Roman" from "Goth."

While I am not arguing that *Titus Andronicus* represents an Elizabethan plea for multicultural tolerance, it does raise questions about the definitions of culture that enable the chain of killing and revenge, and of *sparagmos* and *omophagia* that encircle and define this play. The play begins with a ritual sacrifice, *ad manes fratrum* (I.i.96-101), for Titus's sons who have been killed in battle. This sacrifice is seen as a legitimate demand from the Roman point of view, but not, obviously, from that of the Goths, who (again from the Roman point of view) are both aliens and prisoners of war, and therefore are perfect scapegoats. Their foreign status means that the Roman community is not contaminated by killing or by failing to avenge one of its own. If Alarbus were a solitary prisoner, his sacrifice would have achieved its intended effect, and we would hear no more of him or the Goths. But Shakespeare problematizes the ritual situation by including Tamora and her remaining sons. The "other" that Alarbus represents to Rome is "self" to the Gothic contingent. Moreover, the rite itself is problematic in so far as it is intended as a rite of completion, to answer a killing and to avoid further reprisal; that effect is only possible in the case of communal agreement about its function and operation. For Tamora, it is not a rite but a murder, and therefore demands revenge. Her pleas for Alarbus's life complicate audience response by cutting across national lines of definition: instead of Goths and Romans, the audience is invited by Tamora's lines to consider an undifferentiated human *communitas*:

> Victorious Titus, rue the tears I shed,
> A mother's tears in passion for her son;
> And if thy sons were ever dear to thee,
> O, think my son to be as dear to me!
> Sufficeth not that we are brought to Rome
> To beautify thy triumphs, and return
> Captive to thee and to thy Roman yoke;
> But must my sons be slaughtered in the streets
> For valiant doings in their country's cause?
> O, if to fight for king and commonweal
> Were piety in thine, it is in these.
>
> (I.i.105–15)

Her argument appeals to Titus's sense of piety as well as to the same *romanitas* that informed his own willing sacrifice in war of twenty-one sons for his country. His response turns the argument back upon her.

Patient yourself, madam, and pardon me.
These are their brethren, whom your Goths beheld
Alive and dead, and for their brethren slain
Religiously they ask a sacrifice:
To this your son is mark'd, and die he must,
T'appease their groaning shadows that are gone.

(I.i.121–6)

No compromise is possible: paradoxically, the cycle of revenge that
ritual is designed to prevent is inevitable in the circumstances of
the play. The hard truth of perspective is brought home: what
Lucius calls the "clean" consumption by fire of the *pharmakos*
(127–9) is for Tamora nothing but "cruel, irreligious piety!" (130),
a definition that contradicts Titus's surname, "Pius," noting the
virtue for which he is famous.

These contesting claims for "piety," defined separately by
Tamora and Titus in terms of both "vengeance" and proper burial
rites, illuminate from the very start of the play the crisis of Roman
cultural definition. The question of definitions entailed in ritual
clarity immediately spreads to members of Titus's own family when
he kills and disowns Mutius. In his refusal to allow Mutius's burial,
Titus enacts the definitional crisis, and Marcus identifies it: "Thou
art a Roman; be not barbarous" (I.i.378). Roman values are themselves revealed as the site of contestation. Since one of the hallmarks
of *romanitas* is filial obedience, Mutius's rebellion against Titus in
the matter of remanding Lavinia to Saturninus seems to Titus
nothing less than treason. But Rome's belief in its own laws is
equally compelling, and Lavinia was contracted to Bassianus. In
order to resolve this particular conflict, Titus kills the "traitor" by
first disclaiming kinship: Mutius is deliberately misrecognized,
made an "other," an alien: "Nor thou [to Lucius] nor he, are any
sons of mine. / My sons would never so dishonor me. / Traitor,
restore Lavinia to the Emperor" (I.i.294–6). As an alien, Mutius
can be denied proper ritual burial in the family tomb (I.i.349–54);
but as an Andronicus, he must be so buried, and Titus's refusal is
called by his brother Marcus "impiety" (355), the charge now
coming not from Tamora but from within the family. The violation
of Roman burial rites by a Roman immediately establishes the
pattern of ritual perversion and neglect that continues throughout
the play to the end, when the belated attempt is made to resurrect
Rome from its own scattered seed: Titus and Lavinia are granted

144

proper burial, but Tamora and Aaron will be left to rot at the margins of the city.

The tragedy is set in motion by conflicting ritual observations, a set of relativities, a clash of cultures whose differences reflect their similarities as we can hear in Tamora's pleading. Her maternal plea is dismissed; fittingly she later ignores Lavinia's appeal to "sisterhood." As disturbing as her "unfeminist" treatment of Lavinia is, it is also a strong form of revenge against Titus; as Miola points out, the rape of a daughter "is a flagrant violation of the family and the sacred bonds that tie it together . . . the destruction of her familial bonds has disastrous implications for the order in the city and the hierarchical order in nature itself" (1981: 87). Tamora learns quickly that the Rome Titus embodies has no regard for the feminine (we see this again in Marcus's phallocentric closing invocation), and despite its claims to the contrary, none for the family either unless that family is natively Roman. G. K. Hunter long ago suggested that the "alternative 'household' of Saturninus/Tamora/Aaron with Tamora's assorted children . . . can only be called a 'family' by a radically deformed definition" (1974: 4). However, it should be noted that the vaunted Roman regard for family is shown to be seriously limited in the *paterfamilias* himself. As Shylock says in *The Merchant of Venice*, "The villainy you teach me I will execute, and it shall go hard but I will better the instruction" (III.i.71–3). Since, in this Rome, feminine values are eschewed, Tamora, out of sheer survivalist adaptation, becomes more like the quintessential Roman male, that is, like Titus, one who can kill not only other people's children but his own. Though Tamora never quite manages to kill her own children (she orders her baby's death, but does not execute it), Titus remedies that by making her eat them. In an exchange of behaviors, father-Titus learns to be more like the Gothic (not the neo-Roman) mother-Tamora; his daughter's dismantling teaches him to empathize with the "parents" of a fly. Meanwhile, Aaron, the permanent alien, doubly demonized as "the black man with the Jewish name" (West 1982: 71; Fiedler 1972: 178) teaches everyone what paternity and paternal love really mean when he taunts Chiron and Demetrius about their baby brother and bargains with Lucius to protect his son. Aaron preserves all the characteristics of his theatrical ancestor the Vice (until he steps forward to protect his son); he stays in the margin of Rome and machinates the inversion of all-that-is-Roman to nothing-at-all, an unregeneratable pile of scattered seed.

Rome, as represented by Saturninus, attempted to subvert the alien Goths by incorporating them into Roman citizenship and Roman values by his union with Tamora. But a dismembered polity, "headless Rome" (I.i.186) split from the beginning of the play by opposing brothers, is already fractured beyond any unified set of values. Since gender and racial distinctions are two especially visible options out of a number of tactics for cultural definition, the concretizing of Rome's cultural disintegration in a feminized and racialized dialectic enabled Shakespeare's audience to "see" the consequences to this civilization that allowed itself to let go of its cultural definitions, as Rome indeed had done and as Elizabethan England seemed increasingly in danger of doing (Mullaney 1988: 64; Bartels 1990; Neill 1989).

The definitional crisis spreads in yet another direction when Saturninus establishes Tamora as his empress. Tamora and her sons, former prisoners of war, are absorbed into Roman (or neo-Roman) identity, and the distinction of "Roman" from "non-Roman" is no longer persuasive, no longer even possible. Tamora's empowerment enables her to avenge her son's death, but she does so as a new-made Roman, and the "clean" ritual distinction of *othe*rness is obliterated: for the remainder of the play, except for Aaron, all participants in this internecine slaughter are either Romans or neo-Romans by definition, and the entire community, in a chaos of kin-killing and self-mutilation, turns in upon itself in the ultimate pattern of annihilation.

From the start of the play, little more than half way through the first scene, we see the consequences first of contestation between separate communities; then the arena narrows to a specifically Roman venue, and then the circle contracts to the still smaller arena of a single family. Before the play is over, that arena will contract yet further to its most microcosmic version, the individual: Titus himself becomes the site of contestation, and the divisions we have already witnessed between communities, within a community, and within a family, become manifest in the literal dismemberment of the patriarch and his only daughter and the beheading of two of his three remaining sons. Like Alarbus, Martius and Quintus died from their dismemberment; but the mutilated images presented by both Titus and Lavinia are images of life-in-death, terrifying indistinctions that pollute by their failure to separate the living from the dead, which is the aim and the design of properly conducted, unsubverted, burial rites and mourning practices. Critics have struggled to define Titus's killing of Lavinia in a range of meanings from cruelty to mercy; but within the play, even Saturninus calls him "unnatural and unkind" (V.iii.48). Moral evaluations aside (and who among those present, except perhaps for Lucius and Marcus, is qualified to make any?) Titus completes Lavinia's definition as "dead"; and thus he explains it to Tamora: "'twas Chiron and Demetrius. / They ravish'd her, and cut away her tongue; / And they, 'twas they, that did her all this wrong" (V.iii.56–8).

Ironically, the "headlessness" by which Rome is identified at the opening of the play is filled in by the image of Aaron's punishment at the end of the play. Set "breast-deep," "fast'ned in the earth" (V.iii.179, 183), he appears to be a disembodied head; "planted," he epitomizes the paradox of an unregeneratable polity – his is not the corn or seed Marcus hopes to gather, but as he hopes, his seed, half Moor and half Roman-Goth, will eventually destroy what is left of Rome. By that time, and indeed before the play is over, Rome has lost all vestiges of its political identity. Titus had a hand in that too, when he sent Lucius, "the turn'd forth" (V.iii.109), off to rally the Gothic army to march against what was once his city (a reversion also performed by Coriolanus) and against a woman who was once their queen. Throughout *Titus Andronicus*, both Roman and Gothic cultural distinctions are confounded: early on, Demetrius counseled his mother to wait for the "opportunity of sharp revenge" that would "favor Tamora, the Queen of Goths – / When Goths were Goths and Tamora was queen" (I.i.139–40). By the end of the play, Goths are still not Goths (no more than Romans are Romans); they return with Lucius as his allies. Rome, too, is hybridized by Tamora's marriage to Saturninus; she refers to herself as "incorporate in Rome, / A Roman now adopted happily" (I.i.462–3). After this, her coupling with Aaron and the birth of their interracial child simply extends the blurring of distinctions already set in motion.

All cultural definitions are nullified in this play by the confusion or neglect of cultural markers. Rome, which has long since become a "wilderness of tigers," is in the end identified with the incorporated aliens Tamora and Aaron, each of whom is separately (V.iii.5; V.iii.195) called by Lucius a "ravenous tiger" (Loomba 1989: 46). Marcus's "Let me teach you how to knit again" and Lucius's promise "to heal Rome's harms, and wipe away her woe" (V.iii.148) are taken by some critics at face value (Hunter 1974: 6; D. J. Palmer 1972: 338); that is, they assume that Rome will indeed arise from its "scattered corn." Lucius's first act of "healing" is properly constructed as the re-establishment of funeral rites, which return us to the play's beginning. Funeral rites are part of the set of cultural distinctions that separate "Roman" from "other": Lucius buries Titus and Lavinia in the Andronicus tomb while planting Aaron and leaving Tamora "to beasts and birds to prey" (V.iii.198). Aaron and Tamora are denied such rites not only in revenge but also because there are no rites appropriate to them; as incorporated aliens they remain demonized and marginal.

No regeneration is possible in such a fractured polity. Lucius's attempt to restore cultural unity is undermined by the truth about the bodies he would inter in the Andronicus tomb, once the symbol and locus of ritual integrity as Titus had argued in refusing to bury the son he had killed. The bodies of Titus and Lavinia are fragmented; they are missing parts. Despite Lucius's fiat, then, which is too little and comes too late, the Rome of *Titus Andronicus*, like its historical counterpart under Bassianus and his successors, cannot and could not be re-established, and it never was. By the end of the play we know why and how Rome fell.

POOR SACRIFICES:
A NOTE ON *ROMEO AND JULIET*

The paradoxes inherent in Shakespearean tragedy are unavoidable, embedded in the premises of the genre, arising from contradictions implicit and explicit in the function of the *pharmakos*. In his discourse on the cognate *pharmakon* ("remedy"), Derrida wrestled with its multiple challenges, beginning with the matter of translation. "Remedy," he says, is a "not inaccurate" rendition of *pharmakon*, but it is only half accurate, and "erases . . . the other pole reserved in the word," thereby cancelling the ambiguity *required* for understanding the context:

> When a word inscribes itself as the citation of another sense of the same word, when the textual center-stage of the word *pharmakon*, even while it means *remedy*, cites, re-cites, and makes legible that which *in the same word* signifies . . . *poison* . . . the choice of only one of these renditions by the translator has as its first effect the neutralization of the citational play, of the "anagram," and, in the end, quite simply of the very textuality of the translated text . . . . Textuality . . . is by

nature absolutely heterogeneous and is constantly com-
posing with the forces that tend to annihilate it . . . . There is
no such thing as a harmless remedy. The *pharmakon* can
never be simply beneficial.

(Derrida 1981: 97–9)

Derrida's lengthy discussion suggests two very important basic
points: the first is that, as *Romeo and Juliet*'s Friar Laurence notes
conventionally, "Poison hath residence and medicine power"
within any complex ontological construct such as a flower, and
certainly "in man as well as herbs" (II.iii.24–8). This paradoxical
ambiguity forms the core of the tragic representation. The second
point is that "translation" is interpretation; it has no empirical
force but rather reflects the will, the desire, the apparatus deployed by the translator. Derrida points to the discomfort and thus
the consequent selection on the part of the translator which produces as its own remedy an unambiguous but therefore partial
definition or interpretation of the idea. For these reasons critics
have either demonized or victimized tragic protagonists, as if precisely univocal interpretation could, in fact, "exclud[e] from the
text any leaning toward the magic virtues of a force whose effect is
hard to master" (Derrida 1981: 97). To repeat a point made earlier
in chapter 1, because the conflict (dilemma) represented in a
tragedy occurs between two poles, represented by the protagonist
and the contextual community, and further, because the critical
audience identifies more with that community than with the
protagonist, the victimization of the protagonist replicates within
the audience the situation represented in the play: audiences or
readers see tragic heroes as flawed, wrong, or demonized, because
the communities in the plays have defined them that way as they
must do in order to kill them off. In other words, tragedy works
upon its audience in very much the same way that it works upon its
characters: by producing an inevitable misrecognition of the real
social relations between protagonist and community, with the
protagonist demonized as "other" and the audience/community
ratified as "us." Certain plays – *Macbeth*, for example, or *Coriolanus*
– readily produce this response. Others, like *Romeo and Juliet*,
whose protagonists lead their audiences to a nostalgically or sentimentally selected response, problematize the matter of "sacrifice"
by permitting us to ignore or erase the sense in which these sweet
adolescents are themselves responsible for their own destruction.

149

It is easy to forget that by marrying in secret they prevent their families and their larger community from participating in the marriage rite; as Natalie Z. Davis (1975) and others have observed, from the posting of the banns to the charivari on the wedding night, marriage is a communal affair. It marks, among other things, the change in status from child to adult, from dependency to social enfranchisement, and perhaps most important from the communal point of view, the establishment within the group of a new socioeconomic unit whose accumulated property will eventually be dispersed among legally recognized, that is, legitimate heirs.

As the status between childhood and adulthood entailing these various transitions, adolescence is *de facto* liminality. This is one of the more potent resonances of the epithet "Boy" that Capulet chastizes Tybalt with (I.v.77, 83), emphasizing the latter's misappropriation of authority in Capulet's house. Tybalt in turn spits "Boy" at Romeo (now secretly married) when they fight (III.i.66), and Romeo hurls "boy!" at Paris in the Capulet tomb (V.iii.70). Unlike Romeo, Paris has not married, has not in that sense reached full adulthood. Romeo insists for the sake of his own identity on this difference between them – "Good gentle youth, tempt not a desp'rate man" (V.iii.59) – which has nothing to do with their respective, fictive, ages. This suspension in liminality effaces identity as it effaces adulthood, completion, and thus one's place in the social community: "Boy" is used to the same effect in *Coriolanus* when Aufidius calls the protagonist "Thou boy of tears" (V.vi.100). It will be remembered that, like Romeo (II.ii.50–1; III.iii.106–8) and Juliet (II.ii.33-6), Coriolanus also sought to efface his name and his social identity (V.i.11–13); they all learn fatally that they cannot live nameless, suspended in liminality.

Because ritual is a "direct or iconic embodiment of social 'transitions'" (T. S. Turner 1977: 60), the transformation to adult through marriage and the establishment of a new legal and social unit entails the transformation of the community as well as the individuals. Aided and abetted by Friar Laurence and the Nurse, Romeo and Juliet commit two serious abrogations of community ritual by their secret marriage and by the fake funeral for one not dead. By denying Verona the right to witness and affirm these crucial passages from boy and girl to man and woman, and later from life to death, they violate the ritual processes themselves. That is why Juliet's "contract" with Romeo is, as she says, "too rash, too unadvis'd, too sudden" (II.ii.117–18).

More obviously, perhaps, than in any other Shakespearean tragedy, *Romeo and Juliet* foregrounds the community's culpability. The feud becomes a "plague a' both . . . houses" (III.i.91, 99, 106). "Plague" is never in Shakespeare a mere figure of speech but signals all the uncontrolled virulence of an epidemic, evident in the Prince's inability to stop it (like Richard II's in the jousting debacle), for which he suffers along with the Montagues and Capulets: "And I for winking at your discords too / Have lost a brace of kinsmen. All are punish'd" (V.iii.294–5). The promised golden statues that mark the families' reconciliation are curious monuments whose phallic but inanimate metallurgy denies rather than affirms life. The upright counterpart to the tomb which Romeo apostrophizes as a "womb of death" (V.iii.45), the double statue is a golden erection, meant to symbolize resurrection, that instead commemorates insurrection. Like the "dear love" of Sonnet 124, it "all alone stands hugely politic" (11), witnessed by Verona's "fools of time / Which die for goodness, who have lived for crime" (13–14). Private wedding and faked death may not look like felonies, but when considered as violations of communal interests (recalling Douglas's discussion of ritual observance as the production of "good citizenship" [1966: 3]), they are, and so, more obviously, is the feud interdicted by Prince Escalus. Romeo and Juliet are literally their community's "poor sacrifices" (V.iii.304); they are also, together, the site of its pollution, the subjects who are both the agents and the objects of ritual violations.

If they are not capable of demonization, of misrecognition, then they are not *pharmakoi*. In that case they would be merely victims, and the play would not be a tragedy but a melodrama. The alternative view of the protagonist or *pharmakos* as a microcosm of the community is very disturbing, and that disturbance is one of the principal affects of tragedy. It is one we labor to avoid. Following both Derrida and Artaud, we could say that we avoid it like the plague.

In Artaud's rigorous analogy of theater and plague, we recall, both constitute "a formidable call to the forces that impel the mind by example to the source of its conflicts." The theater is like a plague because "it is the revelation, the bringing forth, the exteriorization of a depth of latent cruelty by means of which all the perverse possibilities of the mind, whether of an individual or a people, are localized" (1958: 30). Artaud continues:

It appears that by means of the plague, a gigantic abscess, as much moral as social, has been collectively drained; and that like the plague, the theater has been created to drain abscesses collectively . . . .

[The theater] invites the mind to share a delirium which exalts its energies; and we can see, to conclude, that from the human point of view, the action of theater, like that of plague, is beneficial, for, impelling men to see themselves as they are, it causes the mask to fall, reveals the lie, the slackness, baseness, and hypocrisy of our world; it shakes off the asphyxiating inertia of matter which invades even the clearest testimony of the senses; and in revealing to collectivities of men their dark power, their hidden force, it invites them to take, in the face of destiny, a superior and heroic attitude they would never have assumed without it.

(1958: 31–2)

But remedy, as Derrida said, is never "simply beneficial"; likewise, for Artaud, plague is never simply destructive. The analogy works for Artaud precisely because the virulence of plague cannot be stemmed or altered by any kind of human intervention; it sweeps away everything that is vulnerable, weaker than itself. Whatever is not destroyed by it is purged, fresh, cleansed, durable. As in the aftermath of a hurricane, a balance is restored, albeit a balance of remainders, of whatever or whoever is left, for whose survival the protagonist's sacrifice has been made.

This function is similar to what Derrida describes in his analysis of Plato's *Timaeus* (89a–d), where Plato recommends that disease itself is a natural thing and therefore should be left undisturbed. In Derrida's account,[15] Plato says that, like every living being, every form of disease has a finite and predetermined duration: "if anyone regardless of the appointed time tries to subdue them by medicine . . . he only aggravates and multiplies them. Wherefore we ought always to manage them by regimen . . . and not provoke a disagreeable enemy" (Derrida 1981: 101). Derrida renders Plato's discourse in one precise fourfold definition:

1 The noxiousness of the *pharmakon* is indicted at the precise moment the entire context seems to authorize its translation by "remedy" rather than poison.
2 The natural illness of the living is defined in its essence as an *allergy*, a reaction to the aggression of an alien element.

152

And it is necessary that the most general concept of disease should be allergy . . . .

3 Just as health is auto-nomous and auto-matic, "normal" disease demonstrates its autarky by confronting the pharmaceutical aggression with *metastatic* reactions which displace the site of the disease, with the eventual result that the points of resistance are reinforced and multiplied. "Normal" disease defends itself. In thus escaping the supplementary constraints . . . the disease continues to follow its own course.

4 This schema implies that the living being is finite (and its malady as well): that it can have a relation with its other, then, in the allergic reaction, that it has a limited lifetime, that death is already inscribed and prescribed within its structure . . . . The immortality and perfection of a living being would consist in its having no relation at all with any outside. That is the case with God (cf. *Republic* II, 381b–c). God has no allergies . . . . The *pharmakon* is that which, always springing up from without, acting like the outside itself, will never have any definable virtue of its own. But how can this supplementary parasite be excluded by maintaining the boundary . . . ?

(1981: 101–2)

Taken together, Artaud and Derrida offer a compelling set of coordinates for the study of tragedy. Through its representation of the *pharmakon* (poison/remedy) or *pharmakos* (agency of both), tragedy functions like a plague, or in Derrida's term, an allergen, an irritant that disturbs and sickens the social organism. The difference between the two formulations is crucial, however. For Artaud the irritation arises from within the community, from the organism's own morbidity; it does not come from outside, although it *is* (in the formulations of Girard, Turner, and Douglas) subsequently marginalized, misrecognized as alien so that it can be excluded and then destroyed. For Derrida's Plato, the allergen is *writing* (the real subject of his essay); for Artaud it is the decrepitude that grows within society itself. As Derrida says, only God has immunity. Mortals do not. If the *pharmakos* is an allergen, then tragedy discloses the operations of a society allergic to itself. Here again, a play such as *Romeo and Juliet* confronts its audience with an uncomfortable truth: violators of structural requirements, of properly observed rites, are carriers of pollution. The fact that in this play they are the most appealing, most attractive, most sympathetic and seemingly innocent representations does not reprieve them from their sacrificial functions for the sake of their plague-ridden community. That fact also reminds us that, like all of Shakespeare's tragic protagonists, they embody at some time or other (as even Macbeth does at the very beginning of his play) the traits the community most values; this paradoxical combination of poison and medicine makes them appropriate *pharmakoi*.

This paradox inheres in tragedy absolutely, but not exclusively. In a widely reprinted essay on Renaissance poetry, "Black and White and Red All Over," Linda Woodbridge observes that such contradictory responses were as deeply embedded in the complexity of Renaissance social practice as in the literature it produced:

> The Renaissance worked against the ritual patterns it set up because it realized that the individual's death blunts any celebration of seasonal regeneration and the race's continuance and because the shock effect of violating ritual with roots deep in European culture creates the dynamic tensions on which art thrives, as varied metrical feet play against a poem's basic beat . . . . Authors drew on a well of readers' unconscious or partly conscious ritual understanding, not seeping through mysterious channels of racial memory but surrounding them daily in popular rites, ritual-linked games, evil-eye superstitions.
>
> (1994: 254)

In many of these rites and games (the sword-dance and St George play, for example), hero and villain are superimposed on or collapsed into each other, so that, as with an Escher print or Gombrich's Rabbit-Duck, perspective determines the thrust of the narrative. The binocular effect, as it were, looking not with one eye or another but with both, gives a third reading, in which both of two oppositional narratives are heard equally and accepted simultaneously. This may not satisfy either esthetic or political biases, but such biases are interpretive concerns, and can only by interpretive selection be ascribed to texts themselves. As *Coriolanus*'s Aufidius says to his lieutenant,

> So our virtues
> Lie in th'interpretation of the time,

And power, unto itself most commendable,
Hath not a tomb so evident as a chair
T'extol what it hath done.

(IV.vii.49–53)

This too is a by-product or consequence of Derrida's *pharmakon*, the embodiment of the binary oppositions of poison and remedy.

BREAD AND CIRCUSES: CORIOLANUS AND ST GEORGE

Nowhere in Shakespeare's tragedies is this more readily seen than in *Coriolanus*, whose protagonist serves his Rome as both scourge and cure. Coriolanus is called a "disease that must be cut away" (III.i.293), his mind "a poison" (III.i.86–7), his former service that of a foot now turned gangrenous (III.i.304–5); he in turn calls the people "those measles / Which we disdain should tetter us" (III.i.78–9). From Menenius's Fable of the Belly (I.i.96–146), through the many references to feeding, starvation, and the well-noted imagery of fragmentation and dismemberment, to its final exhaustion when all that is left of the hero is "a noble memory" (V.vi.153), *Coriolanus* delivers not a single discourse of "the body" but a set of alternative discourses of "bod*ies*."

One such discourse, that of the "grotesque body," has been substantially anatomized in recent critical literature (Adelman 1978, 1992; Bakhtin 1968, 1981; Bristol 1987; Cavell 1987; Stallybrass and White 1986). The discourse of the "grotesque body" is a corollary to that of the "sick body," which figures imbalance, dissonance, or dissent as pathologies invading and threatening a homeostatic ideal body of the state: the body politic "in *Julius Caesar* dies from amputation, in *Coriolanus* from cancer" (Zeeveld 1962: 322). The texts of the "sick body" discourse included, among others, the "Homilee agaynst Disobedience and wylful Rebellion" which posits rebellion of any sort, even against tyranny, as "leude remedies beyinge farre worse then any other maladies and disorders that can be in the body of a common wealth" (1574: 553), Averell's *Mervailous Combat of Contrarieties* (1588: sig. D1v–2), Forset's *Comparative Discourse of the Bodies Natural and Politique* (1606: sig. A2r), Bodin's *Six Bookes of the Common Weale* (1606: 225), and Bacon's essay "Of Seditions and Troubles" (1625 [1985: 103]).

A third discourse embedded in *Coriolanus* is that of the ritual/combat-heroic body, which conflates the protagonist with the patron saint of England and his monstrous opponent, evicted, reincorporated, and finally cut down and annihilated. These three discourses of the grotesque, sick, and ritual-heroic bodies are related not oppositionally but as alternative discourses in different registers of similar social and material concerns; they coexisted in early modern social life just as the mummers' play shared performance spaces and seasons with carnival festivities. Bristol has defined the dualistic forms of *Carême-carnaval* as a "collective balancing and coordination of antagonistic elements within productive life" (1987: 216); in contrast, the ritual-heroic discourse pits the protagonist against the collective antagonist whom his death will presumably save. The coordinates in this discourse are not balanced or equivalent, but their imbalance is countered by the formidable duality of the protagonist as dragon–hero, victim–villain.

If Menenius's commonplace fable expresses the carnivalesque, in which "the lower body stratum continues to assert itself against the imperatives of vertical order and control" (Bristol 1987: 214),[16] Coriolanus's *agon* expresses the alternative tradition of the ritual/combat-hero/*pharmakos*. The crisis represented in the play is thus complicated and multivalent. Instead of clear-cut binary oppositions, the plebs and tribunes on one side and Coriolanus and the patricians on the other, the play orchestrates a multiplex competition of voices, sometimes pairing tribunes with plebs and patricians with protagonist, and sometimes splitting and recombining the strands so that the plebs alternately favor and reject the protagonist; the tribunes (whom Plutarch consistently in the *Life of Coriolanus* calls duplicitous, "seditious," and "the causers and procurers of this sedition" [1967: II: 157, 149]) alternately support and oppose both plebs and protagonist; the patricians collapse into the communal whole when Coriolanus turns against Rome.

The negotiation of the carnivalesque and the ritual/combat-hero discourses expresses the play's ambivalence regarding social structures. In the crucial moment when Coriolanus is required to perform the act of abasement, the public display of his wounds, he rejects the discourse of humility and chooses instead that of the combat-hero, thereby dividing and antagonizing the two previously compatible modes of demotic ceremony. This split is symptomatic of social contingency within the play as well as in the world of Jacobean England. The illusion that informs all such communal celebrations is one of cultural integrity, wherein the "community" comes together as a united whole to celebrate the resolution of crisis. But in *Coriolanus*, as in Jacobean England, there is no such unity, and there is no such resolution (Zeeveld 1962: 327). The play's opening crisis, the issue of plebeian privation and patrician grain-hoarding, is displaced from attention by the war against the Volscians at Corioles (Cavell 1987: 145); Plutarch specifically inculpates the tribunes in creating this diversion, "hoping by the meanes of forreine warre, to pacifie their sedition at home" (1967: II: 157). This focus in turn gives way to an almost obsessive, and certainly unproductive, concern with the hero's intractability. At the end, nothing has changed in regard to the grain supply, and presumably the people are still starving; the tribunes are still serving themselves more than their constituencies, and the patricians have lost their leader. One particularly troubling aspect of the play's problematic representations is the speed with which it displaces attention, or dramatizes the citizens' displaced attention, from the very real, physical threat of starvation, the "destruction of the very material origin of the metaphor of the 'body politic' itself" (Drakakis 1989: 24),[17] to the fetishizing of a single figure, which Bristol (1987: 208), following Max Weber, calls the objectification of "charismatic authority." The citizens' illusion, promoted by the seditious tribunes but which in any case the protagonist himself does nothing to dispel, is that Coriolanus is the primary cause of the people's famine. The making of "charismatic authority" (in this play, as sometimes in real political life) is also and thereby the making of the *pharmakos*.

Coriolanus's illusion is that he can choose his membership in a community, although Rome has made him and he is Roman. If Rome thinks it can reject the product of its own traditions of military and patrician *virtus* for non-compliance in what was in any case a custom devoted to plebeian interests (Plutarch 1967: II: 158), Coriolanus thinks he can "banish" Rome and become a Volscian. But if he is not Roman, he is nothing. As Shakespeare had already shown in *Titus Andronicus*, such shifts are impossible: Coriolanus can no more be a Volscian than Tamora's Gothic family and Aaron the Moor can be Romans or Romeo and Juliet can deny their names. Nor can he be autochthonically independent, "as if a man were author of himself / And knew no other kin" (V.iii.36–7). At the beginning and at the end of his tragic project, Shakespeare dramatized the full cost of such illusions. In

Coriolanus as in *Titus Andronicus*, Rome (arguably a displacement for England [K. Burke 1966: 87; cf. Brockbank 1976: 26–7]), divides against itself, and like Coriolanus, is "task'd to mow / Or all, or lose his hire" (I.iii.36–7). "Rome's self-division can be seen to emanate from the very same 'nature' which binds the Roman body politic together, and the diseased 'body' can only re-affirm its deep structural unity through a displacement of its divisions onto an external adversary" (Drakakis 1989: 36). *Coriolanus* makes it very clear that first the adversary must *be* externalized, moved from the center where he begins, and marginalized, then demonized, then destroyed by an agency exculpated because it has not killed one of its own. This exculpation may be accomplished either by misrecognizing the *pharmakos* (for example, as an alien or a beast, perhaps a dragon) or by the alterity of the killer (for example, as a Volscian rather than a Roman). Either way, and in *Coriolanus* both ways, the illusion of communal purification – its release from pollution – is reinstated, its integrity restored.[18] From this perspective, the play's action is a performance of Jacobean England's own gathering crisis, sprung from an aristocratic illusion of internal coherence (undersigned by the aforementioned contemporary texts of the "sick body" made vulnerable by self-interested factions), but in reality a complex, ambivalent concatenation of voices monarchic, aristocratic, middle-class, and common.[19] The illusion of power so insistently promoted by James and his factions was in time dismembered, indeed beheaded; what was in fact "restored" by the Stuart "Restoration" is merely a rhetorical question.

Coriolanus's heroic complexity conforms to a construct deeply embedded in English cultural memory. In its shape as well as its resonating imagery, *Coriolanus* imbricates the pattern of seasonal entertainments loosely grouped as "mummers' plays," including sword-dances, morrises, and the St George plays, all of which grew over long periods of time out of ancient agrarian rituals of purgation, fertility, and seasonal renewal. The structure of *Coriolanus* is fleshed out upon the bones of popular ritual performances that survived in England well into the nineteenth century.[20] The play finally rejects the Carnival mode in favor of the St George pattern, which in turn it inflects elliptically. Because a tragedy is not in fact a ritual dance, the hero does not rise at the end of the final combat to repeat his battle endlessly. Instead, we are told, he will be memorially reconstructed, preserved in "a noble memory." Unlike ritual which recurs perennially and always implies its own reiteration, and unlike the collective life represented in the drama which, it is understood, goes on, a dramatic work performs, and performs *within*, a finite unit of time. *Coriolanus* isolates and freezes the performance of the mummers' combat, closes it at the protagonist's death, and substitutes "a noble memory" for the promise of the ritual/combat hero's literal resurrection. Except for this matter of closure, however, the ritual battle familiar to the audience is replicated in the play.

The "character" of Coriolanus has been in recent years a favorite site (I am tempted to say "favorite son") for psychoanalytic criticism, some of it very impressive (Adelman 1978; 1992: 147–64; Kahn 1981: 151–72; Barber and Wheeler 1986: 303–5; Sprengnether 1986: 89–111). Exposition of a range of neurotic personal relations in and between the hero and his mother and/or his principal antagonist, however, obscures the play's interrogation of both the dynamic operations and organizational structures of the institutions implicated in the play (Bristol 1987: 219), and the ritual-paradigm function of the hero as *pharmakos*, for which such characters are shaped by those institutions.

The attribution of the ritual/combat-hero pattern to *Coriolanus* needs further explanation, because the modern popular image of St George differs from the one recorded in Shakespeare's day. After the seventeenth century, the figure of England's patron saint became a cartoon-like super-hero, a distillation of aristocratic virtues whose story was told primarily in collections of inspirational tales for children. In the sixteenth and seventeenth centuries, however, in folk custom and prose romance, St George was usually represented as a complicated and ambiguous figure. He was no saint.

His typical play, with only slight variations from town to town, involved formulaic events, motifs, and dialogue. In its basic pattern, the dragon (often represented by a figure called "Slasher") enters, threatens to destroy the community, and challenges all comers to defeat him. George responds and cuts down Slasher with his sword; Slasher is revived by a "doctor," once, twice, or three times, and is joined in a procession out by various other figures from the community, often including a village idiot, a Beelzebub, a local citizen of good repute, and a minor devil, all of whom present themselves for the *quête*, or collection of gifts at the end. In the danced versions, a caller cues the dancers' moves while the community's representatives rhythmically close in upon and back away from the central combatants a number of times, their bodies sometimes blocking from the audience's view the mimed beheading and resurrection. The action always implicates the community as well as the hero. Varying from town to town, the slayer/slain is either the figure of St George or that of Slasher (Chambers 1903: I: 182–227; 1933: 6–10; Tiddy 1923: 224–31; E. O. James 1961: 273–5; Helm 1965). In three transcribed descriptions extant from Warwickshire, George enters first, boasts first, and challenges first: hero and monster are matched in aggressiveness and combativeness. In the version from Ilmington, the caller is "*Mother Christmas,*" and another mother-figure called the Molly (who may or may not be George's mother) lists and reiterates his wounds when he falls. She then tries to prevent the doctor from healing George until her own aches are cured (Tiddy 1923: 226–8).

The ambiguity of the hero–monster, the inconsistency of naming practices, and the peculiar mother-figure are common in the genre of popular entertainments. In what Victor Turner calls "the anthropology of performance" (1982: 13), character name-changes are merely incidents in the spread of ritual performances as they move from one geographical area to another and from one period to another. They are in fact evidence of the continuity of such performances in popular culture, where pattern rather than verbal text is the model. In the case of the mummers' ceremonial, the earliest extant "text" is eighteenth-century; in subsequent recordings, the hero's name undergoes a dizzying variety of changes: St George becomes King George, Prince George, King Robert the Bruce, and even Lord Nelson. Similar changes are found in the names of the co-performers. The folklorist Alex Helm noted that such alterations "develop naturally in the stream of folk evolution, and indeed, had the ceremony been as flourishing now as it was before the First World War, I would expect to find such characters as Winston Churchill, Mr Kruschev, or even Adolf Hitler being used in place of the more familiar St George and Black Prince" (1965: 130).

As the primary (and primal) popular ceremony marking solstitial or seasonal changes (E. O. James 1961: 273), the St George performance is preeminently a communal rite of passage and thus is intrinsically ambiguous. It follows the van Gennep–Turner pattern of separation–liminality–incorporation discussed earlier in this chapter, with the expected emphasis upon the liminal phase and its inherent contradictions. Although most later representations of George figure him as a defender of the faith and one of the "Seven Champions of Christendom," he begins, as in Caxton's 1483 translation of Jacobus de Voragine's *Legenda Aurea*, as an agrarian hero, the rescuer of a princess chosen by lot for sacrifice to a dragon who repeatedly befouled the countryside and destroyed the crops. Following the rescue and the dragon-slaying and dismemberment, George distributes his reward to the poor.

The most popular printed Elizabethan version of George's story discloses a complicated cultural matrix. Richard Johnson's prose romance, *The Most Famous History of the Seven Champions of Christendom* (1596), was reprinted fifteen times in eighty years, that is, with exactly the same frequency as North's Plutarch, and was 'very likely known to Shakespeare.[21] In Johnson's narrative, George's pregnant mother dreams, and his father hears in a confirming prophecy, that she "was conceaued with a dreadfull Dragon." Delivered by Caesarean section, she dies "dismembred of her wombe" (1608 [Q2]: A4r, A5r). George is born with a bright red dragon birthmark on his breast: from the outset, hero is identified with monster. As in Caxton's version, what is at stake, besides the princess's life, is the harvest crop, destroyed by the pestilent breath of the dragon, and therefore the community's survival. The combat is fought in Egypt, at the marginal distance required by the "separation" phase. The boundary-transgressive ambiguity characteristic of both liminality and the Derridean *pharmakon*, as well as the Aristotelian precept for difference within similarity, can be seen in the hero–monster identification, while the "incorporation" occurs in George's victory and distribution of largesse. In Shakespeare's play there is no reintegration of the hero with his community. The movement of the pattern is cut at a critical moment when the hero is destroyed. This moment marks the formal or structural closure that differentiates tragedy from ritual and ritual-based romance, but does not efface the *bricolage* of cultural performance that preserves older forms within the structures of newer ones.

In this archeological sense, the St George play or the sword-dance imbricates an even older ritual pattern;[22] in the same sense it in turn is imbricated in *Coriolanus*. This is evident in several instances. First is the Shakespearean play's concern with plenitude and supply, particularly with the rationing of corn. Then there is the identification of hero and monster, in this play specifically a dragon. Coriolanus is not the first Shakespearean hero to be associated with the figure of the dragon: Lear warns Kent to "come not between the dragon and his wrath" (I.i.122). Much earlier in Shakespeare's career, in *1 Henry VI*, the dead Henry V is eulogized in terms of the same glorious typology: "His arms spread wider than a dragon's wings / His sparkling eyes, replete with wrathful fire" (I.i.11–12). Philip Brockbank calls this figure Shakespeare's "first image of heroic man" (1976: 51), perhaps inspired by Spenser's vision of the Red Crosse Knight's dragon (*Faerie Queene* I: xi: xiv). The dragon in these modes is the valorous double of the hero, as it is in Richard III's attempt to appropriate the image: "fair Saint George, / Inspire us with the spleen of fiery dragons!" (*Richard III*: V.iii.349–50). It is worth noting that such links invariably valorize through analogies of military prowess, glory, and magnificence; they are never derogatory.

Coriolanus is compared to a dragon three times, and in these discrete instances a kind of progression can be seen. Coriolanus himself is the first to mention the analogy, in a speech to his mother:

> . . . though I go alone,
> Like to a lonely dragon, that his fen
> Makes fear'd and talk'd of more than seen – your son
> Will or exceed the common or be caught
> With cautelous baits and practice.
>
> (IV.i.29–33)

Most critics, including Plutarch, charge Coriolanus with willful isolation, but Shakespeare's character represents his isolation as the result of the fear his reputation strikes in his fellow Romans. He finds in the dragon image a pattern for his loneliness. Aufidius says that Coriolanus "Fights dragon-like, and does achieve as soon / As draw his sword" (IV.vii.23–4); the dragon analogue suits Aufidius's sense of a worthy opponent, the supremely skillful warrior. By the time Menenius takes up the image, Coriolanus has become a thing of wonder, transcendent: "This Martius is grown from man to dragon: he has wings: he's more than a creeping thing" (V.iv.12–14).

Coriolanus's ambiguity and transcendence mark him as the Derridean *pharmakon* of ritual action, an identity Girard also proposed in defining ritual as "nothing more than the regular exercise of 'good' violence" (1977: 37):

Blood . . . can stain or cleanse, contaminate or purify. . . .
. . . evil and the violent measures taken to combat evil are
essentially the same. At times violence appears to man in its
most terrifying aspect, wantonly sowing chaos and destruction;
at other times it appears in the guise of peacemaker, graci-
ously distributing the fruits of sacrifice.

(1977: 37)

The ritual hero is feared and admired, isolated and incorporated;
at the center of the heroic/sacrificial *agon*, the hero is collapsed
into the contamination that is to be purged. Coriolanus correctly
identifies as "double worship" the ambivalence threatening the
tradition of aristocratic leadership, dividing Rome and destroying
its integrity. He tells the duplicitous tribunes:

> This double worship,
> Where one part does disdain with cause, the other
> Insult without all reason; where gentry, title, wisdom,
> Cannot conclude but by the yea and no
> Of general ignorance – it must omit
> Real necessities, and give way the while
> To unstable slightness. Purpose so barr'd, it follows
> Nothing is done to purpose. Therefore beseech you –
> You that will be less fearful than discreet;
> That love the fundamental part of state
> More than you doubt the change on't; that prefer
> A noble life before a long, *and wish*
> *To jump a body with a dangerous physic*
> *That's sure of death without it* – at once pluck out
> The multitudinous tongue; *let them not lick*
> *The sweet which is their poison.* Your dishonor
> Mangles true judgment, and *bereaves the state*
> *Of that integrity which should become't;*
> *Not having the power to do the good it would,*
> *For th' ill which doth control't.*

(III.i.142–61, emphasis added)

Coriolanus knows he is the the poisonous–curative *pharmakon*, and
he also knows that the good/ill which he will incorporate is the
prior infection in the integrity of the state. This contradiction
extends beyond the body and character of Coriolanus to that of

Rome itself. There are more fearful monsters in Rome than the winged or armored kind. The play expresses a number of images of cannibalism, as when a citizen complains of the patricians that "If the wars eat us not up, they will" (I.i.85), and when Menenius prays:

> Now the good gods forbid
> That our renowned Rome, whose gratitude
> Toward her deserved children is enroll'd
> In Jove's own book, like an unnatural dam
> Should now eat up her own!
>
> (III.i.288–92)

and again, more grotesquely, when the obsessed Volumnia proclaims: "Anger's my meat. I sup upon myself, / And so shall starve with feeding" (IV.ii.50–1). This last is the most nihilistic of these images; here the body disintegrates, dissolves, and finally disappears. Adelman (1978: 108–24) and Cavell (1987: 152–6) discuss these cannibalistic images as part of the fabric of psychopathology in the play; in her most recent book, Adelman comes close to but finally avoids identifying their context as ritualistic: "in the context of all the cannibalistic images, the mysterious association [between killing Coriolanus and an unlimited food supply] seems to point toward a fantasy in which the people, rather than the wars, will devour Coriolanus" (1992: 154). What Adelman sees as mystifying logic is in fact the logic of ritual sacrifice, in which the *pharmakos* is misrecognized as the cause of disaster and his death as the cure. The fragmentation and dissolution of the ritual body (in this play alternately figured as Coriolanus's and the communal body) is a version of a pervasive disorder, a malformation in the body politic. "Rituals enact the form of social relations and in giving these relations visible expression they enable people to know their own society. The rituals work upon the body politic through the symbolic medium of the physical body" (Douglas 1966: 128). In *Coriolanus*, even the ordinary citizen knows this: "Ingratitude is monstrous: and for the multitude to be ungrateful were to make a monster of the multitude, of the which we being members, should bring ourselves to be monstrous members" (II.iii.9–13). Monsters must be destroyed, in this play as in the sword play, but as Gail Paster (1978: 134–7) astutely notes, it is never quite clear in *Coriolanus* just who is devourer and who is devoured, unless it is the self (in her essay, the "divided self" of the city) devouring itself.

Coriolanus is punctuated throughout with images of fragmentation and dismemberment. In III.i, the tribunes argue that
Coriolanus should be thrown from the Tarpeian Rock and
shattered on the stones below. Disgusted with Rome and Romans,
Coriolanus takes up the cry for his own destruction in III.ii.1–6; in
the next scene, incited by the tribunes, the populace clamors for
his death. His sacrifice would be one in which the entire community, including himself, participates. Earlier, we have already
had a ghoulish exchange between Volumnia and Menenius which
showed a more distinct kind of imaginative fragmentation of the
body, one that is sustained throughout the play. Awaiting the
hero's triumphant return from Corioles, mother and friend enthu-
siastically catalogue the sites of Coriolanus's reported wounds:
"I'th'shoulder and i'the left arm: there will be large cicatrices to
show the people when he shall stand for his place"; "One i'th'neck
and two i'th'thigh – there's nine that I know"; "He had, before this
last expedition, twenty-five wounds upon him"; "Now it's twenty-
seven: every gash was an enemy's grave" (II.i.147–56). The
exchange has the rhythm of a chant and the exaltation of a victory
dance, and recalls the formulaic cadence of the Ilmington Molly:

> King George is wounded through the heart,
> Through the heart and through the knee:
> Ten guineas to a doctor I'll freely gie.
>
> (Tiddy 1923: 227)

Shortly after the inventory by Volumnia and Menenius there are
three separate demands for the custom that the war-hero candidate for consulship display his gaping wounds before an equally
gaping crowd to demonstrate the bleeding through which he has
attained his status (II.i.231–6; II.iii.5–8; II.iii.163–4). This is also
the process by which the community symbolically shares in the
blood of the sacrifice: "If he show us his wounds and tell us his
deeds, we are to put our tongues into those wounds and speak for
them" (II.iii.5–8), despite Coriolanus's warning that they "not lick
/ The sweet which is their poison" (III.i.156–7). In an analogous
moment in *Julius Caesar*, the sharing is actively performed when
Brutus urges the conspirators to "bathe our hands in Caesar's
blood" and Antony asks that "each man render me his bloody
hand" (III.i.106, 184). In the earlier play, wounds and mouths are
linked repeatedly. Decius manipulatively interprets to Caesar
Calphurnia's dream that "from you great Rome shall suck /

Reviving blood" (II.ii.87–8). Antony's soliloquy over Caesar's corpse cites the body's wounds, "Which, like dumb mouths, do ope their ruby lips / To beg the voice and utterance of my tongue" (III.i.260–1). He declines to read Caesar's will to the plebeians, lest "they would go and kiss dead Caesar's wounds" (III.ii.132); he shows them "sweet Caesar's wounds, poor, poor dumb mouths" in order to "put a tongue / In every wound of Caesar" (III.ii.225–9).

Mouths and wounds function differently as respective sites of nourishment and danger. However, they are morphologically identical as orifices through which both contamination and purification can occur, and thus symbolize the body's vulnerability. As Mary Douglas suggests in another context, bodily orifices exude matter (spittle, blood, milk, urine, feces, tears) which is defined as "marginal" precisely because it has traversed the body's boundaries. The identification of a particular body margin as dangerous (i.e., powerful) depends upon the specific situation the body is said to symbolize (Douglas 1966: 121). In Shakespeare's Rome, as we have seen, mouths and wounds are linked as sacramental loci, that is, as ritualistically ambiguous and therefore dangerous and powerful body sites. To bleed for Rome is the duty and honor of the hero; to suck the dead hero's blood is the life-sustaining rite of the populace.

Coriolanus has indeed bled for Rome. In the lines quoted earlier, Menenius counts twenty-seven gashes. Cominius later expands the image: "from face to foot / He was a thing of blood" (II.ii.108–9). At this point in the play, obviously, Coriolanus has not yet been killed and has not yet become the ritual sacrifice. The play leads us to this point gradually, with all the careful preparation of a ritual act itself. The custom requiring the hero to display his wounds is noted several times in the play, in II.ii.136–9 and throughout much of II.iii. Plutarch reports that Coriolanus submits to the custom and is betrayed anyway on the day of election by a fickle populace (1967: II: 158–9). In the *Life of Coriolanus* he explains the custom as a simple show of humility and a display of previous valor, because "offices of dignitie in the cittie were not then geven by favour or corruption. It was but of late time, and long after this, that buying and selling fell out in election of officers, and that the voyces of the electours were bought for money" (1967: II: 158). Plutarch's golden-age nostalgia gives way, however, to cynicism in *Romane Questions* 49, where he discusses the same custom with regard to candidates for "any office and magistracie"; the candidate's nakedness is explained as either the same show of humility and bravery, "because they deemed men woorthy to beare publicke office and to gouerne, not by their birth and parentage, by their wealth and riches, ne yet by their shew and outward reputation, but by their wounds and scarres to be seene upon their bodies," or "because they would seeme . . . in humilitie to debase themselves, the sooner thereby to curry favor, and win the good grace of the commons, even as well by taking them by the right hand, by suppliant craving, and by humble submission on their very knee," or finally, as a way to prevent him from concealing money as bribes for votes (1892: 78–9). Plutarch's explanation mirrors the same crisis of "double worship" in leadership that Coriolanus identified in the lines quoted earlier, where "gentry, title, wisdom, / Cannot conclude but by the yea and no / Of general ignorance" (III.i.144–6).

Shakespeare's Coriolanus shows more consistency, perhaps even more wisdom, than Plutarch's in refusing to submit to a plebeian custom which the plebs themselves (in Plutarch) betrayed. But more important than historical accuracy is Shakespeare's decision to make Coriolanus's refusal the reason for his rejection. For the very private and still very much alive Coriolanus, the public display of his wounds smacks of the fairground side-show, the Carnival (literally *Carne-vale*, the farewell to meat). He is willing to show his wounds privately (II.iii.76–7), but there is more abasement in the public action than he can tolerate (II.ii.145, 148–9; II.iii.51–4, 108–10, 112–24). Carnival operates through such abasements and mockeries of proper rituals. This hero, however, will not turn clown or beggar, will not "idly sit / To hear my nothings mon-stered" (II.ii.76–7). Although he is willing to die for Rome, he will not die in mockery for the sake of custom, no matter how much he wants the consulship.

Moreover, this custom is a plebeian invention, and lacks for Coriolanus the force of either law or ritual. The plebs, as Bristol points out, "characteristically views authority as derived from local custom and from settled ways of doing things . . . . Law takes precedence over decree, but custom takes precedence even over law on this view. The plebs thus acts on the conviction of its own prior authority" (1987: 209). Coriolanus does not share the plebeian view of this prior, appropriated, and restorable authority; as Bristol goes on to say, his is a specifically military sense of hierarchy (1987: 209), in which he himself is set up as its ordering principle. He wants to be a figure of rule, not misrule. In his view such rule, as a codified Roman institution, is unambiguous, uncontaminated, and unproblematical, the Rome of pure military *virtus*. Not for Coriolanus the blurred and messy boundaries and shifting positions of urban life; his first and persistent grievance against the populace is their version of the tribunes' "double worship," inconstancy:

> What would you have, you curs,
> That like nor peace nor war? The one affrights you,
> The other makes you proud. He that trusts to you,
> Where he should find you lions, finds you hares;
> Where foxes, geese. You are no surer, no,
> Than is the coal of fire upon the ice,
> Or hailstone in the sun. Your virtue is
> To make him worthy whose offense subdues him,
> And curse that justice did it. Who deserves greatness
> Deserves your hate; and your affections are
> A sick man's appetite, who desires most that
> Which would increase his evil. He that depends
> Upon your favors swims with fins of lead,
> And hews down oaks with rushes. Hang ye! Trust ye?
> With every minute you do change a mind, . . .
> (I.i.168–82)

Like *Julius Caesar*'s Brutus, Coriolanus confronts "a sick man's" city; the disease carried by what Menenius contemptuously calls "Rome and her rats" (I.i.162) is ambivalence, the "uncertainty" to which he consigns them when he "banishes" Rome (III.iii.123–4). Again like Brutus, Coriolanus is a purist, an idealist, and a conservative, except that, unlike Brutus, he is also a committed hierarchist, and the Rome he wants to conserve, unlike Brutus's Rome, is not in the process of disappearing but no longer exists. It belongs to an historical memory that effaces with the air-brush of nostalgia all trace of ambivalence, that contests the plebeian version of prior authority, and to whose constellation of starry images he will himself at the end of the play be consigned by his Volscian counterpart Aufidius. A Carnival-king has no place in such a pantheon; thus Coriolanus can and must reject that function in favor of that of the militaristic sword-dance hero.

In the play's last moments, Coriolanus invites his newly adopted Volscian army to "Cut me to pieces" (V.vi.111). If the Roman citizenry did not deserve his sacrifice, the Volscian army will. He incites them to frenzy and they do as he asks. The singular Coriolanus – "Alone I did it" (V.vi.116) – is cut down; he will rise only imaginatively in "a noble memory." When he first went over to the Volscian camp, that was all that he wished for: "a good memory / And witness of the malice and displeasure / Which thou should'st bear me. Only that name remains" (IV.v.71–3). Between "a good memory" and "witness of the malice" is all the ambivalence and alternation that disturbs the social reality of the play.

"Name," "memory," and "witness" are paramount signifiers of legitimacy, individuality, and personhood. Coriolanus's banishment creates the critical liminal phase, with its characteristic ambiguity, alternative meanings, and "the emergence of liminal demonic and monstrous figures who represent within themselves ambiguities and inconsistencies" (V. Turner 1982: 113). The central attribute of this phase is the subject's effacement, "stripped of names and clothing . . . . [in] a 'leveling' process, in which the signs of their pre-liminal status are destroyed and signs of their liminal non-status applied . . . . In mid-transition, the initiands are pushed as far toward uniformity, structural invisibility, and anonymity as possible" (V. Turner 1982: 26). Stripped of his Roman identity, banished by decree of the tribunes and the concurring "cry of curs," and in transit to the Volscian camp, Shakespeare's hero renounces his name and his past. Cominius reports:

> I urg'd our old acquaintance, and the drops
> That we had bled together. "Coriolanus"
> He would not answer to; forbad all names:
> He was a kind of nothing, titleless,
> Till he had forg'd himself a name o'th'fire
> Of burning Rome.
>
> (V.i.10–15)

But when Aufidius later reminds him of his non-identity by reinscribing him as a status-less "boy of tears!" (V.vi.100), Coriolanus realizes too late the consequences of this voluntary effacement, and three times hurls the epithet back at the Volscians (V.vi.103, 112, 116), the third time reminding them, himself, and the audience exactly how he acquired the name he once tried to obliterate: "I / Flutter'd your Volscians in Corioles. / Alone I did it. Boy!" (V.vi.114–16).

Pushing his isolation to its furthest extreme, he separates not only from Rome, but from the entire community of human society, to "stand / As if a man were author of himself / And knew no other kin" (V.iii.35–7). Having rejected a point of custom in refusing to show his wounds, he is himself rejected; made nationless, he renounces his nationality. He is a man without normal kinship: his mother, on her knees to him in "this unnatural scene," inverts maternal nurture into behavior "most mortal" to her son (V.iii.184–9). He knows his situation is one that is impossible in nature ("as if") yet true enough in his circumstances: he embodies the paradox of liminality.

In the agrarian diction of the play, the result of this inversion is rot. Coriolanus responds to his banishment:

> You common cry of curs! whose breath I hate
> As reek o' th' rotten fens, whose loves I prize
> As the dead carcasses of unburied men
> That do corrupt my air: I banish you!
> And here remain with your uncertainty!
>
> (III.iii.120–4)

The language deploys the imagery of St George's dragon in the Caxton translation, whose breath killed the crops and whose carcass poisoned the earth. Here the Roman mob shares the role of reeking monster whose pollution is "uncertainty." When Cominius appeals to him to spare Rome for the sake of his friends,

> His answer to me was
> He could not stay to pick them in a pile
> Of noisome musty chaff. He said 'twas folly,
> For one poor grain or two, to leave unburnt
> And still to nose th'offense.
>
> (V.i.24–8)

Ungrateful Rome is figured as a rotting heap of chaff to be purified by fire. This is more than vengeance; it is, or it would be if it were successful, an act of purgation.

In a stable society, such a cleansing would prepare the way for renewal and growth. Here, for a moment, the affirmative return of Volumnia and Virgilia seems to promise just that. The assurance of the messenger who reports their return, "As certain as I know the sun is fire" (V.iv.45), is confirmed with music: "The trumpets, sackbuts, psalteries, and fifes, / Tabors and cymbals and the shouting Romans / Make the sun dance. Hark you!" (V.iv.49–51). Michael Goldman has observed that the music here "is other than martial;

. . . The imagery, too, suggests fertility and abundance to a degree unmatched in any scene," but, he says, "This is a play, for once, in which we must not be allowed the sense of selves breaking out into variety, abundance, or fresh illumination" (1972: 121, 111). Rome is spared, but there is no sense that it will thrive. Its decay might have been averted had Coriolanus prevailed from the start; he was its hero, its heart (*cor*), its integrity. In banishing him Rome destroyed both itself and him; "in such a case," says Menenius, "the gods will not be good unto us. When we banished him, we respected not them; and, he returning to break our necks, they respect not us" (V.iv.31–4).

Some social crises more than others seem to call for sacrificial mediation. When "the social fabric of the community is threatened; dissension and discord are rife. The more critical the situation, the more 'precious' the sacrificial victim must be" (Girard 1977: 18). In *Coriolanus*, the military hero and protector of Rome is scapegoated for a community whose very survival is threatened, not only by war with an external enemy, but first and foremost by manipulated starvation. This crisis, though set aside in the ensuing action of the play, is the whole focus of I.i. It is as early as this scene that Coriolanus is made the target of the plebeians' wrath, which is submerged when the hero conquers Corioles and defends Rome against the Volscians, and rekindled when he defies the custom of public disrobing. Throughout the play's sustained contest for authority, the hunger owed to dearth is never appeased; the central crisis of privation is only temporarily displaced while attention is focused on what Bristol (following Habermas) calls the legitimation crisis (1987: 208). To cure itself, Rome requires a *pharmakos*.

Coriolanus inscribes a moment central to the *agon* of the sacrificial victim: "there comes a point when, fleeing from disaster, he can flee no further. At this point, he turns and faces destruction; and his death is made to seem like an execution, or a sacrificial rite, or something of both . . . . The transformation is of cynosure at once into a victim and a monster" (Holloway 1961: 123). Coriolanus's death "is almost as much a *sparagmos* of the ritual victim by the whole social group as was possible on the stage" (Holloway 1961: 130; also Cavell 1987: 157–65). But in *Coriolanus* there is no sense of a new beginning arising out of the end; the Volscians, led by Aufidius, simply pick up their swords and go home, taking with them the hero's corpse: "My rage is gone, / And I am struck with sorrow" (V.vi.146–7). Rome is not even represented. As in *Hamlet*, the defeat of the hero does not restore the community, whose "rottenness" from the start renders it incapable of redressing its own ills, but remands it to a foreign power. The defeat, in these cases, is not only the hero's but the community's as well.

Coriolanus's movement toward this end isolates a ritual process that in more stable circumstances would not have been aborted. Goldman eloquently identified the process as a "driving pulse of activity" that operates as a "choreography – it allows for a systole and diastole of crowds with Coriolanus at the center" (1972: 115–16). This pulsing choreography of blood-pressure, with the hero/victim at the center, is the sword-dance. The shape of this agrarian practice was still recognized by the Jacobean audience long after its "magical" properties were no longer credited to insure plenitude, and it became, like Hamlet's hobby-horse, "quite forgot." Its ambiguous imagery was no doubt less problematic, less obscure, for Shakespeare's audience than it is for a modern one. Moreover, the play recombines in its hero another set of related figures, the harvester/destroyer, which tightens the connection with agrarian ritual:

> . . . His bloody brow
> With his mail'd hand then wiping, forth he goes
> Like to a harvest man that's task'd to mow
> Or all, or lose his hire.
>
> (I.iii.34–7)

The frenzied harvester is himself cut down, his only resurrection in the language of "noble memory." Whereas in Plutarch Rome rises to victory over the Volscians following Coriolanus's burial, the play ends at his death, toward which it has inexorably driven. The generic difference between ritual and tragedy denies Rome its hero's reintegration, the transformed return from liminality. Instead, Coriolanus defects, but he can only join the Volscian community by dying, and it can only incorporate him by burying him. Aufidius's last word, and the last word of the play, is addressed to this alternative community: "Assist." In Shakespeare as in Plutarch, Coriolanus is buried at Antium, not in Rome, which is denied even its rejected hero's body and consequently the burial rites that would conclude its own *agon* with the hero's. The play ends, but Rome-in-crisis without its *pharmakos* remains suspended in liminality in an unfinished sword-dance.

5

THE HOBBY-HORSE IS FORGOT

Tradition and transition

Critical attention to the transitional (that is, liminal) character of Tudor and Stuart culture has begun to explore the ambivalent relation between the pull of traditional and ritual operations and the manipulation of sociopolitical structures (Cressy 1989; Hobsbawm and Ranger 1984: 1–14; Hutton 1994; Thomas 1971: 3–24). Because it arises within and determines cultural contexts, that ambivalent relation or polarity is manifest in Shakespeare's plays. The signs of tradition indicate the complex interplay of demotic interests. One such sign is the hobby-horse. The line, "For O, for O, the hobby-horse is forgot," occurs twice in Shakespearean drama. In *Love's Labour's Lost* it is part of the banter between Armado and Moth concerning the vagaries of affection.[1] When Hamlet says it, he is mocking Ophelia's reminder that his father died "twice two months" ago, which he hears as "two months" (III.ii.128–31). For him the issue is not chronological accuracy but for how long one should properly remember and mourn his father. Editors of both plays consistently and inadequately gloss the lines as probable references to an unknown ballad on the decline of the morris dance, in which the figure of the hobby-horse was often prominent. Changing times problematize the value of the past, even of a past parent. Nostalgic reference to the forgotten hobby-horse implies the evaporation of old customs: *ubi sunt.* Its reiteration signals both popularity and recognition, evidence of a consciousness among Elizabethans that they lived in a time of perceptible changes.

Such consciousness, or self-consciousness, suggests that adherence to tradition is neither inevitable nor accidental. What is retained is retained deliberately, for a purpose. Eric Hobsbawm argues that the establishment or "invention" of tradition operates, tacitly or overtly, by rules "which seek to inculcate certain values and norms of behaviour by repetition, which automatically implies continuity with the past. In fact, where possible, they normally attempt to establish continuity with a suitable historical past" (Hobsbawm and Ranger 1983: 1). Both the automaticity and the suitability reflect that aspect of the past which the inventors or invokers of tradition wish to recuperate. Thus tradition is politically informed: what is retained, like what is jettisoned, is inscribed within an ensemble of immediate and partisan concerns. Hobsbawm's argument for "tradition" aligns with Moore and Myerhoff's discussion of "secular ritual" (1977: 3–4), wherein ceremony and ritual are appropriated in modern secular affairs to authorize and legitimize particular positions of persons, institutions, events, moralities, world-views, and the like. Tradition valorizes the past in a resistance to change that only occurs when change looms as a loss or a threat. The occasion need not be cataclysmic; any progress, invention, or unprecedented occurrence may send human beings scrambling for the security of the familiar and the comfortable. Conversely, the rejection of a tradition suppresses the full range of values it signals. The complexity of that range is indicated in Hobsbawm's rigorous distinction between "tradition" and "custom," which helps to explain why Hamlet regrets the obsolescence of the hobby-horse and of customs "More honor'd in the breach than the observance" (I.iv.16) in a different register from that in which he contests the play's various maimed rites. These are related forms of neglect, but they are differently weighted:

> The object and characteristic of "traditions"... is invariance. The past, real or invented, to which they refer imposes fixed (normally formalized) practices, such as repetition. "Custom"... does not preclude innovation and change up to a point, though evidently the requirement that it must appear compatible or even identical with precedent imposes substantial limitations on it. What it does is to give any desired change (or resistance to innovation) the sanction of precedent, social continuity and natural law as expressed in history. Students of peasant movements know that a village's claim to some common land or right "by custom from time immemorial" often expresses not a historical fact, but the balance of forces in the constant struggle of village against lords or against other villages.... "Custom" cannot afford to be invariant, because even in "traditional" societies life is not

so . . . . The decline of "custom" inevitably changes the "tradition" with which it is habitually intertwined.

                              (Hobsbawm and Ranger 1983: 2–3)

Despite the appearance of stability, tradition can be "invented" by
permission of custom, and such permission holds for as long as a
particular tradition serves its promoters. On occasion, as
Hobsbawm notes, quasi-historical narratives such as legend and
epic are created to validate changes in custom, which themselves
can be subject to "demotic modification" (Hobsbawm and Ranger
1983: 7). But, he adds, "the strength and adaptability of genuine
traditions is not to be confused with the 'invention of tradition'.
Where the old ways are alive, traditions need be neither revived
nor invented" (1983: 8). These are important observations, because they underscore the dynamic operations of social systems in
defining, changing, or retaining customs and traditions. It is not
always clear under what conditions of influence the modifications
of the "old ways" occur. Such practices are inscribed within the
systems of "operational efficacy" or "social/psychological effectiveness" of secular ritual as distinct from the "doctrinal efficacy" of
religion, which "need merely be affirmed" (Moore and Myerhoff
1977: 12). Because they are not inscribed within an explanatory
doctrine, and because their effectiveness varies among participants, it is difficult to describe their operations precisely; they
cannot always be said to function programmatically, that is, toward
a clearly identifiable goal, nor can their consequences always be
clearly observed: "Exegetical analysis does not help in determining
the unconscious consequences of ritual, consequences that may or
may not occur at all, may occur in every shade of intensity from an
image in the mind, to a slight murmur of the heart, to a profound
ecstasis" (Moore and Myerhoff 1977: 13). Because they cannot be
empirically isolated, they are sometimes denigrated as "mere" or
"simple" folk-lore.

But the *bricolage* of social practices widespread within a population is never a simple matter, and never aimless. Given the often
frustrated efforts of church and governmental officials to suppress
various vestigially pagan folk practices such as the hobby-horse
dance, it would appear that such practices were sustained – where
they *were* sustained – precisely because they were repositories of
self-determination and maintenance for populations lacking other
ways of countering domination by hierarchical agencies. Such

traditions, including traditions of mythological narrative and ritual practice, are evidence of a challenge to a particular hegemonic ideology by one or more counterhegemonies that coexist in any society (Bristol 1987: 210; Foucault 1980: 81–4; Lincoln 1989: 6). They continue regardless of authoritative permission, whether openly or covertly, amalgamated into dominant structures or diminished to what are perceived, not always correctly, within those structures as "harmless" folk amusements.

The complexity of such interweavings in the social fabric, and of their representation in drama, precludes quick and easy assumptions about their operations. In the case of *Hamlet*, for instance, Claudius's revels in the court, as Hamlet explains to Horatio, may be customary, but they are unaccustomed, "More honor'd in the breach than the observance," and in Hamlet's view, not only offensive among several conflations of "mirth in funeral," but also harmful to Denmark's reputation abroad and thus to its political safety. Just as the creation of tradition and custom serve political ends, so too do both the revival and the suppression of tradition and custom. Customary observance can witness a set of communal values without implying unanimity (Goody 1977: 33; Duffy 1992: 12). Ritual behavior signals a variety of positions: sometimes it indicates automaticity, and sometimes compliance as submission without belief, as when participation is politically coerced or when it serves social rather than specifically religious ends. "So too perhaps with rituals of rebellion. . . . Indeed, it is often the rejection of ritual that is seen as revealing the truth; hence its rejection by Protestant and Evangelical sects, as a prelude to creating their own particular interests" (Goody 1977: 33). Goody's call for definitional clarity in both interpretive practice and the language of its discourse (against, for example, the common modern practice of calling any regrettable event a "tragedy") is worth repeating: a refusal to "discriminate between performances of *Hamlet*, the State Opening of Parliament, and the Mass is wasting our time by trivializing the study of social behavior" (1977: 28–9). Such distinctions are needed, but are not to be considered hierarchically: performance of plays, civic occasions, and ecclesiastic events are different modalities of social occasions that are equally important at different moments in a community's social ecology.[2]

As with its enforcement, the rejection of a particular tradition or custom acts to suppress the full complex of values signalled by that tradition or custom. In *Richard II*, when York pleads with King Richard to rescind the suspension of Bolingbroke's inheritance, he argues that the suspension of customary inheritance dismantles the entire system upon which Richard's own kingship rests:

> Take Hereford's rights away, and take from Time
> His charters and his customary rights;
> Let not to-morrow then ensue to-day;
> Be not thyself; for how art thou a king
> But by fair sequence and succession?
>
> (II.i.195–9)

Of course, the question is ironized by the play's conclusion, when Bolingbroke establishes a new dynasty by means other than "fair sequence and succession": such is the consequence of abrogating "customary rights."

HAMLET'S HOBBY-HORSE

The local endurance of "old ways," their retention or rejection, reveals much about the stability or fluidity of a community. Hamlet's complaint that the "hobby-horse is forgot" implies a deliberate rejection rather than a simple erosion over the course of time (Laroque 1991: 126, 130), although as we shall see, the "complaint" registers more as a warning than a dirge; the hobby-horse dance continued well into the seventeenth century (Alford 1978; Hutton 1994: 194). The symbolic content of the reference for Shakespeare's audience entails the play's focus on memory (Alexander 1971: 30–57; Hammersmith 1978); Hamlet's reconstruction of the hobby-horse at once regrets its "forgetting" and amends it. Hamlet relates this figure from the morris dance to his father for very specific reasons; as in his complaint about the "cursed spite" that forces him to set right disjointed time, he thereby situates his political as well as his filial responsibilities. Inadequate remembrance of his father/king is both a political violation and a personal one (Kastan 1987).

The limitations of recorded historiography restrict certain knowledge of the past. Written and preserved documents, which themselves are necessarily partial (in both senses of partisan and incomplete), are usually understood to constitute the only reliable kind of record (Hutton 1994). There are other valid forms of preservation, although these require a more flexible reception

and a more fluid approach to "documentation." Foucault's definition of "subjugated knowledges" serves well to describe the fate of
Hamlet's hobby-horse and all such occluded traditions and
customs. Those "blocks of historical knowledge . . . located low
down on the hierarchy . . . allowed to fall into disuse," and sustained perversely by the strength of their suppression, were concerned
"with a *historical knowledge of struggles*. In the specialised areas of
erudition as in the disqualified, popular knowledge there lay the
memory of hostile encounters which even up to this day have been
confined to the margins of knowledge" (Foucault 1980: 82–3).

The mechanism of suppression first trivializes and then erases
both the specific knowledge and the language that sustains it. By
linking the hobby-horse to his dead father, Hamlet invokes the
"claims to attention of local, discontinuous, disqualified,
illegitimate knowledges against the claims of a unitary body of
theory which would filter, hierarchise and order them in the name
of some true knowledge" (Foucault 1980: 83). In Hamlet's case,
the totalizing body of theory is Claudius's claim to legitimacy as
king and step-father, against Hamlet's own occluded kingship
("popp'd in between th'election and my hopes" [V.ii.65]) and his
mandate to bring both murder and murderer to light. Hamlet is
certainly right to complain; political urgency (his mother's for a
quick remarriage, Claudius's for enthronement, and Denmark's
for a clearly defined political center) – not to mention Claudius's
triple crime – forced the neglect of several traditions and the
privileging of others.

Hamlet's mourning is both personal (for his father) and political
(for Denmark's rightful king); Claudius's marriage and coronation are, for different reasons, equally personal and political. Thus
the play inscribes a complex arrangement of personal–political
and traditional–transitional concerns encoded in the
remembered/forgotten hobby-horse. The figure was specifically a
man dressed in a horse mask and a hoop-like skirt under which he
caught and then released village maids in an aggressively mimed
fertility dance (Alford 1978; Burland 1972; Cawte 1978; Laroque
1991: 126–30 *et passim*; Palmer and Lloyd 1972). The random (and
randy) thrusting of the hobby-horse recurred in an endless oscilla-
tion at various seasonal festivals. The dance signified fertility, and
the more aggressively athletic the better.

Besides this obvious function, the appearance of the hobby-
horse figure aligns it with a pantheon of mythic figures that were

animal–human hybrids. Hamlet himself makes reference to another such hybrid, when he analogizes Claudius to a satyr and his dead father to Hyperion, the Titan son of Uranos and Gaia, heaven and earth, which in fact is Hamlet's expletive two lines later: "Heaven and earth! / Must I remember?" (I.ii.140, 142–3). Hyperion, then, signals the first legitimate "generation," whereas the satyr is nothing more than a minor and debased woodland wanton. Chambers locates the hobby-horse's origin in "worshippers careering in the skins of sacrificed animals" (1903: I: 142); on that view the hobby-horse seems to have combined the ritualized promise of communal renewal and (re)generation with the hybridization of man and beast. In the linguistic framework of the play, this kind of hybridization interpellates much of Hamlet's verbal inquiry into the meaning of "human": "What is a man, / If his chief good and market of his time / Be but to sleep and feed? a beast, no more" (IV.iv.33–5); "O God, a beast that wants discourse of reason / Would have mourn'd longer" (I.ii.150–1). The Ghost's identification of Claudius as "that incestuous, that adulterate beast" (I.v.42) halves the satyr to its bestial component, the Bakhtinian lower-body stratum that, cut off from the counter-discourse of the upper half, makes havoc of the social order. Hobby-horse and satyr are positioned here as binary opposites; although both are human–animal hybrids, they are inscribed within different ethical discourses. The hobby-horse is admitted, indeed conscripted, into the totemic pantheon of early modern social life as a guarantor of fecundity, continuity, and memory; the satyr is excluded as uncivilized, a destroyer of order and structure. Hamlet's hobby-horse is domesticated, owned, a household figure among the *lares* and *penates* of Elsinore as of Elizabethan England. Ejected, "forgot," its promise for renewal is broken.

In the play, the hobby-horse suggests both a forward and a backward glance (Alexander 1971; Kastan 1987). Besides its overtly sexual reminder of fertility against the language and imagery of rot that pervades this play, it also signals a longing for old days and old ways, a nostalgia that would restore what was lost by the king's murder: political and familial legitimacy, those customary and legal guarantors of order and perpetuation. It is no accident that Horatio calls the dead king "buried Denmark" (I.i.48).

The hobby-horse figure has been traced all over middle Europe and back to Greco-Roman centaurs. Its pagan origin is probable, its unruly conduct legendary, and its embrace by significant num-

179

bers of common folk unquestionable. Attempts have been made to pinpoint "the very moment of his transformation from the forbidden pagan animal mask into the village hobby" (Alford 1978: 23). There is a thirteenth century account by a French Dominican in Roussillon of an unruly young man who rode the forbidden hobby-horse right into the church. He came, of course, to a miraculous if bad end, spontaneously combusted in flames that started at his feet, "and burnt him up, him and his horse" (Alford 1978: 23). The clerical reporter's objectivity may be questioned, but not the subsequent popularity of the figure. The problematics of archival research into unhistoricized but long-lived practices make documentation difficult if not impossible, but as Cawte says, "the absence of a record does not mean the absence of a custom" (1978: 10).

Documentation as such begins with a single reference from the fourteenth century, a Welsh poem which translates thus: "The hobby horse was once magnificent, faultless in its appearance, in every throng. Come nearer: it is a miserable pair of lath legs, kicking stiffly. And now, assuredly, there never was a poorer enchantment wrought of flimsy woodwork" (Cawte 1978: 11).

"Once magnificent" suggests that even by the fourteenth century, the figure was known importantly, and had already devolved to something cheaply carnivalized. Thus the hobby-horse in even its earliest recorded description denotes, besides fertility, a debased, diluted caricature. Most fifteenth- and sixteenth-century references come from churchwardens' accounts from a variety of parishes, where the hobby-horse's dance was used to collect significant amounts of money for the church (Cawte 1978: 14–15; Hutton 1994: 61). The occasion for the dance was usually New Year's Day, in apparent keeping with the fertility aspects of the figure (Alford 1978: 1–9; Baker 1974: 41–4; Bucknell 1979: 187). Such accounts continue well into the seventeenth century, evidently stopping at the Interregnum. In London, records show that the hobby-horse was known at Midsummer pageants and at other seasons, in church, city, and court activities (Cawte 1978: 23). The earliest London record is from the churchwarden's accounts of St Andrew Hubbard's in Eastcheap for 24 April 1460, a simple note of payment, 2d., "to Mayers child for dawnsing wt ye hobye hors" (Cawte 1978: 23; Hutton 1994: 61; cf. Alford 1978: 27, situating this entry 1464–5 at Tavistock). Numerous accounts of hobby-horse dances are found for the Midsummer Watch, the annual parade of the city militia, known from 1504 to 1545, and recreated in 1585 "as in tyme past hath been accustomed" (Cawte 1978: 25), by then already a figure of nostalgia. The Midsummer Watch itself disappeared when its main features were transferred to the Lord Mayor's Show in October (Michaelmas), and was later recreated at court under the auspices of the Master of the Revels during the 1550s.

By the 1570s, with the presentation at court of a lost play called *Paris and Vienna* (1572), the hobby-horse had moved into the representational world of the professional stage, while extradramatically it had become associated with Whitsuntide, Shrovetide, Candlemas, and ultimately, Christmas festivities (Chambers 1903: I: *passim*). The records are longer and more detailed from about 1560 onwards. The hobby-horse's ubiquity is evidenced by accounts from various households scattered around the country of payments to troupes of itinerant entertainers whose well-received performances included it (Cawte 1978: 40–2). Once sanctioned by both church and court, the hobby-horse, like other pastimes, came to be "forgot" in part because of those notorious Elizabethan spoilsports, Gosson (1579) and Stubbes (1583), who vigorously condemned all such entertainments. It may be said, however, that their polemics did as much to sustain interest as to discourage it; Stubbes's description of "The order of the Lords of Misrule in Ailgna" is particularly, and invitingly, insistent:

> then they have their Hobby-horses, dragons & other Antiques, togither with their baudie Pipers and thundering Drummers to strike up the deuils daunce withall, then marche these heathen company towards the Church and Church-yard, their pipers pipeing, their drummers thundring, their stumps dau~cing, their bels iyngling, their handkerchefs swinging about their heds like madman, their hobbie horses and other monsters skirmishing amongst the route. . . .
>
> (1583: sig. M2)

They and their sober brethren ultimately won, but not easily and not forever. Although it may have disappeared from streets and church-yards, the hobby-horse was nonetheless "remembered" in the intertextuality of the stage: there are at least twelve works, *circa* 1595–1624, containing some variant of the lament, another nine in which the hobby-horse is represented on stage, including an anonymous *Masque of Hobby-horses* (1574), and nine more allusions to it in plays from 1599 to 1639 (Cawte 1978: 49).[3] The hobby-horse of Hamlet's complaint – originarily liminal, seasonal, and cyclical, collectively understood and communally encountered – when folded into *Hamlet*, becomes part of the authored, continuous, occasionally subversive, "liminoid" (V. Turner 1969; 1982) suburban professional theater. And then the combined configuration of hobby-horse and play becomes both liminal, in so far as it enfolds metalinguistic reminders of the traditional elements of its producing culture (English seasonal ritual), and liminoid, in so far as its "forgetting" reflects upon the legitimacy and sacrality of the political structures interrogated in the play.

Hamlet is in several ways an essay in sustained liminality, which may be the reason for the old commonplace assumption that the play is about a prince who avoids action. Liminality never entails stasis; it is both spatiotemporal and processual, a period and a locus of reflection, isolation, and marginalization during which the emergent identity is established.[4] The violations that generate the play's action also engender a kind of mass separation and liminality for several of its principal characters as the preliminary process of redress. The ghost is, of course, the most obvious example of liminality in the play:

> Doom'd for a certain time to walk the night,
> And for the day confin'd to fast in fires,
> Till the foul crimes done in my days of nature
> Are burnt and purg'd away.
>
> (I.v.10–13)

As he says explicitly here and further on, the crime of Hamlet Senior's death by regicide/fratricide was compounded by the fact that he was

> Cut off even in the blossoms of my sin,
> Unhous'led, disappointed, unanel'd,
> No reck'ning made, but sent to my account
> With all my imperfections on my head.
>
> (I.v.76–9)

This is what is so "horrible! O, horrible! most horrible!" (80). The ghost's extended speech is loaded with the language of putrefaction that Claudius's multiple crime has unleashed: the "foul and most unnatural murther" (25) by a "leprous distillment" (64) that instantly "bark'd about / Most lazar-like, with vile and loathsome crust / All my smooth body" (71–3). And so he hovers in liminal limbo about the ramparts of the castle seeking redress, vengeance that will enable him to complete the transition to his next status. However proper and formal his funeral might have been, it could not resolve his "unanel'd" status, and, furthermore, the funeral itself was "followed hard upon" by the murderer's wedding, thus occluding the distinction of the funeral rite itself.

"Doubtful" deaths, "obscure" funerals, remembered erasures: *Hamlet* is a play whose "indirections find[s] directions out" (II.i.63) by directing our attention to the inevitable disintegration of a community that neglects its rites of distinction. Elsinore is indeed an unweeded garden, an indistinct place of decay; inside its boundaries nothing can be seen clearly. The "proof more relative" than the word of a ghost, the "evidence" of Claudius's reaction to "The Mousetrap," would not have held up in a court of law: Claudius might have risen from his seat because he saw a representation of his crime, or he might have risen because he saw a nephew murdering an uncle. In fact after the performance he tells Laertes that Hamlet is out to kill him (IV.vii.4–5). While the audience is assured that Claudius did in fact murder his brother, Hamlet does not hear the "confession"; if he had heard it, he would have known that it too was an aborted rite, Claudius confessing but not repenting (III.iii.66, 97–8). But Hamlet thinks he sees Claudius "in the purging of his soul, / . . . fit and season'd for his passage" (III.iii.85–6). Only away from Elsinore can Hamlet begin to see through the fog of indistinction.

Other characters as well are removed from Elsinore in order to return transformed: Laertes goes off to France believing that he has his father's blessing as well as the king's (but he hasn't: Polonius sends Reynaldo after him to monitor his behavior), and returns abruptly, like his adversary–double Hamlet, to avenge his father's murder and supplant the present king.[5] In this regard, his separation from Elsinore prefigures and foregrounds that of Hamlet, whose transformation is completed – and only can be completed – during his journey to and from England. It is of central importance that Hamlet traverse a body of water, where national boundaries are blurred, marked only (if at all) on maps, those stylized representations of arbitrary and arbitrated distinctions. The sea of Hamlet's separation and liminality concretizes his experience: a body of water between two land masses, two countries, two *states*, is itself a liminal and ambiguous space. The actual boundary that distinguishes Danish from English sea is indeterminate. Literally suspended, on the ship, between two states, Hamlet's experience is perfectly liminal; only via a condition of complete liminality can Hamlet finally see the way forward – "the interim's mine" (V.ii.73) – and come home.

His transformation contrasts ironically with that of Ophelia, who likewise completes her dramatic trajectory suspended (and finally submerged) in a body of water:

> Her clothes spread wide,
> And mermaid-like awhile they bore her up,
> Which time she chaunted snatches of old lauds
> As one incapable of her own distress,
> Or like a creature native and indued
> Unto that element. But long it could not be
> Till that her garments, heavy with their drink,
> Pull'd the poor wretch from her melodious lay
> To muddy death.
>
> (IV.vii.175–83)

Like Hamlet, but for a much shorter time on a much smaller body of water, Ophelia completes the passage to which the play's events consign her. Like Hamlet's, her transformation ends in death, but unlike Hamlet, Ophelia never emerges into new consciousness. Gertrude's description represents Ophelia not only as unaware ("incapable of her own distress"), but indeed no longer even completely human. Like Claudius, she is hybridized, "mermaid-like," and "like a creature native and indued / Unto that element." Ophelia's death, like the place where it occurs, is "muddy" (Crapanzano 1992: 309).[6] It is permanently indistinct, like her burial, and like Gertrude's account, which apparently is not much credited in the play by anyone who hears it. If it were, it would have clarified Ophelia's death as accidental and removed the taint that necessitated the "maimed rites." Gertrude reports that Ophelia fell into the water while "on the pendent boughs her coronet weeds / Clamb'ring to hang" (IV.vii.172–3). The priest nevertheless suspects suicide: "Her death was doubtful" (V.i.227). And no one thinks – or dares – to ask what Gertrude's activity might have been while Ophelia slowly floated, other than carefully observing and reporting.

Hamlet himself cannot explain the mystery of his reclamation from the sentence Claudius has placed upon him in the packet carried by Rosencrantz and Guildenstern:

Rashly –
And prais'd be rashness for it – let us know,
Our indiscretion sometime serves us well
When our deep plots do pall; and that should learn us
There's a divinity that shapes our ends,
Rough-hew them how we will.

(V.ii.6–11)

Fortuitously, Hamlet has his father's royal seal to legitimate and guarantee the sentence: "Why, even in that was heaven ordinant" (V.ii.48), and the plan is neatly symmetrical with the play's initiating events: the betrayers will be "put to sudden death, / Not shriving time allow'd" (46–7). Hamlet's acquiescence to or rather his collaboration in a process beyond his comprehension completes the frame begun with Horatio's early prediction at the ghost's appearance, "Heaven will direct it" (I.iv.91). These appeals to the mystery of divine agency, culminating in the "special providence in the fall of a sparrow . . . the readiness is all . . . . Let be" (V.ii.219–24), mark Hamlet's very brief reincorporation in Denmark as its legitimate leader empowered to appoint Fortinbras his successor. The Norwegian's nomination suggests Denmark's reintegration as an undivided, unpolluted, but also un-Danish, community. In tragedy the closure of the cycle of violence is never what it is in ritual-observant societies where the completion of the process is a mark of restored order. Hamlet's attempt to redress all the maimed rites of his community cannot redeem the loss of that community to itself.

It should be noted that the voyage outward as a separation from the site of regicidal pollution belongs only to those who are themselves not guilty of that pollution: the victim-king, Laertes, Hamlet, and in so far as her madness is a kind of separation from the community, also Ophelia; like the sea, the river and graveyard too are away from the castle locus. Laertes and Ophelia might be called adjunct or preliminary sacrifices; the principal *pharmakos*, fully conscious of his role, is Hamlet. The polluters, in contrast, remain spatially embedded, confined deep within the castle: in Claudius's court chambers, in the room where he kneels in incomplete and ineffectual prayer, in Gertrude's closet, in Polonius's hiding place behind the arras.[7] This spatial embeddedness expresses a contradiction opposite to liminality. Situation within the castle, behind the arras, in the queen's closet would seem to afford

185

the greatest protection from retributive action or assault. But at the same time and by the same means, those who are so embedded are also hemmed in, hedged around, incapable of alteration, transformation, and thus like Claudius at his aborted prayer, of purification.

The pollution of Denmark from the center of its center, Elsinore, and the redress beginning at the margins, inverts the relation of center and margin, placing in question not only the function of authority but that of communal integrity and identity as well. In *Hamlet*, as in all of Shakespeare's tragedies, the safety and integrity of the community are at risk from the first moments. Denmark's monarchy at the beginning of the play rests on a deception and a "murder most foul"; at the end of the play it is hegemonized by a foreigner (Hawkes 1986: 93). The improper habitation of Danish kingship makes the monarchy a sham, with Claudius the player-King out-playing the Player-king of Hamlet's fiction. Claudius interprets accurately Fortinbras's reason for moving against Denmark: "thinking by our late dear brother's death / Our state to be disjoint and out of frame" (I.ii.19–20), which it is. Not for Hamlet alone is Denmark a prison, the time out of joint, the earth a sterile promontory, the heavens a foul and pestilent congregation of vapors, and man the quintessence of dust.

With so much rotten in the state of Denmark, all signifying distinctions are erased, inverted, or completely nullified. As both Hawkes (1986) and Evans (1989) have argued, the end of the play forces us back to its beginning. In Evans's words, "[In *Hamlet*], Saussure's analogy of the signifier and signified as different but indivisible, like the opposite sides of a sheet of paper, is extended into a Möbius strip in which end and beginning, 'inside' and 'outside' are not finally distinguishable" (1989: 130; also Hawkes 1986: 94–6). In this pool of indistinction, Horatio's intention to see "your father's funeral" is inverted immediately: "I prithee do not mock me, fellow student. / I think it was to see my mother's wedding" (I.ii.177–8); the "funeral bak'd meats" that "did coldly furnish forth the marriage tables" are more than just parodic signs of inversion or, as Hamlet quips, of "thrift." Their conflation erases the distinction that funerals and weddings mark in culture: the passage from one state of being or social condition to another. Gertrude's neglect of a proper period of mourning to signify her widowed status occluded the liminal distinction that would have permitted her subsequently to marry again into a new identity. The "o'erhasty marriage," the conflation of mirth and dirge that took place before the action of the play began, was only one of several "maimed rites" that eventually uncreate Denmark. Her failure to observe the proper ritual functions erased the distinctions necessary for communal well-being. Denmark's political exigency for a designated male ruler, Gertrude's desire for a husband, and the agreement of the assembled lords at Elsinore addressed in Claudius's opening remarks (I.ii.1–16), all conspire through the conflation of "mirth in funeral and dirge in marriage" (I.ii.12) to commit a serious violation of culturally requisite ritual distinctions. The breach widens throughout *Hamlet* to encompass not only the "maimed rites" of Ophelia's funeral, itself an inversion: "I thought thy bride-bed to have deck'd, sweet maid, / And not have strew'd thy grave" (V.i.245–6), but also all the others. Thus it is not just in mockery that Hamlet calls Claudius "dear mother" as he is sent off to England; corrected by Claudius, Hamlet insists: "My mother! Father and mother is man and wife; man and wife is one flesh; and so, my mother" (IV.iii.49–51). The identifying distinctions of kinship and even gender dissolve in a context that fails to honor the rituals that protect them.

Behind and antecedent to these ritual inversions is, of course, the one that "hath the primal eldest curse upon't, / A brother's murder!" (III.iii.37–8). Claudius's rank offense that "smells to heaven" spreads all over Denmark. Hamlet is the first to nose it out; the world seems to him "an unweeded garden / . . . Things rank and gross in nature / Possess it merely" (I.ii.135–7). The language of rot and pollution invades the play: one can nose Polonius's corpse on the way up the stairs to the lobby; Yorick's smelly skull makes Hamlet's gorge rise; "hell itself breathes out / Contagion to this world" (III.ii.389–90). Given the extremity of Claudius's crime and Gertrude's ritual neglect, Denmark has no possibility of retaining its distinction from Norway and no royal Dane survives to retain it.

The function of ritual is, as I have noted, "to prevent the fiend and to kill vermin" (*King Lear* III.iv.159); that is, to preserve spiritual and physical health. Like all social constructions, ritual operates in a framework of relations, intrinsically and in connection with the community that sustains it. Its hierarchy is designed to reflect that of the social order. Because they mirror the hierarchical mechanisms of the social structure, rituals are able to regulate social situations (T. S. Turner 1977: 61–2). But as Foucault reminds us, ritual, or indeed any system of rule, may be managed by members of any social or political group powerful enough to seize its control:

> This relationship of domination . . . is fixed, throughout its history, in rituals, in meticulous procedures that impose rights and obligations. It establishes marks of its power and engraves memories on things and even within bodies. It . . . gives rise to the universe of rules, which is by no means designed to temper violence, but rather to satisfy it . . . .
>
> The nature of these rules allows violence to be inflicted on violence and the resurgence of forces that are sufficiently strong to dominate those in power. Rules are empty in themselves, violent and unfinalized; they are impersonal and can be bent to any purpose. The successes of history belong to those who are capable of seizing these rules, . . . controlling this complex mechanism, they will make it function so as to overcome the rulers through their own rules.
>
> (1977: 150–1)

A society's rituals, therefore, constitute the enacted double of the social structure itself. They are contestable, and if they are neglected or abrogated, so consequently is the social structure. As the first act of *Hamlet* makes abundantly clear, several crucial ritual operations and relationships have been violated or ignored before the action of the play begins; the resultant tragedy is not silence (which only comes when all the royal and noble Danes are dead and Denmark becomes Norwegian territory) but the inexorable shaking out of the consequences. Shakespeare was clearly interested in the dynamics and the iconic values of such situations: the implication of fratricide closed *Richard II* some five years earlier, and a remarkable number of situational echoes (open graves, midnight watches, political restructuring) are retained for *Hamlet* from its immediate predecessor, *Julius Caesar*. In the Girardian "sacrificial crisis," the disappearance of ritual entails the collapse of distinctions between "impure violence" (in this case, regicide and fratricide) and "purifying violence" (revenge). In such situations, "purification is no longer possible and impure, contagious, reciprocal violence spreads throughout the community" (Girrard 1977: 49). Girard's thesis applies to the ritual abrogations in *Hamlet.*

When the religious framework of a society starts to totter, it is not exclusively or immediately the physical security of the society that is threatened; rather, the whole cultural foundation of the society is put in jeopardy. The institutions lose their vitality; the protective facade of the society gives way; social values are rapidly eroded, and the whole cultural structure seems on the verge of collapse.

(1977: 49)

As Hamlet says, "Seems . . . ? nay, it is" (I.ii.76). His refusal to call Claudius "father" or to allow Gertrude's reference to Claudius as his father is but a minimal effort to retain the distinction of kinship that ought to inhere in the word. With the time wrenched out of joint by the untimely death of the king, all such distinctions are erased. It falls to Hamlet to set right the structures that previously bound his world. His tragedy is that he cannot.

Claudius's rank (double) offense, compounded with incest and the neglect of ritual propriety, bring Denmark to the verge of collapse. The first to feel it are the guards, Bernardo and Francisco, on watch against Fortinbras's invasion. They direct their gazes outward, as soldiers on watch should do, mounted up on the castle walls, external to the site of the central action of the play within and below. Up on Elsinore's ramparts, they occupy a liminal position. Neither what they were nor what they will be, they have no certain identity during the period of liminality that is the play. This, aside from the dramatic "fact" of darkness and cloaks muffling faces against the cold, accounts for their failure to recognize each other by appearance or voice when the play opens. "Who goes there?" "Nay, answer me." "Long live the King": always a safe answer, whoever the king is. These opening exchanges constitute what Stephen Booth, in another context, called "ceremonies of safety" (1983: 85); they are the play's earliest evidence of unease, confusion, danger, indefinition, liminality.

The guards do not know exactly why they have been placed on "this same strict and most observant watch" (I.i.71); the confusion that runs through the play begins with them. It is not unusual for ordinary soldiers to be kept ignorant of the cause in which they labor (witness the long and moving discussion between Williams and Bates in *Henry V*, IV.i), but it is difficult, to say the least, to guard effectively when one does not know against what one guards. Although the ghost has already appeared on two previous nights, it is not the reason for the watch. The compulsion to explain it only elicits Horatio's vague answer, "This bodes some strange eruption to our state" (I.i.69), which is followed immediately by Marcellus's more urgent question:

> Good now, sit down, and tell me he that knows,
> Why this same strict and most observant watch
> So nightly toils the subject of the land,
> And why such daily cast of brazen cannon
> And foreign mart for implements of war;
> Why such impress of shipwrights, whose sore task
> Does not divide the Sunday from the week.
> What might be toward, that this sweaty haste
> Doth make the night joint-labourer with the day?
>
> (I.i.70–8)

The division of Sunday from the week and of night from day are biblically mandated distinctions. Their erosion itself marks "some strange eruption," and leads to questions at least as urgent as those about the ghost. Horatio's explanation that Fortinbras seeks to reclaim his father's lands has no authority beyond speculation and rumor: "At least the whisper goes so" (I.i.80). The need for clarity shows up even in the way in which the late king is identified: for Bernardo (I.i.41, 43, 110) and Marcellus (58), he is "the King," evidently the only one they recognize by that title; for Horatio, who had come home to see the funeral (I.ii.176), he is "Our last king" (I.i.80). For the guards as for Hamlet, the distinction of the separation rites, the funeral *and* the requisite period of mourning, is blurred or missing altogether. Thus the opening scene with its cast of minor characters suggests the impact upon the community at large of the crisis that propels the play's central action. That impact is preeminently the erasure of the traditions on which Denmark's structures are built. The guards feel it, even if (or especially since) they do not know how to articulate it, for articulation, discourse, requires and demonstrates some clarity or definition to begin with.

The first act of *Hamlet*, then, sets up precisely the Girardian "sacrificial crisis"; its resolution takes the form of the quest for certainty in which the hero is engaged throughout. As is widely recognized, Hamlet's goal is not simply revenge but clarification, demystification; not only justice but "setting right" the disjunctions of time and every other kind of order in his world. His language consistently reflects this effort, whether he is quibbling with his mother over the word "father," or attempting to define the "piece of work" that man is or the qualitites that distinguish "woman," the assignment of shapes to a cloud formation, how to distinguish sanity from madness, proof from assumption, seeming from truth, or a hawk from a handsaw. With all known distinctions thrown into question, the ultimate question emerges: not only "what a piece of work is a man," but indeed, "*How* noble in reason! *How* infinite in faculties!" (II.ii.303–4; emphasis added).

Time too, as a primary construction of order in civilization, has no meaning here. It is "out of joint," its divisions unobserved, and Hamlet's confusion/conflation matches his disordered context. In his first soliloquy, we hear that his father has been "But two months dead! Nay, not so much, not two" (I.ii.138); then "a little month" (I.ii.147); later, settling by Ophelia to watch the play-within, he claims, "my father died within's two hours," which she corrects to "twice two months, my lord," and he hears as "die two months ago," and comments ironically "and not forgotten yet? Then there's hope a great man's memory may outlive his life half a year" (III.ii.127–32). The relation of time to life and memory enters the inquiry: "How long will a man lie i'th' earth, ere he rot?" (V.i.163); in the graveyard, historical memories (Caesar's and Alexander's) coexist with personal ones of Yorick and the dominant one of the dead king. As Susan Cole has aptly noted, "In Claudius's court, memory is a kind of revenge" (1985: 47). It is also an appropriate form of ritual redress, and the only one left to Hamlet.

Hamlet himself does not survive this redress; he becomes instead the sacrifice necessary for completion. Hamlet's death provides the play's only occasion for ritual completion, including as it does both public and private witness, mourning, and epitaph (Cole 1985: 60). But the violations of ritual have cut too deep to permit complete healing: there will be no renewal of "buried Denmark" as a nation. Hamlet's concern at the moment of his death is that the rites of mourning, the passage of rule, and his own memorialization be managed properly, as they never were for his father: "O God, Horatio, what a wounded name, / Things standing thus unknown, shall I leave behind me!" (V.ii.344–5). He and Laertes exchange forgiveness, and three times he asks Horatio to "report me and my cause aright" (V.ii.339), "Absent thee from felicity awhile, / And . . . tell my story" (347–9), and, approving Fortinbras's election, again, "So tell him, with th'occurrents, more and less, / Which have solicited – the rest is silence" (357–8). The telling memorializes him, in both senses of mourning and recollection. Unfortunately, Fortinbras's well-intentioned ceremony for Hamlet, "The soldiers' music and the rite of war" (V.ii.399), is based on a guess: "he was likely, had he been put on, / To have prov'd most royal" (397–8). Royal, certainly, but not necessarily a soldier, although for Fortinbras these two estates may be identical. Even at the very end, the wrong rite is performed.

As Cole and others have noted, none of the other characters receives a fully proper funeral either. Ophelia's rites are "maimed." Polonius's "hugger-mugger" burial was, as Laertes says, "obscure": "No trophy, sword, nor hatchment o'er his bones, / No noble rite nor formal ostentation" (IV.v.215–16). Ophelia's raving is the nearest thing to a memorial for Polonius, although it is unclear whether she laments the loss of her father or her lover (Cole 1985: 56–7). Polonius's unshriven death and ritually incomplete burial as well as the drive to revenge make Laertes Hamlet's double. Yet at the end we are concerned only with Hamlet's funeral; no mention is made of Claudius, Gertrude, or Laertes, other than "Take up the bodies" (V.ii.401). The neglect of ritual that has propelled this play from the start continues through to its end (Cole 1985: 60; Danson 1974: 24–5; Holleran 1989; Holloway 1961: 32).

The commands of tradition and ritual processes run through *Hamlet* like the understage voice of the ghost. Remembering these signs and patterns resists the selective neglect of cultural structures. As Hawkes observes, in this regard the function of tradition is identical with that of theater itself:

> Hamlet's promise to the Ghost to " . . . Remember thee! / Aye, thou poor Ghost, whiles memory holds a seat / In this distracted Globe" (I.v.95–7) . . . hints at such a theatre's immense but informal educative function in an oral culture as an institution serving to *remind* its members of accepted common values . . . almost as a unifying and preservative act of *anamnesis*, of "bringing to mind".
>
> (1974: 125)

Memory indeed "holds a seat" in the theater that houses the play as in the skull that houses Hamlet's recollection.

The traditional hobby-horse dance was likewise a theatrical performance, an enacted narrative confirming a transgressive/

permitted sexuality that promised communal renewal. Instances of its suppression in Elizabethan England implicitly denied both that renewal and the social and political agreements expressed in communal festivity. Conversely, whenever its suppression was noted, as in Hamlet's lament, such notice effectively reversed that suppression by "bringing it to mind." By enfolding the hobby-horse into the narrative text of his play, Shakespeare accomplishes a double feat of *anamnesis* for both the traditonal dance and Hamlet's father.

This signifies a much greater zone of reference than a nostalgia for a buried past or a soft tribute, "caviary to the general" (II.ii.437). The specifically sexual symbology of the hobby-horse locates its occlusion/remembrance in a combat arena where legitimacy itself is confirmed or denied. The promiscuity signalled in the hobby-horse dance denoted a type of social transgression, but at the same time, by its communal complicity, it paradoxically also denoted legitimation and permission (that is, until it was suppressed). Moreover, in so far as transgression itself is always a reminder of the "right rule" being transgressed, both license and legitimacy were simultaneously interrogated every time the hobby-horse danced. Thus, Hamlet "re-members," not only by recalling but also by restoring the image of the dancing hybrid along with the dis(re)membered image of his father. His *agon* is a contest for legitimacy against Claudius's rewriting of history, which would suppress, and would have everyone else forget, the dead king. What is at stake is nothing less than Denmark's legitimacy, its succession, its potency, and its political and cultural integrity.

> What the individual remembers tends to be what is of critical importance in his experience of the main social relationships. In each generation, therefore, the individual memory will mediate the cultural heritage in such a way that its new constituents will adjust to the old by the process of interpretation . . . ; and whatever parts of it have ceased to be of contemporary relevance are likely to be eliminated by the process of forgetting.
>
> The social function of memory – and of forgetting – can thus be seen as the final stage of what may be called the homeostatic organization of the cultural tradition . . . .
>
> (Goody and Watt 1968: 30)

By invoking the hobby-horse, Hamlet locates this issue in a figure that resonated vibrantly for Shakespeare's audience. It hardly matters, in this regard, that his effort is ultimately futile: succession will be by designation, not dynastic inheritance. At the end of the play, Denmark's political identity is something else no longer present and intact, like the old king and the occluded hobby-horse, and indeed like Hamlet himself, who remands his "story" to his trusted friend Horatio. As a metalinguistic instance of a Foucaultian "subjugated knowledge," the hobby-horse signals a forgotten discourse which Hamlet re-members by complaining that it is "forgot," and with it, his father (whose command, "Re-member me," weighs equally with the command to revenge) and himself as well. By the end of the play, Hamlet has revoked his earlier wish in the first soliloquy to uncreate himself, to "melt, / Thaw, and resolve . . . into a dew" (I.ii.129–30) – echoed soon after in the Ghost's "adieu, adieu." Instead he reclaims and re-integrates himself into the community of Denmark by identity with both his father (Kastan 1987: 111; Hammersmith 1978) and the state. Just as his father before him was "buried Denmark," Hamlet at the end names himself by naming his nation: "This is I, / Hamlet the Dane!" (V.i.257–8), thereby reversing the gestures of denial and isolation we have seen in *Romeo and Juliet* and in *Coriolanus*. Also like his father before him, his final wish is to be remembered. It is thus only through "remembering" that identity survives, whether that identity is personal, communal, or national.

In the figure of the hobby-horse remembered, all such survival is signified and legitimated. As Goody and Watt emphasize, "the existence of mnemonic devices in oral cultures . . . offer some resistance to the interpretative process . . . . – all such factors may shield at least part of the content of memory from the transmuting influence of the immediate pressures of the present" (1968: 31).[8] The identification of traditional elements within Shakespearean tragedy discloses a purposeful frame of reference whose impact on the Elizabethan audience was doubtless considerably greater than it is for a modern one. Among those experiences of which Hamlet reminded his original audience was their participation in a transitional culture, a culture in the process of change. Homeostasis is contested by change; change is resisted by memory. Thus, the discourse represented by the forgotten hobby-horse signifies continuity contested by suppression, while its remembrance signifies resistance to change. The old joke redefining the "golden rule" – "the one who has the gold makes the rules" – applies as well to the ones who have control of cultural processes. Intent upon reclaiming tradition and all that it implies for legitimacy, both *Hamlet* and its eponymous hero spoke to the full range of Shakespeare's audience, who knew the hobby-horse, its periodic suppression, and the paradox of remembering by acknowledging forgetting. Custom may have been honored more in the breach than in the observance during this time of social and political change, but it was certainly not "forgot."

Arguments such as those by Moore and Myerhoff, Hobsbawm, and Foucault, noted earlier, address the opportunism of new or renewed secular operations in reviving the structures and referents of older ways to establish contemporary legitimacy and force. But these are not the only occasions for using tradition. Tradition, as the term indeed implies, is what is retained ongoingly, not only to be invoked as needed but persisting despite transition and change. That is, to renew or re-create suggests an attempt to recuperate something that has died out or is moribund. But certain aspects of the traditional life of early modern England, including Hamlet's regretted hobby-horse, never completely died out, and vestiges remain even now. One of the salient features of tradition and ritual is their tenacity, which is doubtless the source of the power they appear to have for groups or individuals who invoke them in the first place. It is not only to the past that such groups revert in ritualizing or traditionalizing action, it is to the orderly natures of ritual and tradition themselves. A hallmark of transitional cultures like early modern England – the term "early modern" itself signals transition – is their persistence in certain traditional practices while simultaneously instituting or relinquishing certain others. Often the traditional practice itself is valuable enough to resist obliteration. Factional power interests, busy perhaps with acquiring or retaining position, may sometimes lose control of traditions and then seek to recall them, but in demotic populations, tradition and ritual form the cement that supports their ordinary lives, and the ordinariness of those lives is precisely what is valuable.

IN DOUBLE TRUST: STRUCTURES OF CIVILIZATION IN *KING LEAR* AND *MACBETH*

It is necessary to recall briefly the Aristotelian definition of tragic action as the violation of specific social bonds:

Now if an enemy does something to an enemy there is nothing piteous . . . . Nor . . . when the two are neither friends nor
enemies. But . . . when killing or something else of this sort is
either done or about to be done by brother to brother, son
to father, mother to son, or son to mother, these the poet
ought to seek.

(Else 1967: *Poetics* 1453b18–23)

For Aristotle, the essence of tragic action was the violation of
kinship and thus of community.

A community is a dynamic organism; it grows and changes, and
in this sense is subject to the same kinds of "rites of passage" and
endures the same kind of *agon* we have come to associate with
protagonists. Both *Macbeth* and *King Lear* present a society in a
liminal moment, in transition from one type of structure to another.
It is possible to forget, while engaged in Macbeth's treachery or
Lear's suffering, that their respective communities are also in
upheaval. At the beginning of *Macbeth*, the external threat posed
by the Norwegian invasion is compounded by the interior treasons
of Macdonwald and the Thane of Cawdor. Scotland's feudal
government is transformed by the end of the play into a specifically
English hierarchy when Malcolm constitutes his courtiers as "Earls,
the first that ever Scotland / In such an honour nam'd"
(V.ix.29–30). Similarly, from the division of the kingdom at the
beginning to Albany's attempt to install Edgar and Kent in a dual
kingship at the end – "Friends of my soul, you twain / Rule in this
realm, and the gor'd state sustain" (V.iii.320–1) – *King Lear* enacts
the rupture of Britain, for which Lear's disintegration throughout
the play is a sustained personified emblem. In both plays, though
differently in each, the structures Victor Turner labelled "hierarchy" and "communitas" are themselves made subjects; that is,
both hierarchy and communitas *per se* are contested, not only in
the sense of who occupies and instantiates their various strata, but
as coordinates of structure altogether. Both plays interrogate the
possibility, the viability, of ordered civilization: can it survive human interference? How much interference? Does its shape alter?
If so, does its name change? Whereas Hamlet's Denmark and
Coriolanus's Rome are absorbed by other recognized nations,
Lear's Britain and *Macbeth's* Scotland (like *Titus's* Rome) change
their identities by a kind of internal combustion. These later plays

represent the subjectivity, the subjection, and through it, the precariousness of political/cultural identity.

In discussing the relation of social structure and discourse, Bruce Lincoln describes the 1917 *débacle* within the Society of Independent Artists in New York over Marcel Duchamp's *Fountain* (the famous inverted urinal), one of the more exquisite statements of "symbolic inversion" in modern art, which led to the defection from the society of both Duchamp and his patron Walter Arensberg. This event, says Lincoln, is generally understood by art historians as a turning point in the development of the New York avant-garde (1989: 143). Following Victor Turner, Lincoln argues that in such instances of profound cultural alteration, "a previously latent cleavage within the group was called into focus"; following failed attempts to resolve the resultant crisis, "schism followed along the lines of the preexisting cleavage . . . . What is of paramount interest . . . is that the initial violation was nothing other than an act of symbolic inversion" (1989: 144). Symbolic inversion is as powerful as, and sometimes more powerful than, active revolt in moving social change. When the symbols that signify important relations in culture are tampered with, ruptures occur along faultlines whose integrities those symbols are meant to insure: "Any structure of ideas is vulnerable at its margins" (Douglas 1966: 121).

The vulnerability of identity at the margins, the boundaries of bonds, is a focal concern of *King Lear* and *Macbeth*. Both plays interrogate virtually every kind of human interrelatedness and definition of identity: feudal, familial, spousal, national. In *Lear* most obviously, the inquiry begins with a concrete objectified symbol of identity, boundaries, and margins, the map of Britain.

Elizabethan audiences had heard, perhaps with some amusement, the bickering for Britain among the rebels Hotspur, Glendower, and Mortimer in *1 Henry IV* (III.i.71–139). Hotspur thinks he can move the boundary-river Trent as easily in reality as on a map – "a little charge will do it" (114) – but he is quickly diverted from his course in the debate by Glendower's shift to the topic of music, and finally gives up the game: "I do not care . . . / But in the way of bargain, mark you me, / I'll cavil on the ninth part of a hair" (135–8). Hotspur is a complicated representation, and it is difficult to know whether the debate over the map proves him mad or merely contentious. In the event, it had no serious consequence in the play, and the Trent flowed on undisturbed.

Doubtless Jacobean audiences, some eight years later, heard Lear's map-altering command in a very different register, despite the similar language used in both plays: "Come, here's the map: shall we divide our right / According to our threefold order ta'en?" (*1 Henry IV*, III.i.69–70); "Give me the map there. Know that we have divided in three our kingdom" (*King Lear*, I.i.37–8). In the latter event, the consequences are a "gor'd state" and the rest of the tragedy.

A map is a symbol of both structure and communitas, replacing "the discontinuous, patchy space of practical paths by the homogeneous, continuous space of geometry" (Bourdieu 1977: 105); its lines inscribe fissures along which crisis occurs, and like Duchamp's urinal, its inversion interpellates other cultural definitions. Thus, in *King Lear*, when the fundamental inscription of known national identity is altered, the definitions of all relations are destabilized, including (as in *Hamlet*) the definition of "human." At the spatial center of the play is the question of what that word means, and with it the definition and possibility of civilization. Lear's "unaccommodated man" is "a poor, bare, forked animal" (III.iv.106–8) who, as the Fool notes with relief, had "reserv'd a blanket, else we had all been sham'd" (III.iv.65). The nearly naked Edgar appears as liminal man, in transit from his animal origins; the shame from which "we all" are saved by his rags is that of confronting a beastly kinship. Lear looks through the "loop'd and window'd raggedness" to an undifferentiated communitas in the company of Edgar/Tom, Kent, Gloucester, and the Fool – statusless outcasts like himself, momentarily related in the liminal locus of the heath. Man is "no more than this," and the tangled bestiary of the play's animal imagery – from dogs and tigers to pelicans and centaurs – implies the fragility of civilized veneers. Lear's cartographic gerrymandering makes Britain the object of a contest for ownership that contextualizes both Edmund's scheme ("Well then, / Legitimate Edgar, I must have your land" (I.ii.15–16)), and the proprietorship that allows Goneril and Regan to shut their doors against the king. It creates the statusless limbo of liminality which dissolves all the security of familiar social structures.

The world of *King Lear* is circumscribed by several kinds of boundaries, all of which are breached at the start of the play. Gloucester acknowledges the violations of his marriage vows and jokes about it; the king vivisects his kingdom and abdicates, while somehow hoping to "retain / The name and all th'addition to a king" (I.i.135–6), as if that were possible. Lear sets up the testy game between his daughters in order to give the "third more opulent" (I.i.86) part of Britain over to a foreigner, France or Burgundy, whoever marries Cordelia, as if Britain were Lear's personal estate, and not a nation. He disowns his loving daughter, while the other two compete for Gloucester's bastard son. Lear and Gloucester act as if social roles were unrelated to social contracts.

Marxist critics were perhaps the first to notice that the play repeatedly interrogates the strength of the bonds that linked the constitutive elements of feudal society, and that alterations in these bonds were the specific "forces of change at work in the kingdom" (Delany 1977: 432). Like Richard II, Lear and Gloucester "are addicted to precedent and ceremony" (Delany 1977: 433), and the old forms on which they rest are contested by a swelling bourgeois acquisitiveness and social functionalism, represented by Goneril, Regan, and Edmund (Delany 1977: 433; Selden 1987: 146–7). The battle between old and new (or old and young) is real enough in this play; but however repulsive and dangerous Edmund, Goneril, and Regan appear to be, Shakespeare makes it clear that the fathers broke the rules first by violating the same "traditional" bonds whose loss they come to regret: Gloucester broke his marriage vows in fathering Edmund, though he retained the tradition of endowing his legitimate elder son; Lear violates his royal obligation to protect the realm, and also the custom of primogeniture in promising the "third more opulent" portion of the land to his youngest, not his eldest, daughter. The encroachment of bourgeois "functionalism" is symptomatic of the play's variously represented violations, enabled by the gap in social processes created by the dysfunctional guardians of traditional feudal codes.

One problem that arises in Marxist readings of *King Lear* such as Delany's is the tendency to valorize the actions of Goneril, Regan, and Edmund for working against the economic and social inequities of the feudal system. That view leaves us with something of a moral problem, because however pragmatic and progressive their levelling efforts may seem, neither their actions nor their motives aim toward the common good, nor do they result in anything but the destruction of order. Delany acknowledges that they do not intend to replace the old order with a new egalitarian structure and that the outcome of the struggle is "too dark and bloody to be redeemed by the vapidly moralistic Edgar" (1977: 437). Others (Selden 1987; Patterson 1989) have read Lear's "poor naked wretches" speech (III.iv.28–36) as a kind of proto-Marxist self-criticism on Lear's part about the inequities of a feudal economy. Patterson's analysis particularly exemplifies a failure to distinguish the reader's reading from the text's explicit content. Finding a charitable message in the passage, she says:

> the play as a whole does not remain faithful to that message, not, at least, at the deep structural level of socioeconomic analysis. For Lear *recovers* from his wisdom-as-madness, and takes nothing from it into his reconciliation with Cordelia that is not a purely domestic intelligence . . . .
>
>   Is this, then, to be construed as Shakespeare's . . . conclusion that the hope of changing places is, after all, a delusion from which we should recover? I doubt it. Such a conclusion is barely compatible with his most transgressive strategy so far, to make the king his own most powerful social critic. [The] play retreats finally into the domestic and familial, as a shelter from sociopolitical awareness . . . .
>
> (Patterson 1989: 116)

Patterson is not the first critic to locate a potential interpretive trajectory in a single line and then criticize the play's infidelity to that trajectory, or to find a thinly veiled "irony" in the play's "failure" to deliver the message that the critic would like to see delivered. The play "does not remain faithful to that message" because the message is not the play's but the critic's. Lear's reconstructed domesticity in Edgar/Tom's hovel does not constitute a retreat "from sociopolitical awareness" but the consequence of that awareness, an elliptical rather than a circular return to the focus of his original violations. As for the "poor naked wretches" who immediately elicit Lear's apparent transformation, as Jonathan Dollimore observes, the play offers us no view of the large population of Jacobean poor. The actual wretches Lear sees before him were, are, and remain members of the court: the King, his Fool, and an Earl, joined a few moments later by a Duke and then that Duke's legitimate son who survives at play's end to assume the king's throne.

> In a world where . . . a king has to share the suffering of his subjects in order to "care", the majority will remain poor, naked and wretched. The point of course is that princes only see the hovels of wretches during progresses (walkabouts?), in flight or in fairy tale . . . . So, far from transcending in the

name of an essential humanity the gulf which separates the privileged from the deprived, the play insists on it.

(Dollimore 1989: 191–2)

Lacking accommodations, the hovel's refugees are the "unaccommodated man" Lear sees in Poor Tom. And they are the only ones he sees. None of them ever goes home again – even Edgar will presumably move to new, royal, quarters.[9]

The play not only interrogates a moribund feudal–aristocratic system; it also exposes the structures of civilization *per se* as system, articulated in relationships that require careful, consistent protection by *some* structure of hierarchy and communitas. The feudal structures of *King Lear* are the particular instantiations of "system" in general. Cordelia loves Lear "according to [her] bond" (I.i.93); Kent persists throughout the play in the duty of serving his master; the Fool performs his professional role of tutoring the king; Edgar remains bound to his father. It is Edmund, whose "bonds" as he rightly says were severed by and under the conditions of his birth and who therefore stands outside both structure and communitas, who identifies the crux:

> Thou, Nature, art my goddess, to thy law
> My services are bound. Wherefore should I
> Stand in the plague of custom, and permit
> The curiosity of nations to deprive me . . . ?
>   . . . Why brand they us
> With base? with baseness? bastardy? base, base?
> . . . .
> Our father's love is to the bastard Edmund
> As to th'legitimate. Fine word, "legitimate"!
>
>   (I.ii.1–18)

Unlike Edgar, born "by order of law" (I.i.19), Edmund recognizes, as only one excluded by structure can do, that "legitimacy" is merely a matter of civil law, the "curiosity of nations." Thus his bond is properly to Nature, as bastards are "natural" children; only by Nature's law is his existence recognized. Edmund's rejection of (and by) the "plague of custom" ironizes Edgar's later quip as lunatic Tom when mad Lear asks him about his "study": "How to prevent the fiend and to kill vermin" (III.iv.159). For Edmund custom is a plague; for everyone else in the play, custom is plagued.

201

King Lear pushes Hamlet's citation of ritual crisis to an extreme: here custom is not "More honor'd in the breach" (I.iv.16); it is entirely breached. As a new-made outcast, sharing to some extent Edmund's permanent condition, Edgar can identify what all of the play's principal characters neglect, and what I have argued throughout this book is the prophylactic and curative function of ritual.

The fissures that weaken structure can best be seen from the outside, and only Edmund begins from that position. Very quickly after the play begins, Lear's court is vacated and the principal characters move outside to the liminal heath, but instead of leaving behind the structure to which they subscribe and within which they are themselves inscribed, they remain in important ways bound to it. That is why, as Dollimore notes, the play "insists" on the gulf created by hierarchy.

> In, boy, go first. – You houseless poverty –
> Nay, get thee in; I'll pray, and then I'll sleep.
> Poor naked wretches, wheresoe'er you are,
> That bide the pelting of this pitiless storm,
> How shall your houseless heads and unfed sides,
> Your loop'd and window'd raggedness, defend you
> From seasons such as these? O, I have ta'en
> Too little care of this! Take physic, pomp,
> Expose thyself to feel what wretches feel,
> That thou mayst shake the superflux to them,
> And show the heavens more just.

> (III.iv.26–36)

Having expelled Cordelia and Kent, and then having been himself evicted by Goneril and Regan, Lear becomes the victim of his own diaspora. He is what Gaston Bachelard calls the "dispersed being" (1969: 7) without a stable point of reference, unable to re-cognize the once-familiar.

> I fear I am not in my perfect mind.
> Methinks I should know you, and know this man,
> Yet I am doubtful: for I am mainly ignorant
> What place this is, and all the skill I have
> Remembers not these garments; nor I know not
> Where I did lodge last night.
> (IV.vii.62–7)

202

However, contested social structures do not necessarily provide the safety and security one seeks in them. Lear hesitates before Tom's hovel, ostensibly because he is distracted by what the thunder says, by recent memories of his displacement by his daughters, and by a paternal concern for the well-being of his Fool. A hovel is precisely *not* the kind of domicile Lear is accustomed to. A king's entry into such a structure entails the annihilation of his status as king, his deconstruction along with that of all that monarchic structure implies. It is precisely the action and the locus required in Turner's definition of liminality, and if this action were performed in the context of a properly ordered Swazi ritual (see above, chapter 4) instead of a Jacobean tragedy, the king's lesson in lowliness would assure his and his kingdom's renewal.

In order to take refuge in the hovel, Lear must first do battle with all the constructs of his courtly microworld. The larger universe, represented by the heath and its inhospitable weather, offers a space in which the hypocrisies and abuses familiar at court – those of the simp'ring dame, the rascal beadle, the corrupt judge – are exposed and challenged. "O, I have ta'en / Too little care of this" is a massive understatement. Simplistically read, Lear's "revelation" might result in a radical re-ordering of the play's social structures. But when we see what in fact happens, we see too that such a re-ordering does not occur, and indeed may not be possible. Wherever they go, people carry with them the positions they have occupied in the social structure; these are imprinted as "dispositions which are so many marks of *social position* and hence of the social distance between objective positions"; consequently, they are "reminders of this distance and of the conduct required in order to 'keep one's distance' ... (by ... 'knowing one's place' and staying there)" (Bourdieu 1977: 82).

Bourdieu's commentary helps to locate Lear's behavior before the hovel not as a demolition of hierarchy but as its perpetuation, and not because Lear wills it so but because of the conditions set by what Bourdieu calls "habitus," the complex social principle in which individuals "wittingly or unwittingly" produce and reproduce social meaning: "[Each agent's] actions and works are the product of *modus operandi* of which he is not the producer and has no conscious mastery .... It is because subjects do not, strictly speaking, know what they are doing that what they do has more meaning than they know" (Bourdieu 1977: 79). The situation represented in *Lear* III.iv entails just such a misrecognition: among the band of refugees, two (Kent and Edgar) are disguised from the rest and from each other; when Gloucester first enters the scene, he does not recognize and is not recognized by the others. Moreover, the refuge itself is illusory: there is no lunatic's hovel because there is no lunatic, and the shelter of the hovel is in any case a one-night stand. Lear, the Fool, Kent, Gloucester, and Edgar are dispossessed of their habitual homes, which in each case was previously the court and its substructures.

By the operation of "habitus," once he has installed himself, nested, in the hovel, Lear can only reconstruct himself regally, ordering "Come, unbutton here" (III.iv.109); two scenes later he establishes a moot court and arraigns his daughters *in absentia*.[10] Lear can no more jettison the hierarchic structures of his former life than Edgar can become Tom o' Bedlam. The Fool's earlier analogy of Lear and a snail was more than a witty criticism:

FOOL.   . . . I can tell why a snail has a house.
LEAR.   Why?
FOOL.   Why, to put's head in, not to give it away to his
        daughters, and leave his horns without a case.
                                                (I.v.28–31)

Social man carries his house with him. Even the birdcage haven Lear imagines with Cordelia (V.iii.8–19) is a home for retired courtiers gossiping about their former domain; it would not be mistaken for a farmhouse or a hovel. It belongs to the same social structure as does Lear himself. To be wrenched out of one's home, displaced, dislocated, dispossessed by any agency whatsoever, even oneself as Lear is in the very first instance, constitutes a genuine and profound threat to identity, and therefore to social existence. As Lear says, "home" is not a matter of physical comfort or simple protection from elemental weather, but of "habitus," the full set of relationships, hierarchies, and ordered activity that the word signals. Tormented by the loss of those relationships, he does not feel the weather's fury:

When the mind's free,
The body's delicate; this tempest in my mind
Doth from my senses take all feeling else,
Save what beats there – filial ingratitude!
Is it not as this mouth should tear this hand
For lifting food to't? But I will punish home.
                                                (III.iv.11–16)

"Home" in this passage carries two meanings: "on target," and the domain of all that is, or would be in a *mundus rectus*, socially constructive. It is a Foucaultian "heterotopia," a "kind of effectively enacted utopia in which . . . all the other real sites that can be found within the culture, are simultaneously represented, contested, and inverted. Places of this kind are outside of all places, even though it may be possible to indicate their location in reality" (Foucault 1986: 24). Lear's "homes" in the hovel and the birdcage are in this sense "heterotopias," where hypocrisy, though it prevails, is also arraigned; where poverty and misery are not relieved but are at least shared.

In this play, however, as in *Macbeth* and *Hamlet*, "real" homes, specifically castles, are sites of violations. In Lear's case these violations are mixed in with the political or stately issues of the division of the kingdom and the early retirement of the king.[11] The subplot allows us to focus more particularly on the specifically domestic dissolutions. When Regan and Cornwall arrest Gloucester and blind him, the first point that penetrates his mind is the fact that this is occurring in his own house. He is more horrified by the violation of his role as host than by the denial of his authority:

> What means your Graces? Good my friends, consider
> You are my guests. Do me no foul play, friends.
> . . . .
>   . . . I am your host,
> With robber's hands my hospitable favors
> You should not ruffle thus. What will you do?
>   (III.vii.30–41)

He invokes the same code that is perversely cited by Macbeth in his moment of conscience before Duncan's murder and by Lady Macbeth's false horror afterwards:

>   He's here in double trust:
> First, as I am his kinsman and his subject,
> Strong both against the deed; then, as his host,
> Who should against his murtherer shut the door,
> Not bear the knife myself.
>   (I.vii.12–16)

LADY M.   Woe, alas!
          What, in our house?
                    (II.i: 87–8)

The fact that Macbeth casts regicide in the language of inhospitable behavior signals the weight of that code for Shakespeare's audience. These concerns, however ironically voiced, are recognizable retentions from the Anglo-Saxon code of *comitatus*, the system in which the most prominent relationship was a lord's protection of his followers, and the most prominent locus for that relationship was the mead-hall, where all significant social operations were defined. As Bourdieu observes:

> Inhabited space – and above all the house – is the principal locus for the objectification of the generative schemes; and, through the intermediary of the divisions and hierarchies it sets up between things, persons, and practices, this tangible classifying system continuously inculcates and reinforces the taxonomic principles underlying all the arbitrary provisions of this culture.
>
>   (1977: 89)

Comitatus was more than a matter of hospitality, or rather, hospitality meant in this context something more than it would mean today. The code itself persisted well through the late medieval period as well, although as social life became more centralized, the term *comitatus* gave way to the medieval *familia*; both terms specifically signalled the full complex of relations and obligations implicit and explicit in the word "hospitality." It was not an optional manifestation of polite behavior, but an absolute requirement of aristocracy (Keen 1990: 169).

Noting that "Regan's neglect of hospitality is a fault which has at least as wide a significance as her want of filial respect" (1987: 148), Selden locates the "corruption of hospitality" (149) in the play by reviewing Elizabethan vagrancy statistics and legislative debates regarding the disposition of "rogues, vagabonds, and sturdy beggars" created by enclosures and other consequences of increasing urbanization (1987: 150–2; also Underdown 1985: 34–6). But he omits the Tudor legislation, and especially Elizabeth's Poor Relief Act of 1598 (reissued in 1601), that had made support of the poor a legal obligation of every parish. In regard to *King Lear*, the two most interesting stipulations of these acts are the one requiring "That the parents or children of every poor, old, blind, lame, and impotent person . . . shall at their own charges relieve and maintain every such poor person . . . upon pain that every one of them to forfeit 20s. for every month which they shall fail therein" (39 Eliz. c.3: VII, in Tanner 1940: 491), and the opening statement of the 1598 document: "Be it enacted by the authority of this present Parliament, That the Churchwardens of every parish, *and four substantial householders there* . . . who shall be nominated yearly in Easter week, . . . shall be called Overseers of the Poor of the same parish" to establish and administer provision of work, shelter, and cash donations (in Tanner 1940: 488–9; emphasis added).[12] Two points thus emerge: the first is that Goneril's and Regan's behavior is not only a filial fault; it is also illegal; the second is that ordinary (albeit "substantial") householders, not just the aristocracy, specifically were made responsible for maintaining the homeless. In view of these statutory provisions, the social violations performed by the various characters in *King Lear* are inflected not only against early modern "Christian" morality but also against established law. It is not only the aristocracy or the government who failed in their social obligations but persons of various social and economic strata, including even solvent parents or children of the poor. The legislations of 1598 and 1601 indicate at least a formal recognition of the "partnership" (an ideologically utopian heir to *comitatus*) required for a stable society, however much that recognition (then as now) was more honored in the breach than in the observance. Such a recognition began long before Elizabeth's reign, and long before the kind of entrepreneurial urbanization to which the critics I have noted attribute the social dissolution reflected in the play; in fact, legislation concerning beggars began in the mid-fourteenth century (Tanner 1940: 469) and by 1531, in a statute recognizing the difference between able-bodied ("sturdy") poor prohibited from begging and "aged, poor, and impotent persons" permitted to do so, the population Lear categorizes as "houseless poverty" was officially recognized not as a social anomaly but as a demographic reality.

Selden's essay suggests that *King Lear* should be read as a reflection of the specific consequences of urbanization, enclosure, etc., none of which is mentioned in the play as a cause of homelessness or of anything else. Even Edgar/Tom's recitation of the causes of his "condition" (III.iv.85–98), aside from being entirely made up, is a litany of abuses committed by, not upon, him: whoring, gamb-

ling, drinking, pickpocketing, borrowing, and generally aspiring
to live beyond his means. Moreover, before he launches his recitation, he counsels obedience to biblical commandments specifically
in regard to family relations: "Obey thy parents, keep thy word's
justice, swear not, commit not with man's sworn spouse, set not thy
sweet heart on proud array. Tom's a-cold" (III.iv.80–3). Lear's
born-again concern for "wretchedness" springs first from his insistence that no one could fall to Tom's condition unless he had
"give[n] all to thy two daughters" (III.iv.49). Family relations,
domestic relations, the relations of *comitatus*, appear to be the
focus in these scenes. Anglo-Saxon elegies such as *The Wanderer*,
The Husband's Message, *The Wife's Lament*, and *The Seafarer* remind
us that homelessness existed long before capitalism. We follow
Lear and his mini-court of vagrants, but we never learn what
happens to his "hundred knights,"[13] presumably also left homeless,
who were "riotous" even under Goneril's roof, that is, before they
were dismissed and dispersed. We can assume that they met a fate
quite similar to the one recited by Tom. "The vagrant was the
extreme case of that much-feared menace, the 'masterless' man or
woman. A society held together by the cement of the household
required that everyone have a parent or a master" (Underdown
1985: 36). If Shakespeare addressed contemporary developments
in economic practices, as Selden and others suggest, he did so in
the context of the breakdown in family relations and codes of
loyalty and reciprocal responsibility.

The liminal heath, in *King Lear* as in *Macbeth*, stands as the
antithesis of all that words like "home," "court," and "civilization"
normally signify. Such marginal loci are distinct places contextu-
ally reserved in ritual for actions that cannot (properly) occur
within the bounds of normal life. "Physical space helps to structure
the events which take place in it" (P. Burke 1978: 108). Roberto Da
Matta, an anthropologist investigating the Brazilian *Carnival*,
writes at length about the social expectations and appropriations
of open and closed spaces:

> The category "street" indicates the world with its unpre-
> dictable events, its actions and passions. The category
> "house" pertains to a controlled universe, where things are in
> their proper places . . . .
> The distinctive feature of the domain of the house seems to
> be control over social relations, which implies a greater inti-

macy and a lesser social distance than elsewhere . . . . but the
street implies a certain lack of control and a distancing
between self and others . . . . It is an area of confusions and
novelties, where robberies occur and where it is necessary to
walk carefully, suspicious and alert. In sum the street, as a
generic category in opposition to the house, is a public place,
controlled by the government or by destiny – those impersonal forces over which we have minimal control.

In this sense the street is equivalent to the category scrub
land (*mato*) or forest (*floresta*) of the rural world, or to the
"nature" of the tribal world. In each case we are speaking of
a partly unknown and only partly controlled domain peopled
with dangerous figures. Thus it is in the street and in the
forests that the deceivers, the criminals, and spirits live –
those entities with whom one never has precise contractual
relations.

(1984: 209–11)

Da Matta's distinctions illuminate Shakespeare's heath, which encompasses some of the same social operations as the Brazilian
"street" (or scrub land or forest). It too is a place of uncertain
social relations, imprecise contracts, dangerous figures. It is of
course a symbolically liminal space, but symbolic terms do not
adequately convey the real, physical, material dangers of social
annihilation. In a society that recognizes the primacy of the house
and of households, to be homeless is to be inhuman, even less than
animal:

> This night, wherein the cub-drawn bear would couch,
> The lion and the belly-pinched wolf
> Keep their fur dry, unbonneted he runs,
> And bids what will take all.

(III.i.12–15)

Domesticity in this sense adumbrates a law of natural behavior that
gives wild animals the sense to come in out of the rain. Against
those forces that would thus annihilate them, Shakespeare's outcasts establish domesticity wherever they find themselves, even in
a hovel on the heath. This kind of domesticity, it should be said, is
in one sense quite distinct, and in another sense difficult to separate, from material issues of property, land, and the ways in which
land is bound up in the operations of ideology. In *King Lear* those

209

issues are most clearly articulated in the Gloucester–Edmund–Edgar constellation, though they are also present in Lear's focus on the enfranchisement of Goneril and Regan and disenfranchisement of Cordelia (Dollimore 1989: 199–201). The domestic and the ideological are in this context reciprocal interventions. Nevertheless a distinction can be made between land as commodity, with all the attributes of "power, property and inheritance" (Dollimore 1989: 197), and land as a site for the affective emotional operations of domestic life. Lear's imagined haven with Cordelia in a birdcage-prison does not seem so crazy when we realize that birdcages, like some asylums and some prisons, are meant to protect their inmates from predators.

The primacy of domestic structure as well as of such "feudal" customs as monogamy, intrafamilial obligations, and the reciprocal duties of monarchy were not immediately eradicated by the rise of an individual-centered bourgeois system. The multiple breaches of order in *King Lear* are rooted in the several failures by half of the central characters, and especially the ones invested with power, to guard any idea of interconnectedness. Those who retain and embody socially constructive values must do so by dissembling (Edgar, Kent, and in his own way the Fool) or in exile (Cordelia). In the face of such rivings and rivalries as we see in this play, no civilization can survive, let alone flourish.

Because the play attends at length to Lear's painful *anagnorisis* and Gloucester's and Kent's abiding loyalty, it permits a degree of sympathy toward "a sight most pitiful in the meanest wretch, / Past speaking of in a king" (IV.vi.204–5), and a degree of righteous satisfaction at Goneril's poisoning, Regan's suicide, and Edmund's relatively honorable death by duel. The play's characters assign a certain traditional logic to its fatalities: "This shows you are above, / You justicers, that these our nether crimes / So speedily can venge! But, O poor Gloucester" (Albany, IV.ii.78–80); "The gods are just, and of our pleasant vices / Make instruments to plague us" (Edgar, V.iii.171–2) and Kent's apocalyptic question about the "promis'd end" (V.iii.265) suggest that divine justice has been served. Even the cynical Edmund, whose goddess was "Nature," dies acknowledging a tidy cosmology: "The wheel is come full circle, I am here" (V.iii.175). But there is something unconvincing, unsatisfying, about such lip-service to supernatural order near and at the end of a drama that repeatedly insists on human rather than divine interventions as the causes of disaster. Abstract and malleable concepts of justice, whether human or divine, have no practical consequence for a state "gor'd" – that is, covered with blood (from the Old English *gor* or filth, recalling Douglas's "matter out of place") and also split, pierced, triangulated (from the Old English *gara*, a pointed triangular piece of land, and *gar*, spear). Kent is wise to reject Albany's suggestion that he and Edgar jointly "sustain" it, not only because, as a faithful feudal retainer, he will soon join his lord in death (V.iii.323), but also because a dual kingship replicates the division of the kingdom that constituted the play's initial rupture. The play's end implies no restoration or resurrection. The image of "sustaining" a "gor'd state" is that of holding together the edges of a gaping wound until time's sutures can reconstitute the flesh. Shakespearean tragedy consistently concludes with a wish that such a healing might occur extra-dramatically, in some unrepresented future time, and simultaneously represents that wish as impossible. The "promis'd end / Or image of that horror" is the total dissolution of both structure and communitas.

In *Macbeth*, a loyal thane violates the "double trust" of his kinsman/king and guest. Duncan more than once counted on the trust mandated by *comitatus*; before he placed it in Macbeth, he had similarly relied on Cawdor: "He was a gentleman on whom I built / An absolute trust" (I.iv.13–14). With the king's "most sacrilegious murther" (II.iii.67) – the violation of more than his trust – comes statuslessness, liminality, the negation of all structures and definitions; "nothing is / But what is not" (I.iii.141–2). Such moments are dangers against which the instantaneous succession in the formula "the king is dead; long live the king" is posed, and are to be avoided – except in drama, where they are explored in the safety of a hypothetical question: what if?

Macbeth moves by and is built around questions. The first four scenes and II.i all begin with interrogatives. The opening question, the Weird Sisters' "When shall we three meet again?" quickly establishes the perhaps surprising fact that a disciplined order governs their world: they will meet again, at a specific time and place, according to a plan. We see that same careful attention to detail in the list of the caldron's ingredients. The question Duncan asks in the first line of the second scene offers a disturbing contrast: "What bloody man is that?" The bloody sergeant appears as a man turned inside-out, an inversion that emblematizes the whole play. There will be a good deal more blood turned outward before the play ends. The grooms' faces will be smeared with blood; so will

Macbeth's and his wife's hands. Macbeth tells Banquo's murderer: "There's blood upon thy face . . . . / 'Tis better thee without than he within" (III.iv.13–14). Lady Macbeth mutters as she sleepwalks, "Yet who would have thought the old man to have had so much blood in him?" (V.i.39–40). Indeed, how much blood is within is something we are never expected to know unless the body's boundaries are breached. "Blood" in this context (or out of its proper context) is Douglas's "dirt," defilement, pollution, like the "gor'd state" that remains at the end of *King Lear*. The bloody sergeant instantiates a discourse of inversions that signal confusion and disturb rational clarity: the man turned inside-out is not a pretty sight. The image appears again when Macbeth sees Banquo's ghost: "the time has been, / That, when the brains were out, the man would die, / And there an end; but now they rise again" (III.iv.77–9).

Inversion is inextricable in this play from paradox and contradiction. The musical cadences of the Sisters' chant, "fair is foul and foul is fair" (I.i.11), contrast sharply with Macbeth's chilling citation of paradox in *his* first scene, after Duncan's envoy names him Cawdor and proves half of the Sisters' prophecy. His mind turns to kingship and the means of achieving it:

My thought, whose murther yet is but fantastical,
Shakes so my single state of man,
That function is smother'd in surmise,
And nothing is, but what is not.

(I.iii.139–42)

Paradox signals the permeability and thus the contamination of logical boundaries and definitions: "To be King / Stands not within the prospect of belief, / No more than to be Cawdor" (I.iii.73–5). The impossible is the only truth.

It is in this context that the play represents Scotland's transformation to a structure modeled on English hierarchy, when Malcolm declares to his followers at the end of the play, "My thanes and kinsmen, / Henceforth be earls, the first that ever Scotland / In such an honor nam'd" (V.ix.28–30). Culture, too, is turned inside-out in *Macbeth*. Its structure is derived by way of human anatomy; the play's definition of culture, like *Hamlet*'s and *Lear*'s, waits upon its definition of "human," which is predominantly, in this play, collapsed into definitions of (mostly masculine) gender. Macbeth claims that he "dare do all that may become a man; /

212

Who dares do more is none"; his wife replies, "What beast was't then, / That made you break this enterprise to me?" (I.vii.46–8). Later, explaining why he killed Duncan's grooms, he says, "who can be wise, amaz'd, temperate and furious, / Loyal and neutral, in a moment? No man" (II.iii.108–9). To be human, he suggests, is to live in clarity, without contradictions, but that idealistic notion too is overturned in this play of paradoxes. It is interesting that the opposite of "loyal" here is "neutral," not "treacherous"; there are some words Macbeth can not say. Still later, he reasons with the men he hires to kill Banquo, seeking their personal commitment to the murder; evidently he does not rely on mercenary contracts. He asks if they will submit to Banquo's suppression of their advancement; they reply, "We are men, my liege," like the soldier in *Lear*, ordered by Edmund to hang Cordelia, who says, "I cannot draw a cart nor eat dried oats; / If it be man's work I'll do't" (V.iii.38–9); but, as Lear said, the distinction between human and animal is sometimes difficult to locate: "Man's life is cheap as beast's" (II.iv.267). Macbeth presses for further distinction, saying that there are men and men, as there are all kinds of dogs in the canine catalogue (III.i.91–100). The definition of "man" in these instances is derived by slight degrees of differentiation from an animal. Lady Macbeth thinks that manhood is fearlessness: "When you durst do it, then you were a man" (I.vii.49), but fearlessness or fierceness is the woman's part in this play, and in any event, the play's debate over gendered behavior is doubly interpellated by both the Weird Sisters' androgynous appearance and Macduff's insistence on his right to grieve for his dead wife and children: "I must also feel it as a man" (IV.iii.221). When Macbeth is frightened by Banquo's ghost at the banquet (III.iv), Lady Macbeth can easily mock her husband's manhood; the ghost does not, after all, appear to her. His defense is that he would not fear what he could fight: a Russian bear, a Hyrcanian tiger, an armed rhinocerous. Man to man or man to beast, "what man dare I dare" (III.iv.98–100). Human and animal are in very close relation here, and that relation is fundamentally combative. What may finally distinguish human from bestial, as in the case of Edgar as Poor Tom, is the fact that human beings wear clothes.

Simultaneously with even the most rudimentary forms of civilization, costume became a cultural artifact, the robe encoding the role. Costume is as central to ceremony and ritual, to all the forms of order that identify culture, as to the stage and the court. In the early modern period, dress not only signified role, but also was dictated by it; as Lisa Jardine has noted, Sumptuary Laws, beginning "within a year of Elizabeth I's accession," and culminating in the elaborately detailed legislation of 1597, marked "the tension between the old, outgoing feudal order and the new mercantile order" (1983: 141–2); they were evidence of the acute anxiety produced by changing social structures. Stephen Orgel points out that when monarchs appeared in masques at court, they "were revealed in roles that expressed the strongest Renaissance beliefs about the nature of kingship" (1975: 38–9). In the masque, a theatrical form saturated with sumptuousness, the monarch's costume was even more sumptuous than the rest; Elizabeth reportedly had difficulty walking in her gowns, and their elaborate patterns iconographically told volumes' worth. Even in the earliest cultures, clothes made the man, and decoration was designation: hunters and priests put on the skins of their animal victims as a sign that they had absorbed and become fully identified with the power of the slain.

Early in the play Macbeth asks Ross, who has just hailed him as Thane of Cawdor, "Why do you dress me / In borrowed robes?" (I.iii.108–9). Lady Macbeth thus prods her husband to action: "Was the hope drunk / Wherein you dress'd yourself?" (I.vii.35–6). New regimes call for new uniforms, and the governed must wear them as well as they can, as Macduff cryptically warns when he announces Macbeth's accession: "Adieu, / Lest our old robes sit easier than our new" (II.iv.37–8). Macbeth's new robes fit worse than Macduff's: "Now does he feel his title / Hang loose about him, like a giant's robe / Upon a dwarfish thief" (V.ii.20–2). Shakespeare's frequent derision of courtly fondness for borrowed style is represented only once in this somber play by the Porter's remark about French hose (II.iii.14). In *Lear*, too, costume marks social differentiation: "If only to go warm were gorgeous, / Why, nature needs not what thou gorgeous wear'st" (II.iv.268–9). On the liminal heath, Lear's robes represent "superflux," "lendings" he would tear off (III.iv.35, 108). Distinctive clothing is an inscription of structure, and it is inextricably woven in with the ceremonies and rituals that bind the elements of particular cultures.

Those ceremonies and rituals are not neglected in *Macbeth*, but the attention given them reverses expectations. The formal ceremonies of court are quickly dispensed with; Duncan's burial is reported in three lines (II.iv.33–5), while Macbeth's coronation

gets one and a half: "He is already nam'd, and gone to Scone / To
be invested" (II.iv.31–2). These stately rituals are clearly not what
the play examines. Far more attention is paid to the banquet in
Macbeth's palace and to the Sisters' dance around their caldron.
The formal banquet is a rite of confirmation, and marks – or
should mark – the acceptance of Macbeth as king. It is therefore
very important that formal procedures and rules of hospitality be
observed. Early in the day set for the "solemn supper," as Banquo
enters the court, he is announced by the king as "our chief guest";
Lady Macbeth epitomizes the discourse of hospitality: "If he had
been forgotten, / It had been as a gap in our great feast, / And
all-thing unbecoming" (III.i.11–13). The code of hospitality protects the social order; its violation heralds anarchy. But as both
Duncan and Banquo learn fatally, hospitality at the Macbeths'
takes perverse forms. At the banquet itself, Lady Macbeth struggles
to play the perfect hostess, cover Macbeth's lapses, and maintain
the required order. The entire scene (III.iv) oscillates between the
signs and processes of order and those of chaos. Macbeth calls his
guests to the table: "You know your own degrees, sit down . . . . /
Our hostess keeps her state; but in best time, / We will require her
welcome" (1–6). Lady Macbeth speaks more truth than the guests
realize: "to feed were best at home; / From thence, the sauce to
meat is ceremony" (34–5); her husband adds, "Now good digestion
wait on appetite, / And health on both" (37–8). Almost immediately the illusion of order is undone by Macbeth's vision of
Banquo's gory locks.

Banquets began in civilization as the communal breaking of
bread, bonding by feeding the body politic.[14] They came to be
formal, institutionalized rituals, processes of statecraft in which
hierarchy was encoded in seating and food-distribution plans.
Such a visible encoding of the social order not only celebrated,
confirmed, and perpetuated the *status quo* but, by reifying it, also
exposed it to possible contestation (Lincoln 1989: 81). Hierarchy
thus informs and shapes hospitality, and hospitality, although it
often looks like the instantiation of egalitarian *communitas*,
ratifies structure: "You know your own degrees, sit down."

From the start of his career, Shakespeare was interested in
dining as a constitutive element in the ecology of social life: in *The
Comedy of Errors* V.i.73–6, Aemilia meditates on the dangers of
disrupted dining; in *Titus Andronicus* there is the perverse culinary
intervention of a manic cook and a Thyestean pie. In *Macbeth*, the

215

concern for peaceful eating (and sleeping) extends on all sides, and signals anxiety in regard to both personal and political health: a nameless lord tells Lennox that he hopes, with God's help and Macduff's, "we may again / Give to our tables meat, sleep to our nights, / Free from our feasts and banquets bloody knives, / . . . All which we pine for now" (III.vi.33–7). In an earlier scene, Macbeth would "let the frame of things disjoint, both the worlds suffer, / Ere we will eat our meal in fear, and sleep / In the affliction of these terrible dreams, / That shake us nightly" (III.ii.16–19). Dining and repose most famously intersect again in

> . . . the innocent sleep,
> Sleep that knits up the ravell'd sleave of care,
> The death of each day's life, sore labor's bath,
> Balm of hurt minds, great nature's second course,
> Chief nourisher in life's feast.
>
> (II.ii.33–7)

But in this play's discourse of inversion, where fair is foul, sleep provides the occasion for Duncan's and the grooms' murders; the hapless sailor whose wife insulted the Weird Sister is punished with eternal waking (I.iii.19–20); Macbeth will sleep no more, and Lady Macbeth sleeps walking.

The biological need for food and sleep was satisfied in early societies by appeal through ritual to divine powers (gods, spirits, demons, or totems); hunting and farming in particular were invested heavily with sacred functions.[15] In modern societies where these needs are supplied by technology and commerce, secular and social rituals retain some of their vestigial meanings. Certainly the food supply was still a matter for concern in Shakespeare's day, when natural disasters such as drought and plague combined with human interventions such as war embargos, grain-hoarding, price manipulations, and speculation (see the Porter's line about the farmer "that hang'd himself on th' expectation of plenty" [II.iii.4]), and kept these commodities from being taken for granted.

Against that anxiety, the fullest image of plenitude in the play occurs in the ingredients list for the Sisters' caldron. Like Lear's band of refugees, these outcast, marginal women with beards set up housekeeping on a heath. Persistently demonized, the Weird Sisters ironically live the most ordinary and orderly of domestic lives. This is especially evident in comparison with the Macbeths, whose domesticity is a perversion, and the Macduffs, whose domesticity is shattered. The caldron (a uterine symbol?), the receptacle and vessel for their mysterious recipe, is the locus of their power; they are "the most fertile force in the play" (Eagleton 1986: 3). Who in the audience did not wonder – and who could ever admit to knowing – what that famous recipe produced? They are the first characters we meet as the play begins, where in an expression of absolute, even academic, order, they plan their next meeting and announce the play's dominant paradox: "Fair is foul and foul is fair" (I.i.11). We must wait until IV.i to see the women more intimately at their kettle.

Even the appearance of the Sisters is paradoxical and baffles Banquo: "you should be women / And yet your beards forbid me to interpret / That you are so" (I.iii.45–7). Old women with facial hair, the Sisters typify the mysterious folk in rural places who gather herbs and practice healing, and who are believed to be able to tell the future. In most of Celtic folklore, they did not curse or cause evil except in retaliation for harm or slander done to them, as they do to the hapless sailor whose inhospitable wife denied one chestnuts and called her a witch. The sailor's wife's remark is the play's only spoken instance of the epithet, although the Folio speech prefixes and stage directions, as well as much subsequent critical discussion, have literally demonized them. They are, as Kenneth Muir pointed out, "the kind of old women who, because of their appearance, get credited by the villagers with possessing supernatural powers – and if a cow dies or if a child falls sick they get the blame for it" (K. Muir 1962: 238). The seventeenth century's view of "witches" was by no means stable or consistent: while James I's belief in witchcraft was well known, it was not universally shared, and was countered by the sceptical positions of Reginald Scot's *Discoverie of Witchcraft* (1584), which James ordered burned, and Samuel Harsnett's *Declaration of Egregious Popish Impostures* (1603) (Monter 1983: 32). Simon Forman's description of the 1611 performance of the play refers only to "3 women feiries or Nimphes" (K. Muir 1962: xiv). Holinshed describes them as "three women in strange and wild apparell, resembling creatures of the elder world . . . . either the weird sisters, that is . . . the goddesses of destinie, or else some nymphs or feiries, indued with knowledge of prophesie by their necromanticall science, bicause everie thing came to passe as they had spoken" (Bullough 1973: VII: 494–5). Travellers among the audience might have seen a resemblance to Italian *benandanti*, who were called witches and warlocks by Church inquisitors, but who saw themselves as "anti-witches," procurers of good, practicing specifically agrarian fertility rites to insure and protect crops (Ginzburg 1983: 4, 22). Or the Sisters' appearance might have signalled to the more learned in the audience the hermaphrodite figure in alchemical iconology, which coincidentally represents perfect harmony and synthesis out of seeming paradox (Heninger 1977: 3, 188–90). Exotic (literally excluded, alien) power, like that of the *pharmakon*, works as both poison and cure; "it is an idea, before it is a phenomenon . . . [and] may include inversions of any of the positive values peculiar to a given society" (Larner 1981: 2). In any case, Larner argues, the European phenomena of witch-hunting and witch scares had abated by the end of the sixteenth and beginning of the seventeenth centuries, and did not take hold in Scotland and England until the 1620s (1981: 18). Moreover, variant Protestant (Lutheran, Anglican, and Puritan) distinctions of "witchcraft" from other forms of "magic" and "superstition" (Monter 1983: 28–32) radically problematize the Sisters' contemporary reception in Shakespeare's play. We cannot be sure what these women would have signalled to their audience. They are not accounted for in the play's conclusion; they simply disappear after IV.i.

What we do know about them is that in the dialogue they are called "Weird." In the earliest, that is, the First Folio, printing, the word is spelled "weyard" (Acts III and IV) and "weyward" (Acts I and II). The *OED* defines it, even in the notable spelling, as: "having the power to control fate or destiny, or dealing with it, or partaking or suggesting of the supernatural." But the Folio spelling for Acts I and II obviously suggests reading "weyward" as "wayward," "by the wayside," beyond the social pale; in other words, marginal and liminal. Thus the Sisters stand as foils to Lady Macbeth (Belsey 1985: 185), who begins within the social domain and willfully moves outside it. Their beards make their gender ambiguous, unknowable, and therefore dangerous, like Lady Macbeth whose famous wish to be unsexed is affirmed in her husband's "Bring forth men-children only! / For thy undaunted mettle should compose / Nothing but males" (I.vii.72–4). Women who subvert standard social definitions of the "feminine" tend to be demonized by those for whom alterity is otherwise unintelligible (Belsey 1985: 185; Larner 1981: 20).

In a play that gives a great deal of attention to domestic dysfunction, the Sisters paradoxically present the nearest thing we have to "normal" domesticity. The probably interpolated figure of Hecate provides a mistress for their household: she praises their management of the caldron (IV.i.39–43), and when they transgress, as they appear to have done in the first of her two scenes, she promptly scolds them as "saucy and overbold" (III.v.3). Thus chastened, they turn to their kettle and stir things up. The marginal liminal heath where the Sisters live is the appropriate locus for them, as it is for Macbeth in his transformation from loyal thane to murderer and tyrant. In the open, undomiciled space of the heath, again inversely, public becomes private and unbounded "waywardness" is domesticated.

Liminality does not force transformation; if it did, Banquo would have been similarly changed. But it is required when such changes are taking place; it provides the space between what was and what will be. In *Hamlet, Lear, Richard II*, and *Coriolanus*, the dramatic action begins at the center (the court, the city) and moves outward, respectively, to England, to the heath, to Wales, to the Volscian camp. In *Macbeth*, where all structure is inverted and fair is foul, two of the first three scenes take place on the heath and the other in "a camp near Forres." We do not see the inside of a castle until the fourth scene. The action moves from marginal to central space, but in this play, the space inside structure is more dangerous than outside. There is no safety in castles. There is no reincorporation of the hero who is also the villain. There is no reintegration of Scotland, which instead is transformed to a version of English hierarchy. What that transformation registered for an audience whose monarch was a Scot turned English is a speculative matter: on the one hand, it looks like a confirmation of English political structure; on the other, it discloses the arbitrariness, the instability, of political/cultural definitions inscribed within the play's discourse of inversion.

The force of transformation – "the first that ever Scotland / In such an honor nam'd" (V.ix.29–30) – is the fiat of nomenclature, the ordering system of signifiers. The play's action moves through a lexical progression from things that cannot be named, as when Macbeth could or would not say "treacherous" as the opposite of "loyal," to those that must. Lady Macbeth, early on, says, "Glamis thou art . . . and shalt be / What thou art promis'd" (I.v.15–16); she does not say what that is. Macbeth cannot say "Amen" (II.ii.26). Throughout most of the play, Duncan's murder is simply called "the deed," especially after the fact; regicide is unspeakable.

219

Macduff cannot say it either: "Tongue nor heart / Cannot conceive, nor name thee!" (II.iii.64–5). Macbeth asks the Sisters what they do; they reply, "A deed without a name" (IV.i.49). Malcolm refuses to say Macbeth's name; it blisters his tongue (IV.iii.12) until he links it with the word "treacherous" (18), the word Macbeth would not say. That word marks the turning point, after which names emerge steadily as ordering forms of differentiation. Ross calls Scotland not "our mother, but our grave" (IV.iii.166). Malcolm says that Macbeth smacks "of every sin / That has a name" (IV.iii.59–60). Finally, the naming comes to closure when, as noted above, Malcolm re-names his "thanes and kinsmen" as the first Scottish Earls, signifying with that naming the absorption of one cultural structure into another. Names are always signifiers, indicating identities and relationships when they are assigned. But when they are used, spoken, vocally inflected, they signal a range of possibilties, from affirmation to deception (Eagleton 1986: 6). Naming is magical invocation: after Marlowe's Faustus signs his contract, Mephistopheles is forbidden to name "who made the world" (II.ii.67–73). Inversely, in the parodic scenes, Faustus, Wagner, and even the clown Robin can invoke by naming major and minor demons at will. Traditional Judaism uses the Tetragrammaton to mask the true (and unspeakable) name of God; conversely, in Islam, "the ninety-nine names, or epithets, of God, comprising all the divine attributes, may be written on paper (or simply repeated) in order to produce far-reaching effects" (Goody and Watt 1968: 227). The study of cultures, from Freud (1950) to Lévi-Strauss (1966), Goody and Watt (1968), and Foucault (1970) is in large measure the study of names.

Macbeth as hero/villain remains one of the most vexing definition-defying constructs in Shakespearean tragedy. His status as villain, as "butcher," poses no difficulty, but if he is not at the same time the tragic hero, then he is the only titular protagonist in Shakespearean tragedy (except perhaps for Julius Caesar) who is not. Derrida's model of the bivalent *pharmakon*, poison and cure, reconciles this interpretive dissonance. So too do Girard's early theories of mythic process and the "sacrificial crisis." He notes the "conflictual aspects in the narrative elements at the beginning of many primitive myths [which] suggest violent disorder rather than a mere absence of order, primordial or otherwise. We often have a confused struggle between indistinguishable antagonists" (1978: 185). Eliminating one of the antagonists permits differentiation of character, which represents the differentiation of human thought, which, in turn, in Girard's view, is the birth of cultural order. Differentiation, i.e., separation, alienation, is served by scapegoating, for which a given myth provides the narrative context. Scapegoating requires motive; thus the goat is invested with "a truly fantastic and superhuman power to harm the community" (Girard 1978: 187). We have already seen how these distinctions apply to Bolingbroke and Richard in *Richard II*. They apply equally well to the Weird Sisters and the Macbeths. The malefactor/victim is presented as someone special, either alienated from the community from the start or one who moves outside it. The Sisters and Lady Macbeth may serve as the most obvious figures of separation and alienation, but ultimately it is Macbeth who is "sacrificed" as malefactor and victim. The difficulty of seeing Macbeth as victim, sacrificial or otherwise, except of a will to power, is offset by recognizing that as a constructed subject Macbeth embodies all that is feudal Scotland at the start of the play. Scotland is full of contradictions: its values of bravery and fealty are already threatened by the first Thane of Cawdor, the traitor whom Macbeth in every respect replaces. Its structure of monarchic succession is unclear until Duncan names his successor. Like Macbeth's, its "single state" is "shaken"; its function is "smother'd in surmise / And nothing is but what is not" (I.iii.140–2). "There's no art," says Duncan, "To find the mind's construction in the face" (I.iv.11–12); it resides deeper. Macbeth is Scotland's "monstrous double"; he replicates its contradictions, its feudal values and the violence that sustains them. From loyal thane, "brave Macbeth," "valiant cousin! worthy gentleman" (I.ii.16, 24), he is quickly turned around, or rather, like the bloody sergeant's appearance, turned inside-out. And he in turn is doubled and inverted by Malcolm.

Just before he announces his virginity to Macduff, Malcolm prepares himself for heroic function, in Girard's terms, by identifying himself completely with Macbeth. This long passage (IV.iii.50–100) is more than just a test of Macduff's loyalty to Scotland. Reciting a catalogue of extraordinary vices, Malcolm makes himself more dangerous to Scotland than Macbeth:

> It is myself I mean; in whom I know
> All the particulars of vice so grafted,
> That, when they shall be open'd, black Macbeth
> Will seem as pure as snow; and the poor State

Esteem him as a lamb, being compar'd
With my confineless harms.

(IV.iii.50–5)

In a complicated process of repeated inversions and identifica-
tions, Malcolm turns himself inside-out, "open'd," exposing vices
in comparison with which Macbeth appears as "a lamb," the
emblem of innocence and sacrifice. The ritual subject identifies
with his opponent and becomes what must be destroyed, and then
redifferentiates himself as he emerges newly forged, new born.
The next coronation at Scone, Malcolm's, will doubtless be fully
and properly attended, except, perhaps, for his brother
Donalbain. Duncan's other son disappeared from the play after
II.iii, even earlier than the Weird Sisters. His last ominous line,
"the near in blood, / The nearer bloody" (140–1), suggests the
possibility of another cycle of treachery and kin-killing.

The play ends with only an illusory order emerging out of
paradox and contradiction. When Macbeth hears that "none of
woman born / Shall harm" him (IV.i.80–1), he believes that there
is no such thing and thus misrecognizes Macduff's threat. The
symbolic contradiction entailed in the Sister's prophecy likewise
appears to bring about, but in fact problematizes, Scotland's
rescue by Macduff, not "born of woman" and left childless, and its
restoration of "measure, time, and place" (V.ix.39) by Malcolm,
"yet / Unknown to woman" (IV.iii.125–6). Like Marcus Andronicus's ironic promise to knit the "scatter'd corn" of a Rome im-
agistically left without women, Malcolm's and Macduff's
combination of unusual birth, childlessness, and virginity suggest
no potential for procreative renewal. The hope that "Things at the
worst will cease, or else climb upward / To what they were before"
(IV.ii.24–5) is shattered by the end of the play, when it is clear that
"things" will not return "to what they were before." Scotland will
not be restored; it will be reconstructed in the image of its
southern neighbor.

Arguing for Macbeth's status as tragic hero, Kenneth Muir
wrote:

> We cannot divide the world into potential murderers and
> those who are not. It consists of imperfect human beings . . . .
> If they commit evil it is because they hope thereby to avoid
> another evil, which seems to them for the moment to be

worse, or obtain another good, which seems attractive if only because it is not in their possession.

(1962: lxix)

Once again, Tom o'Bedlam's formulation says this better: he studies "How to prevent the fiend, and to kill vermin" (*Lear* III.iv.159). Warding off spiritual harm and preventing disease are exactly the functions of ritual practice. Rites of passage specifically are defined as prophylactic rather than purgative. They clarify and decontaminate entrance to a new status, and they emphasize the permanence and value of all societal classifications (Douglas 1966: 56). In representing the processes of alienation, identification, and scapegoating, *King Lear* and *Macbeth* represent the basic processes of civilization-under-construction and the difficult and problematic birth of structure and hierarchy.

Writing about *King Lear*, Stephen Greenblatt notes the "intense and sustained struggle" at the juncture of Elizabethan and Jacobean England "to redefine the central values of society . . . . At the heart of this struggle . . . was the definition of the sacred, a definition that directly involved secular as well as religious institutions" (1985: 165–6). He concludes by saying that Lear's concerns are still ours:

> Because the judicial torture and expulsion of evil have for centuries been bound up with the display of power at the center of society. Because we no longer believe in the magical ceremonies through which devils were once made to speak and were driven out of the bodies of the possessed. Because the play recuperates and intensifies our need for these ceremonies, even though we do not believe in them, and performs them, carefully marked out for us as frauds, for our continued consumption.
>
> (1985: 183)

He thus reasserts the appeal to systems of order through ritual and ceremony. Nevertheless, the nihilistic images of their violations peep out from under these plays in performance, reminding us that cultural structure is always held in a delicate balance. "Double, double, toil and trouble." Like Duncan approaching Macbeth's castle, we are always "here in double trust."

223

CONCLUSION
wRiting / Lost in translation

A text is not a text unless it hides from the first comer, from the first glance, the law of its composition and the rules of its game.

Jacques Derrida, "Plato's Pharmacy"

Representations such as *Macbeth*'s Weird Sisters and their marginal-yet-familiar domain complicate the ways in which we comprehend the operations of ritual action in Shakespearean tragedy. Though they live somewhere nameless, unspecified except as "a heath," their arena is domestic: their curses concern the comforts and discomforts of ordinary life rather than the state of someone's soul. The second time we meet them, in the opening lines of I.iii, they rehearse their activities in the immediate past and future. One has been killing swine; another begged chestnuts from the sailor's wife, and will avenge her slighting by turning the hapless (and blameless) sailor into Coleridge's Ancient Mariner, a Flying Dutchman, sleepless and homeless for nearly two years, "a man forbid, / Weary sev'nights nine times nine" (I.iii.21–2), indeed like Macbeth, whom Eagleton calls "a floating signifier" (1986: 3). Their caldron too invites a closer look. One-third of the items listed are of the most exotic and improbable origins: scale of dragon, liver of blaspheming Jew, nose of Turk, and so on. But the remaining two-thirds are ordinary animals, or parts of them: toads, fenny snakes, newts, frogs, bats, dogs, owlets – easily recognized, domestic, familiar, all cooked up into a "gruel thick and slab" (IV.i.32). These are the commodities in which the Sisters traffic. This domesticity, it seems to me, is important: their domain is that of the material, not the spiritual, world, and their crimes, as Ginzburg has suggested, were characterized not in theologically defined terms, but in material terms of "the destruction they brought to harvests and famine, and the sorcery they worked on children" (1983: 27). Like Puck in the comic mode, they undid domestic work, spoiling crops, souring milk, sickening livestock, defiling home, field, and harvest (Thomas 1971: 519). The domestic imagery in which so much of the language of *Macbeth* is cast is the demotic language of a non-aristocratic audience. It intervenes in a play about kingship, disturbs its monarchic focus, blends its homely voice with those of elite and courtly interests, and serves as a reminder of the communal whole that is the play's ultimate subject. Critical neglect of these domestic ritual discourses may be related to a general linkage of "domestic" with "female," and a general dismissal of both from serious consideration. As Linda Woodbridge and Edward Berry have observed:

> Studies of ritual tend to stratify along gender lines: "male" rites such as ceremonies of political power, male initiation, war, and ceremonies of international diplomacy draw most theorists' attention, while "female" rites promoting human and agrarian fertility now languish in neglect, after a period of virulent scholarly attacks . . . . The exclusion of fertility from serious attention, the defining of ritual as rites of power, is the preference of a male-dominated society.
>
> (Woodbridge and Berry 1992: 8)

This view interpellates a challenge that Shakespeare's festive tragedies answer by their explicit concerns with rites of fertility, seen as rites of survival and perpetuation, as well as communal rites of passage. It may be that such rites in the context of festive tragedy are appropriated by "male-dominated" interests: that would certainly be a plausible view. Or it may be, as the quotation marks around the terms "male" and "female" suggest, that latter-day interpretation has artificially split ritual concerns into hierarchically gendered domains. That too would be a plausible view. When survival rather than honor's at the stake, when the whole community or polity is at risk, gender-specific job-descriptions are unaffordable luxuries. As Lear says, "When the mind's free, / The body's delicate" (III.iv.11–12).

Without reference to gendered domains, Moore and Myerhoff painstakingly distinguish secular from religious ritual and ceremony:

> When religious rituals are situationally specific (the funeral of a particular person, the marriage of two individuals) by

implication they link these specific occasions to all deaths and all marriages . . . and eventually to the religious doctrine itself. When secular rituals are situationally specific, they also may link the immediate with a larger reality, but they do not, even in a vague way, invariably attach to a total explanation.

(1977: 12)

In Elizabethan and Jacobean England, some secular rituals were indeed attached to religious doctrine, for example, rituals concerned with monarchy, owing to the manufactured doctrine of Divine Right and the Church's involvement with ceremonies of coronation and royal weddings, births, and funerals, which by their very occasions linked the political with the religious domain. Some of what Moore and Myerhoff would label "secular rituals" were appropriated by both ecclesiastic and political interests as the means by which a particular kind of "order" was maintained in both the home and the state, as in Hooker's 1593 *Laws of Ecclesiastical Polity*, which asserts that social disorder begins with domestic strife and adduces the example of Cain and Abel (Hooker 1975: I,x,3), and the "Homilee agaynst Disobedience and wylful Rebellion" (1574), which similarly conflated domestic, political, and ecclesiastic hierarchies. Francis Dillingham's *Christian Oeconomy or Household Government* (1609) makes the same connection: "A great cause of disorders, both in church and Commonwealth, is a disordered family" (quoted in Selden 1987: 147).

Many Elizabethan and Jacobean "secular rituals" were attached to belief systems that preceded those of the Christian Church in England, that were once called pagan, and now politely called "folklore." Hamlet's hobby-horse belongs to that category, as do traditional dances, morrises and sword-dances, effigies, masks, maypoles, harvest-homes and other agrarian or seasonal practices not specifically absorbed by the Church. Because they are not inscribed within a totalizing doctrine, and because their practice varies among participants, it is difficult to describe, much less assert, precisely how they work or why they persist. To the extent that they persist outside centers of power, that is, among demotic segments of a population, their aims are not always clearly identifiable. Moore and Myerhoff have reminded us that ritual produces a variety of consequences, some that are unconscious, and some "that may or may not occur at all, may occur in every shade of intensity from an image in the mind . . . to a profound ecstasis"

(1977: 13). That is why field workers in anthropology and folklore, to the extent that they lack the "thick description" that permits the reading of the "acted document" that is culture (Geertz 1973: 6, 10), often relegate such practices to the domain of "pastimes," simple merriment for simple folk.

But sustained social practices among any population or segment of a population are never simple matters, and never aimless. Goody reminds us that "ritual observance" sometimes signals automaticity, and sometimes, as in the Greek city states or among the maranos of Spain and Arab lands, compliance without belief (Goody 1977: 33); when coerced, it manifests dominant communal values without unanimity. Goody's remark about the difference "between performances of *Hamlet*, the State Opening of Parliament, and the Mass" (1977: 29) is a well-placed caution, given the loosening of definitions that informs some of the studies in Moore and Myerhoff's volume (which includes Goody's essay), Hobsbawm and Ranger's (1984), and Robert Bocock's (1974). If categoric definition fails because of popular variables, and if ecumenical indefinition fails because it is indiscriminate, then the best function of a book such as this one is to note the presence of the past in the present, as it were, and the resonances of both inclusion and occlusion where they occur.

But there is more. We can distinguish the natural, often unconscious, automatic, or merely compliant occasions of ritual in "real life" from deliberate insertions in plays. Shakespeare's characters do this by noting the absence of custom or ritual where it might do some good, and by signalling its omission, violation, or perversion. Hamlet explicitly does this; so do Richard II, Titus, the parents and prince of *Romeo and Juliet*, and several personae in *Julius Caesar*, *Macbeth*, and *King Lear*.

Given the efforts (and frequent failures) of church and governmental establishments to suppress "folk" customs in early modern England, it may fairly be said that such practices were sustained (where they were sustained) precisely because they were repositories of self-determination and maintenance for populations lacking other ways of countering domination by hierarchical agencies, "employ-[ing] thought and discourse, including even such modes as myth and ritual, as effective instruments of struggle" (Lincoln 1989: 7). Such practices continue regardless of hierarchical permission, openly or covertly, amalgamated into dominant structures or diminished by those structures to "harmless" or "simple" folk amusements.

Identifying traditional and ritual elements within Shakespearean tragedy is rewarded not only in the domain of interpretation but also in the disclosure of a context that persistently recedes from modern view. To see the extent of this traditional thread is to supplement the endless and sometimes inconclusive attempt to historicize the plays' original performative conditions and their impact. Early modern culture was unarguably infused at innumerable junctures with tradition and ritual. Some, as I have noted throughout this book, were honored more in the breach than in the observance, but like Hamlet's hobby-horse, they were never "forgot." They persisted in social practice and in the commemorative performances of Shakespearean tragedy.

Tragedy has always been festive in its origin as well as its signification: it began in the West with the Aeschylus–Sophocles–Euripides triad, whose plays we know primarily because they won prizes at the Dionysian festivals where they were first performed. They were preserved as monuments of their producing cultures. The descriptive record of Aristotle's *Poetics*, with its meticulous analysis of the processes of catharsis by the hero's agency, depended on those texts in much the same way as we who write about Shakespeare's some four hundred years after their original performances depend upon negotiated texts culled variously from quarto and folio inscriptions.

Performance written down, flattened on the pages of a book, represents a static version of a play-as-performance. When that performance imbricates another, as a play imbricates forms of ritual action, the difficulty of finding a language in which to talk about it, or write about it, or represent it in a way that does not betray it out of all useful understanding, increases exponentially. Writing about writing in "Plato's Pharmacy," Derrida wrestles with a passage from Plato's *Phaedrus* on related matters of authorship in myth, in *logos*, and in art. His words point to the arena beyond "book": beyond his book, beyond this book, beyond Hamlet's book, and beyond Shakespeare's book:

> Books, the dead and rigid knowledge shut up in *biblia*, piles of histories, nomenclatures, recipes and formulas learned by heart, all this is . . . foreign to living knowledge and dialectics . . . . Not that logos *is* the father, either. But the origin of logos is *its father* . . . . *Logos* is a son, then, a son that would be destroyed in his very *presence* without the present *attendance* of

his father . . . . Without his father, he would be nothing but, in fact, writing . . . . The specificity of writing would thus be intimately bound to the absence of the father . . . . [Socrates insists that] " . . . It always needs its father to attend to it, being quite unable to defend itself or attend to its own needs."

(Derrida 1981: 73, 77)[1]

It is perhaps for this reason that Hamlet, reader of books and authored author of both his father's closure and his own, entrusts the next tale to (H)*oratio*, the speaker, although "the rest is silence." Writing, says Derrida's Plato, is "repeating without knowing" (1981: 74). Both ritual and performance are finally transformed and betrayed by writing about them. In the end, says Derrida,

> The magic of writing . . . is like a cosmetic concealing the dead under the appearance of the living. The *pharmakon* introduces and harbors death. It makes the corpse presentable, masks it, makes it up, perfumes it with its essence . . . . Death, masks, makeup, all are part of the festival that subverts the order of the city, its smooth regulation by the dialectician and the science of being. Plato . . . identif[ies] writing with festivity. And play. A certain festival, a certain game . . . . The pharmacy is also, we begin to perceive, a theater.

(1981: 142)

Yes. But. To proceed from this pharmacy to performance, or rather to theatrical performances that modern Western audiences can recognize as such, and then to the pages of printed texts that attempt to anchor them, requires a very long and circuitous journey indeed. "[The] literary work is both the analogy of a knowledge and caricature of customary ideology" (Macherey 1978: 59). Consigned to and constrained by writing, ritual (an embodiment of "customary ideology") is "undone" in the performance, and then again in the text, of a play. What Macherey calls the "liberating violence" of interpretation then further "dismantles the work in order to be able to reconstruct it *in the image* of its meaning, to make it denote directly what it had expressed obliquely" (1978: 76). And yet, he says, "To recoil from the task of an interpretation is to accept failure or to vanish into the work; it is to privilege the inessential, out of a care for false objectivity; it is to refuse to listen to a fundamental and haunting image" (1978: 77).

Wole Soyinka also recognizes the transformational interpretive analogy of tragic and ritual protagonists as a diminution in scope, tailored to contemporary concerns, "a mere extraction of the intellect, separated from the total processes of being and human continuity" (1976: 36). Soyinka's post-colonial perspective of both Nigerian and Western drama discloses critical relationships that may be less accessible from a unitary cultural position. He analogizes the Western critical endeavor to "a steam-engine which shunts itself between rather closely-spaced suburban stations," picking up various loads of freight along the way: allegory, "nature truths," "naturalism," surrealism, absurdism, "until it derails briefly along constructivist tracks and is towed back to the starting point by a neo-classic engine" (1976: 37–8). Now, of course, the freight loads would also include post-structuralism, historicism, feminism, and psychoanalytic approaches. In any case, in 1976 he inveighed against this literary train-spotting as:

> a form of esoteric enterprise spied upon by fee-paying strangers, as contrasted with a communal evolution of the dramatic mode of expression, this latter being the African. Of far greater importance is the fact that Western dramatic criticism habitually reflects the abandonment of a belief in culture as defined within man's knowledge of fundamental, unchanging relationships between himself and society and within the larger context of the observable universe.
>
> (1976: 38)

His emphasis here is on Western dramatic criticism rather than on Western drama itself: the "stations" in his railway journey through Western literary apprehension are the various and temporal theoretical perspectives of the last several generations. The drama itself is not at issue in his critique, but rather the ways in which that drama is received and used, which may ultimately be only the (or the only) ways in which we can talk about art of any kind. The belief he calls for is probably irretrievable in both African and Western cultures because it is predicated on "unchanging" social and cosmological relationships. But his nomination identifies a cultural vestigialism already growing in Shakespeare's time – the first early modern age of "fee-paying strangers" – that permits a glimpse of the communal interests of tragedy sustained in the face of increasing individualism and social fragmentation. If literacy grows at the expense of memory, as Goody and Watt argue (1968), a parallel loss occurs in the development of Western culture, as what Victor Turner called "communitas" (1969) shrinks and shrivels. What is left is what Aufidius promises for Coriolanus: "a noble memory." In Shakespeare's festive tragedy, the anxious legacy of communal ritual insists upon itself; it too demands a "noble memory."

NOTES

1 FESTIVE TRAGEDY

1 Recent works treat the subject of ritual in the comedies with tighter definition: Berry (1984), following van Gennep ([1909] 1960), focuses on rites concerning birth, initiation into adulthood, marriage, and other family matters; Marcus (1986) works in the political arena. For these and other studies, including mine, Barber's book unquestionably prepared the way.

2 Frye (1957) established an archetypal pattern for the analogy of the major literary genres to seasons of the year, which he later (1965) elaborated for Shakespeare's comedies. (See Berry 1984: 13–14, for a brief discussion of the relation between Barber and Frye on the comedies.) In his companion piece on the tragedies (1967), Frye could not sustain the seasonal analogy, but still insisted that tragedy "revolves around the contract of man and nature, the contract fulfilled by man's death" (1967: 4). This view led to an inescapable conflation of tragedy and irony, with which he struggled throughout this later work because, like most of his contemporaries, he could not move beyond a view of the protagonist as the essential subject of tragedy; that is, he could not see the hero as a representative of his community.

3 Phyllis Rackin's admirable candor exemplifies this reflexive aspect of current study:

> The questions I ask are the products of my own historically specific concerns; the answers I recover, even when couched in the words of sixteenth-century texts, are the products of my own selection and arrangement. The history I write, like the Renaissance history-making it describes, takes its shape from the pressures of a world where rapid cultural change has given the study of history a new urgency and an academic setting where the practice of historiography has become a subject of intense controversy and radical transformation.
>
> (1990: ix)

4 Hutton exemplifies how a well-intentioned but rigid commitment to

printed records can collapse an argument. He rejects claims for some performance practices in the absence of a specific documentary instance; e.g., he argues that the Mummers' combat play, for which the earliest textual record is a 1738 chapbook, cannot be assumed to have been performed before then, let alone in an identifiable format (1994: 8); he argues similarly regarding wassail customs (1994: 14). At the same time, he "surmises" continuity for other seasonal performances, assuming very early, even pagan, origins for eighteenth-century and later representations (1994: 7–8). Hutton privileges written documents, especially aristocratic household and official parish records, as evidence of performance. But performances by and for an illiterate peasantry are not likely to be recorded in such documents.

5 I disagree, however, with Laroque's claim that "festivals, poor and rich alike, draw upon the same mythical and imaginary stock" whose recognition "could blow apart the watertight compartments set up by ideologies and call into question the idea that the class struggle is universal. . . . Festivity is profoundly ambivalent and, for that reason, tends to repel dialectical interpretations" (1991: 5). It is precisely this complicated ambivalence that summons dialectical analysis. Moreover, as Laroque himself notes, the idea of "merry England" was a Stuart construction, designed as a very specific and politically laden construct that glorified a past as Stuart interests would have it remembered. Such institutional "nostalgia" might be called "the politics of distraction." (On nostalgia as a political construct, see Rackin 1990: 86–145.) Here again the application of "thick description" is important in order to sort out, where possible, the component resonances.

6 The terms "liminal" and "liminality" are Victor Turner's, in what is now a widely recognized formulation derived from van Gennep ([1909] 1960). For a full discussion of liminality, see V. Turner (1969), especially chapter 3, "Liminality and Communitas."

7 Although I have consulted an edition and translation different from his, I owe the Bede reference to Laroque 1991: 16.

8 Averell's critique is especially vivid: "a lawlesse Lord . . . alwayes crauing and euer commaunding, still feeding, and neuer leauing, thou art a bottomlesse whirlepoole of all gluttonie, an unsatable sea of ceaselesse gourmandie, . . . that rather bestowe more upon Cookes to fill the belly, than on the learned to instruct the mind" (1588: sig. C1v). My thanks to John Drakakis for sharing with me his unpublished essay, "Writing the Body Politic: Subject, Discourse, and History in Shakespeare's *Coriolanus*" (1989) in which he cites and discusses these texts.

9 In an apparent effort to avoid a modern or western ethnocentrism, some anthropologists and literary critics substitute terms like "preliterate" or "preindustrial" for the word "primitive." I find such substitution artificial, awkward, and misleading. Tribal cultures are certainly "literate" within their own developed forms of written or pictorial language, and they are certainly "industrial" in terms of their own mechanical or technological requirements. In other words,

"preliterate" and "preindustrial" are also value-laden western terms. I therefore apply the term "traditional" as a distinction implying a strong degree of communal coherence and limited governmental differentiation lost to "modern" cultures.

10 See, for instance, d'Aquili, Laughlin, and McManus (1979), especially "Ritual and Human Cognition" ([McManus] 216–48). McManus distinguishes four developmental stages of cognition as information processing. Barring individual differences in consistency between internal models and sensory data (225), the four stages are: 1) relatively fixed perceptions of hierarchical organization; 2) emergence of alternative perceptions of the same dimensions; 3) complex rules for simultaneously comparing and relating perspectives; and 4) generation of complex relationships among rules of comparison (217). It is this last which enables cognitive translation of disparate cultural phenomena.

11 Soyinka's commentary is worth quoting at length:

> Sango's "tragic fall" is the result of a hubristic act: the powerful king throws himself in conflict not simply with subjects or peers but with the racial fount of his own being. Weak, vacillating, treacherous and disloyal, the human unit that constitutes the chorus of his downfall is, in Sango's drama, the total context of racial beginning; the ritual metaphor communicates this and the poetry is woven into its affirmation. Yet side by side with acceptance of the need to destroy this disruptive, uncontrollable factor in the moral community, the need to assert the communal will for a harmonious existence, is recognition of the super-human energies of an exceptional man. . . . Of course we may also . . . [see] this act of apotheosis in the opportunistic light of the self-entrenching priesthood. Duro Ladipo's play *Oba Koso* indicates quite clearly that Sango did commit suicide, that it was the priests who quickly got together, hushed the wailing of the women and rebuked them for revealing that Sango took his own life. The body conveniently disappears and his elevation is attested. The king is dead; long live the god! And why not indeed? Economics and power have always played a large part in the championing of new deities throughout human history.
>
> (1976: 11–12)

3 THE RITUAL GROUNDWORK

1 Bocock (1974), working from a sociological rather than an anthropological argument, discusses ritual as "non-rational action" in modern industrial England, and includes what he calls "aesthetic" (i.e., dance, theater, music) as well as religious domains. Although he cautions against stretching the parameters of "ritual" to include the most mundane activities, he nevertheless includes such transitory activities as "pop" festivals, athletic events, labor strikes and political rallies. From an anthropological perspective, Bocock's approach is problematic

because it privileges activities common during the decade in which he was writing that have diminished since that time, for example, "pop festivals" and other so-called "counter-culture" gatherings specific to one or at most two generations. Part of the difficulty of analyzing ritual in the twentieth century is the extreme fragmentation of culture itself. Unlike ritual in traditional cultures, what Bocock identifies as those of modern times do not link past, present, and future. They are not designed to ensure survival beyond the moment and are often random or spontaneous occurrences.

2　Dumouchel makes the important point that "societies, though they have always resulted from human actions, have almost everywhere conceived of themselves as instituted by the sacred: by powers beyond the reach of humanity" (1988: 17).

3　In a footnote to this rhetorical maneuver Greenblatt acknowledges the "intensified ambiguity" of the remark, but he clearly intends the implication of the play's immediate threat to stand. An alternative, and ironic, speculation is suggested by W. Gordon Zeeveld at the end of his essay on *Coriolanus*: "Had Shakespeare's audience been able to foresee the course of seventeenth-century history as clearly, the upheaval some forty years later might have been averted" (1962: 334). A theater that can spark revolution can also avert it; but it appears in Shakespeare's case to have done neither. See also Marcus 1988: 27–9.

4　That is, it has been obscured in recent criticism. The connections between Shakespeare's play, Hayward's book and the Essex plot are debated at length in Albright 1927, Heffner 1930, and Albright 1931.

5　In a Royal Shakespeare Company production of the play some years ago, the actors did in fact freeze the moment for several seconds in a tableau. To underscore the reciprocal identity of the two kings and kinsmen, the actors playing Richard and Henry switched roles on alternate evenings throughout the run of the play.

6　Besides the obvious biblical source, Shakespeare and his audience would have known the dramatizations of the Cain and Abel story in the cycle plays at Coventry and elsewhere, which continued, despite various statutory suppressions during the Reformation, through the 1570s (Laroque 1991: 56; Cox 1989: 22, 39), and possibly until 1591 (Ingram 1981: xix).

7　Personal communication.

8　For an extensive annotated bibliography of studies in Shakespeare's classical sources, see Velz (1968b). More specific studies include, notably, Barroll (1958), Starnes and Talbert (1955), and Spencer (1964).

9　Granville-Barker's famous identification of the "spiritual problem of the virtuous murderer" (1927: 53) still makes sense, but it reduces Brutus's character to that of a monolithic idealist, completely out of touch with reality, and surely *not* one with whom to mount a serious political effort. The problem with such a view is that no one *in the play* seems to see Brutus as a starry-eyed dreamer; indeed, his reputation for good sense and proper action makes him trusted by everyone. Even Antony must call him "honorable" (although what that word

NOTES

comes to mean through rhetorical repetition is another matter).
Brutus's idealistic vision is grounded in a very real traditional political
structure, the Rome that is, was, and he hopes ever shall be.

10 I might add that Plutarch is no great defender of Antony on the other
side; while the conspirators are called "hunters," in the same passage
Antony and Lepidus are called cowards: "But Antonius and Lepidus,
which were two of Caesar's chiefest frends, secretly conveying them
selves away, fled into other mens houses, and forsooke their owne."

11 Neither Plutarch, who is the only ancient writer to report it, nor any
modern commentator can explain the origin or significance of this
part of the rite. Frazer thought it was a ritual "of death and a new
birth. By touching the lad on the forehead with the knife . . . they
symbolicaly slew him as a goat, and . . . brought him back to life again
as a kid . . . fed on its mother's milk. The lads testified their joy . . . by
laughing" (1929: II: 340–1). More recently, Dumézil calls this part of
the rite merely "enigmatic," and does not attempt to explain it (1970:
I: 56, 348).

12 The need for such foresight in leaders seems to be an urgent one in
Shakespeare's view. King Henry and Warwick discuss this idea in *2
Henry IV*, and Warwick's lines prefigure Brutus's reflections on the
"tide in the affairs of men" (IV.iii.218):

There is a history in all men's lives,
Figuring the nature of the times deceas'd;
The which observ'd, a man may prophesy,
With a near aim, of the main chance of things
As yet not come to life, who in their seeds
And weak beginnings lie intreasured.
Such things become the hatch and brood of time.

(III.i.80–6)

13 Rabkin has also noticed the double meaning of this phrase (1967:
115–16), but thinks the act that initiates the repercussions of revenge
is Brutus's "crime against the established order." Actually it was
Caesar who acted against the *established* order of the Republic, and
what Brutus acts against, as Rabkin says further on (1967: 147–8, n.
23), is never fully established.

14 Burckhardt's further remarks are worth recall:

A tragedy . . . is a kind of sacrifice brought to purge the world of
some disorder and restore it to its natural harmony. . . . It is this
comforting theory that the clock tolls into an irrecoverable past.
For it rests on a no longer tenable faith in an underlying universal
order . . . that may be temporarily disturbed but can, by the
proper purgatives properly administered, be reestablished. . . .
Once the time is out of joint, sacrificial tragedy is no longer
possible.

(1968: 19)

15 The Feast of St Michael and All Angels (29 September, or 10 October
for Old Michaelmas) may have coincided with the premiere

performance of *Julius Caesar*. Although the date of the performance is uncertain, it is generally agreed that it occurred early in the autumn of 1599, largely on the evidence of the letter by Thomas Platter, a Swiss travelling in England between 18 September and 20 October, which refers to a play about the death of Julius Caesar performed at a thatch-roofed theater near the Thames.

4 COMMUNITAS, HIERARCHY, LIMINALITY, VICTIMAGE

1 Ritual can, of course, be used to create social change, but this happens rarely and requires a complex set of operations: a competing actor or group of actors may claim control over a particular ritual identified as the source of power, as did both pre- and post-Reformation interests throughout Europe (Cressy 1989: xi–xiv; Duffy 1992; Hutton 1994: 69–110); a competitive set of rituals may be portrayed as more powerful than a traditional set, as occurred generally in missionary activities under colonialism; or a non-ritual power source may be introduced to supplant a traditional ritual, as happens when advancing technology insures greater crop yields, or when "modern" medicine replaces healing rites. In these cases, however, it is not the ritual that leads to change, but the altered application or replacement of ritual that is co-opted by a competitive party. See Burns and Laughlin, "Ritual and Social Power" in d'Aquili, Laughlin, and McManus (1979: 275–77).

2 In their comprehensive analysis of ritual using the theory of bio-genetic structuralism (an empirical study of human behavior based on brain function in human beings and other mammals and on the interaction between the organism's central nervous system and its environment), d'Aquili, Laughlin, and McManus identify

> a set of neural constraints we may term the *cognitive imperative*. This concept refers to the drive in man, other mammals, and birds to order their world by differentiation of adaptively significant sensory elements and events, and to the unification of these elements into a systematic whole. . . . Frustration of the imperative due to unyielding environmental novelty may lead to anxiety and eventual system breakdown. The brain of higher organisms tends to strive for a balance between novelty and redundancy in the environment. Too much novelty or complexity is met by attempts to classify it into simpler categories, to reduce it to meaningful bits of information. Too little novelty, on the other hand, leads to boredom, restlessness, and attempts to seek or create greater uncertainty or complexity.
>
> (1979: 10)

This unifying theory accounts for several things: the ubiquity of systems and structures among human beings; the biogenetic imperative of order in increasingly complex environments as well as the breach of order in the face of intolerable stasis; and the apparently global occurrence of ritual to manage cycles of order and breach.

3 For documentation of Shakespeare's fascination with monstrous births, see Orange (1976), and Gaines and Lofaro (1976). The latter note the popularity of the subject of "various grotesqueries which we would today classify as birth defects. Between 1561 and 1609, twenty-two ballads dealing with monstrous births were recorded in the Stationers' Register. There must have been at least an equal number of prose pamphlets on the same topic" (1976: 180).

4 At the end of his chapter on "Group Psychology and the Primal Horde," Freud explains:

> The uncanny and coercive characteristics of group formations . . . may therefore with justice be traced back to the fact of their origin from the primal horde. The leader of the group is still the dreaded primal father; the group still wishes to be governed by unrestricted force; it has an extreme passion for authority; . . . The primal father is the group ideal, which governs the ego in the place of the ego ideal.
>
> (1955: 127–8)

Elaborating Freud's idea, Kenneth Burke underscored the notion of transference, while distinguishing the "ritualistic" from the "pseudo-scientific" scapegoat:

> the delegation of one's burden to the sacrificial vessel of the scapegoat is a giving, a socialization, albeit the socialization of a loss, a transference of something, deeply within, devoutly a part of one's own self. . . . An *explicit ritual* of such transference may, paradoxically, often be the best way of protecting the individual from the deceptions of this pseudoscientific objectivity. . . . A ritualistic scapegoat is felt both *to have* and *not to have* the character formally delegated to it – but a pseudoscientific scapegoat, endowed by "projection" without an explicit avowal of the process, is felt purely and simply *to have* the assigned character.
>
> (1957: 39)

5 Although Scythian invasions of the area around the Black Sea, where the Greeks encountered them, apparently ceased by the end of the second century, B.C.E., their reputation for barbarism was easily conflated with that of the various "Goths" who were active during the first several centuries, C.E.

6 *The history of Herodian.* Subsequent English issues are from 1629 and 1634–5, too late for Shakespeare. The extremely popular, anonymous *Scriptores Historiae Augustae* was known throughout Europe in Latin codices (six editions from 1475 to 1518), including ones owned by Petrarch and Erasmus, but was not translated into English until the twentieth century. Its details differ from those in Herodian: it does not mention Saturninus, it diminishes Julia Domna's role (although she is identified as a notorious adulteress), and it underemphasizes

the conversion of Rome to Syrian religion (Magie 1921, 1924: I and II). Herodian's history is the only contemporary record known to have existed in English during Shakespeare's lifetime. For a detailed account of Shakespeare's use of Herodian and its implications for reading *Titus Andronicus*, see Liebler 1994a.

7 Both Maxwell (1961) in a line gloss at IV.ii.20, and West (1982: 70) note the reference to "Moorish javelins" in the line from Horace's *Odes* that Titus inscribes on the bundle of arrows presented to Chiron and Demetrius, and both think this a glance at Aaron. But it is just as likely that the Moorish reputation for javelin-throwing was already inscribed within Shakespeare's conception of Aaron, derived from Herodian. Horace provided additional support.

8 Echols reminds us that Herodian was himself a Syrian living in Roman exile (and, interestingly, writing in Greek), and adds that "his early association with the Syrian dynasty at Rome would account for the amazing 'Romanness' of his outlook. Herodian is so thoroughly patriotic and so Romanized that he can speak of his fellow non-Romans as barbarians, and can offer an analysis of his fellow Syrians that is thoroughly unflattering" (1961: 5).

9 It is important to recognize that modern interpretations of "Elizabethan" attitudes may be more modern than Elizabethan. As Bernal argues, "For 18th- and 19th-century Romantics and racists it was simply intolerable for Greece, which was seen not merely as the epitome of Europe but also as its pure childhood, to have been the result of the mixture of native Europeans and colonizing Africans and Semites" (1987: I: 2); in the Renaissance, "no one questioned the fact that the Greeks had been the pupils of the Egyptians, in whom there was an equal, if not more passionate, interest" and who were "deeply respected for their antiquity and well-preserved ancient religion and philosophy" (1987: I: 23–4). If Elizabethan England inherited the Classical period's acceptance of the Afroasiatic roots of Greek culture, we may need to re-evaluate our assessments of Shakespeare's representations of his Moors – not only Aaron, but more obviously Othello and Portia's Moroccan suitor in *The Merchant of Venice* – all of whose noble traits are misrecognized by their Italianate fellow characters. Bernal's thesis has been challenged, not only on points of historical accuracy but also on its failure to recognize a distinction between "objective" and "subjective" ethnicity. The former is "a biological category which defines groups of human beings in terms of their shared physical characteristics resulting from a common gene pool," whereas the latter identifies "the ideology of an ethnic group by defining as shared its ancestors, history, language, mode of production, religion, customs, culture, etc., and is therefore a social construct, not a fact of nature" (Hall 1992: 185). Herodian's history (along with Dio's and the *Historia Augusta*) establishes as certain that Rome between 183 and 236 was governed by an Afroasiatic dynasty, in terms that satisfy Hall's important distinctions of "objective" as well as "subjective" ethnicity. How the Elizabethan heirs to this history interpreted that ethnic admixture is a question requiring further

careful investigation; see Loomba (1989); Neill (1989); Bartels (1990).

10 Julia Domna's extraordinary influence during Bassianus's reign is generally acknowledged by historians and translators of Herodian. See Echols 1961: 5, and Whittaker 1969: II: 367n.

11 Electra's relative passivity is sometimes considered evidence of the "patriarchal" (i.e., misogynist) nature of both Aeschylean and Senecan tragedy (Figes 1990). Presumably a more even-handed treatment of social formations would have allowed Electra to do more than pour libations, curse, and wait for Orestes to do the filthy deed of matricide; but then, a less even-handed treatment would not have allowed Clytemnestra to wield the knife against her husband.

12 Cox underscores the Stoic Roman nature of Titus's infanticide, arguing that such a view of "romanism" had a long and solid following among Elizabethans (1989: 173–6). This is a fair enough reading, but Titus's extraordinary suffering might have been represented through any of a variety of dramatic events. The play's persistent focus upon violence and ritual, it must be said, figures something else besides a fascination with Roman Stoic values.

13 Laroque identifies the pie as:

> the transgression of a triple taboo. The first, clearly, is cannibalism; the second and third are indicated by the use of the word "daintily" ["Whereof their mother daintily hath fed" (V.iii.61)]. "Dainty" was also a term currently employed to refer to the testicles, which suggests that two other major taboos have also been transgressed – those of castration and incest, for Tamora has taken in and consumed her own sons' reproductive organs. Born from their mother's body, they re-enter it through a different orifice.
>
> (1991: 275)

This identification of the triple taboo, it seems to me, is a better claim than the limited Freudian one which sees the cannibalistic feast as "oral vengeance" of the "catastrophically perceived preoedipal mother, who threatens total dismemberment and destruction (the devouring mother)" (Willbern 1978: 171). However, the issue of *omophagia* in the context of a formal banquet is more problematic than either Laroque or Willbern represent; it is simultaneously a ritual act of regeneration and an act of pollution, and in its inherent ambiguity it expresses the contestational and contradictory nature of foundation myths in general. For a provocative discussion of *omophagia* in Greek tragedy, see Kott 1973: 186–230.

14 White argues that Lavinia's rape and mutilation implicitly condemn a Rome where justice is constructed as male, self-destructive, revenge even when instituted by a woman such as Tamora (1986: 26–35; cf. Willbern 1978: 161; Tricomi 1974: 17). However, apart from a brief imagistic suggestion at the beginning (I.i.9–17) and another one at the end (V.iii.73–6), the crisis in Rome is represented throughout the

play as a masculine ethos compromised by Tamora's Asiatic-feminizing influence, an issue Shakespeare explored again later in *Antony and Cleopatra*.

15 This is extremely problematic, as both Derrida and his translator acknowledge. Derrida used Robin's "authoritative French trans-lation" (1981: 71) of Plato for most of his essay's quoted material. Derrida's translator, Barbara Johnson, used yet a different edition of Plato in English, with supplemental reference to several different English translations which, she says, she "sometimes partially adopt-ed" (1981: 66n.). Thus the difficulty of linguistic access is not only thoroughly explored in this essay; it is also thoroughly exemplified.

16 Lincoln suggests a significantly tangent view of the Fable's referential domain: without mentioning *Coriolanus*, he discusses the narrative from Livy, II.32, the "Apologue of Menenius Agrippa," where, he says, debt and its punishment are the major issues. "Unable to win con-cessions from the patricians . . . the plebs are said to have physically withdrawn from the city and established themselves as an independ-ent community on the Aventine Mount, leaving the patricians to tend their own needs without the support of plebeian labor" (1989: 145–6). Lincoln argues that Livy's account has been contested as an inflected discourse effacing the dependence of the patricians on the plebs; in Livy, the Fable persuades the plebs to end their secession and return to the city, reconciled. Subsequently and consequently, the office of *Tribuni plebis* was created to provide protection for plebeian interests by officers elected from the plebs themselves. This revisionist reading raises questions about Shakespeare's selection of material: there is no hint in the play of so autonomous a plebeian move as secession, or of a threat of *patrician* starvation without plebeian labor. Apparently unaware of *Coriolanus*, Lincoln concludes his section on Menenius: "this discourse was still being employed as late as 1594, when the lieutenant general of the Cahors court, in condemning the Croquant rebels, posed as a rhetorical question: What would happen if the members of the body should rebel against the stomach and refuse to feed it?" (1989: 148). What makes this interesting for readers of *Coriolanus* is the play's interpretation of the plebs as hungry and complaining, but dependent upon patrician "generosity," and endangered both by its absence and by seditious tribunes. The question of source-reception, the "genealogy" through which the "Apologue" reached Shakespeare – whether directly from Livy, or perhaps via Machiavelli's version in the *Discourses*, which supported the principle of *vox populi* (Zeeveld 1962: 323–4) – inter-pellates its appropriation for the play. The idea of a plebeian power to secede, absent from the play, reconfigures the play's initial conflict and raises questions about the scapegoating of Coriolanus to both plebeian and patrician interests.

17 John Drakakis has very kindly given me permission to quote from his essay on *Coriolanus* (cited above, chapter 1, note 8). Among his valuable interventions in this essay is his suggestion of yet another "body" discourse, the economic body.

18 In "*Coriolanus* and the Delights of Faction," Kenneth Burke offers an Aristotelian reading of victimage that inculpates any audience watching the play. We (Burke insists on "we," rather than restricting response to a Jacobean collective) "pity him even while we resent his exaggerated ways of representing our own less admirable susceptibilities. . . . Thereby we are cleansed, thanks to his overstating of our case" (1966: 89, but the point is reiterated throughout the essay: 81–94). He reminds us that the play is concerned "drastically" with class distinctions, recalling that "in earlier medical usage, a 'drastic' was the name for the strongest kind of 'cathartic.' Also, the word derives etymologically from the same root as 'drama'" (1966: 82).

19 The 1607 Midlands Uprising and other revolts against Enclosure Acts, which not only destroyed livelihoods but also re-drew, and in some cases erased, village maps, may have been more a symptom of growing unrest than a cause, "more often to have followed the abandonment of holdings than to have caused it" (Keen 1990: 72); in some cases tenants rather than landlords did the enclosing (Keen 1990: 73). Such enclosures actually began as early as the thirteenth century. Pettet's (1950) essay linking the date of *Coriolanus* with the 1607 Insurrection is now generally dismissed for occluding the long history of enclosures and their pernicious consequences all over England and over several centuries. Pettet seems to have ignored his own cited evidence, relegating to a footnote Stow's report in the *Annales*: "that of very late years there were three hundred and forty towns decayed and depopulated" (quoted in Pettet 1950: 40, n. 6). By Shakespeare's time, enclosure and redistricting had made the metonymy of land as an inviolable integrity (so eloquently lamented in Gaunt's famous speech in *Richard II* II.i.40–66), an illusion, or at least a very distant nostalgia.

20 As late as the early twentieth century, Sharp noted the "sudden" lack of support for local morris teams in the counties, which he attributed in part to "the enclosure of the common lands, and the creation of a proletariat, which led to a general migration of labouring men from the villages to the towns in search of work, the disruption of the social life of the village," and other ills; but, he added, "Whatever the reason of its decay, the Morris dance . . . flourished almost universally in the Midland counties as recently as fifty years ago" (Sharp and McIlwaine 1912: 19). E. O. James (1961) and Helm (1965) found recent evidence of its survival, although Helm thinks it is finished as a serious endeavor, relegated as it was by the 1960s to entertainment at school-term festivals. Curiously, morris and sword dancing have seen increasing popularity in the United States at festivals celebrating British culture and during intervals at regional performances of Shakespearean plays; there are at present considerable numbers of active professional and amateur morris teams, including an all-female team, the Ring o' Belles, who perform in the New York metropolitan area.

21 Chambers briefly mentions this text, although his suggestion appears to have been subsequently ignored. He credits Johnson with having

"brought together the scattered legends of the [other six] national heroes" (1903: I: 221), and notes that "the mummers' play follows Johnson" (1903: I: 221, n.2), that is, Johnson supplies an authentic narrative.

22 The dragon, says Chambers, was probably "the representative of the hardness of the frost-bound earth in winter" (1933: 178); thus the St George play, in his view, adumbrated the old seasonal ritual battle of winter and spring. He implies that the dragon directly symbolizes natural, i.e., climatic, elements that threaten plenitude and fruition, which might seem now to be a naive critical stance. Shakespearean demons are invariably human, and in so far as these cultural figures derive from solidly entrenched customs and practices, it might be more accurately said that the dragon figure, separately and as collapsed into the figures of both George and Coriolanus, represents a range of human and other forces inimical to communal life.

5 THE HOBBY-HORSE IS FORGOT

1 Marcus correctly argues that this instance is more than a quaint reference to an outmoded form of celebration; the minor characters' lament for the hobby-horse is itself a dislocation, a marker for the abrogation of customary social practices at several moments in the comedy (1991: 169–71). Her point about the hobby-horse lament, however, rests on an incorrect assumption that the hobby-horse and other such pastimes mentioned in *Love's Labour's Lost* "are somewhat out of place at Yuletide, being more strongly associated with maying customs in the spring and early summer" (1991: 170). The hobby-horse dance was certainly a May-time practice, but it was also regularly performed at the New Year because of the figure's association with sexual energy and fertility, and thus was part of the Yuletide celebration as well (Alford 1978: 1–9; Baker 1974: 41–4; Bucknell 1979: 187; Chambers 1903: I: 258).

2 Marcus makes a related point: "The impact of textual levelling upon our analysis of Shakespearean folk customs and topography should be clear, since it is a corollary of the method itself: we will be less able ... to talk in terms of archetypes and large ritual patterns, more able to talk about historical particularity and local difference" (1991: 178).

3 Besides *Love's Labour's Lost* and *Hamlet,* Cawte (1978: 48–51) lists Kemp's *Nine Daies Wonder* (1600), Jonson's *Entertainment at Althorp* (1603), *Bartholomew Fair* (1614), and *The Gypsies Metamorphos'd* (1621), Breton's *A Poste with a Packet of Mad Letters* (1606), Weelkes's *Ayeres* no. 20 (1608), *Old Meg of Hereford-shire* (anon., 1609), Cooke's *Green's Tu Quoque* (1611), Ford, Dekker, and Rowley's *The Witch of Edmonton* (1621), and Drewe's *The Duchess of Suffolke* (1624). He also notes nine instances of the hobby-horse's presence in stage plays from 1572 to 1639: the anonymous *Paris and Vienna* (1572) and *Masque of Hobby-Horses* (1574), another "performance of hobby-horses at court" (1575), Nashe's *Summers Last Will and Testament* (1592),

Ruggles's *Ignoramus* (1615), Holyday's Τεχνοραμια (1618), Fletcher's *Women Pleas'd* (1620), *The Witch of Edmonton* (again), Jonson's *Masque of Owls* (1624), and nine more allusions to it: Jonson's *Every Man Out of his Humour* (1599), Beaumont and Fletcher's *Knight of the Burning Pestle* (1607), Middleton and Dekker's *The Roaring Girl* (1608), Fletcher and Shakespeare's *Two Noble Kinsmen* (1613), Webster and Rowley's *A Cure for a Cuckold* (1625), Sampson's *The Vow Breaker* (1625), Massinger's *A Very Woman* (1634), Shirley's *The Lady of Pleasure* (1635), and Cavendish's *The Varietie* (1639). Alford includes a sketchier list with several inaccurate dates, but adds the following insightful observation: "At the very zenith of his popularity, when composers wrote and madrigal singers sang of him, when stage plays brought him trotting on, when street scenes were full of allusions to him, at that moment he was said by everybody to be 'forgot'" (1978: 29).

4 Although perhaps most clearly observed in reports about tribal or traditional communities, liminality persists as a recognizable experience in modern life. Such moves are commonly made and are recognized in physical gestures and words in weddings, funerals, graduations, bar mitzvahs, and the like. Occasionally there is a report about a modern community that has retained strong ties to its traditions. On 17 January 1991, an article appeared in the Newark (New Jersey) *Star-Ledger* about a 65-year-old professor of nutrition at the University of North Carolina at Chapel Hill who had been summoned home to his village of Asaba in Nigeria to assume the role of king. After such preparations as purchasing typewriters, fax machines, and telephones for his administrative duties, he was to be crowned on 5 March.

> During the traditional ceremony, the elders will confer on him the secrets of Asaba. . . . According to tradition, he'll be confined to a room for 30 days before the coronation to contemplate the past and plan for the future. "You have this period for yourself," he said. "It's a period of dedication and reflection on what you're going to do to fit into your new position. . . . I tried to argue my way out of it. I told them that in my job as a professor, I was continually thinking and reflecting. I said, 'Do I need it?' and they said 'Yes, we think so.'"

5 The doubling of experience between enemies is a form of brotherhood or twinship that often accompanies instances in myth and legend of fratricide. In so far as they share the status of avenging sons (not to mention the possibility of their relation as brothers-in-law had Ophelia lived and married the prince), Laertes and Hamlet constitute each other's doubles who, in the final duel, commit reciprocal fratricide. The difference between theirs and the play's initial brother-murder is its ritualized format as a legitimate duel, and of course, their exchange of mutual forgiveness at the moment of death. It is a mark of "setting right," or at least of ending the chain of violations. On the widespread pattern of double-adversaries and fratricide, see Girard (1977).

6 Crapanzano, an anthropologist much interested in *Hamlet*, further

observes that the alliteration of "melodious" and "muddy" "suggest a merging of song and death, of discrimination, as in melody, and the absence of discrimination, as in 'mud.' . . . Without discrimination, without [Derridean] *differance*, with the merging of the signifier and the signified, sign and reality, there can only be an absence of consciousness – death" (1992: 309).

7 Polonius's inculpation is suggested by Claudius's remark to Laertes that "The head is not more native to the heart, / The hand more instrumental to the mouth, / Than is the throne of Denmark to thy father" (I.ii.47–9). Irving Ribner (1966) glossed these lines as a hint that "Claudius is obviously indebted to [Polonius] for assistance in procuring his election as King." Gertrude's complicity in the crime(s) has also been disputed, but the ghost gives several hints that she may have begun her affair with Claudius before her husband's death: the lust of his "most seeming-virtuous queen," he says, "Will sate itself in a celestial bed / And prey on garbage" (I.v.46, 56–7).

8 Goody and Watt also take up the relation of writing and reading to the preservation or alteration of memory. One of the "consequences" of literacy is that a notion of "social relevance" selects what memory will store (1968: 31). When writing enters culture, oral transmission and memory "are no longer man's only dialogue; and in so far as writing provides an alternative source for the transmission of cultural orientations it favours awareness of inconsistency. One aspect of this is a sense of change and cultural lag. . . " (1968: 49). Further study of *Hamlet* in regard to these issues of change and resistance would need to examine how much of the dialogue is also concerned with "reading" and "writing" and how many times we see Hamlet holding a book, a project partly considered by Goldberg (1988).

9 The variant assignments of the play's closing lines in Quarto and Folio texts do not affect this supposition. Regardless of whether Albany or Edgar speaks "The weight of this sad time we must obey," the penultimate lines, "Friends of my soul, you twain / Rule in this realm" are delivered *to* Edgar and Kent, the latter declining.

10 These "mock trial" lines occur in the Quarto version, but not in the Folio.

11 The commonplace Renaissance analogy of state and family is implicit here, of course, and has been thoroughly explored in recent critical texts, e.g., Selden 1987. Selden's argument, like that of his Jacobean textual citations, focuses on the "family" as a social unit, and not upon the physical structure it occupies.

12 The following stipulation of Section II of the 1598 document might have interested Shakespeare: among those specifically to be "taken, adjudged, and deemed rogues, vagabonds, and sturdy beggars, and [to] sustain such pain and punishment as by this Act is in that behalf appointed" were

all persons calling themselves scholars going about begging, . . . all fencers, bearwards, common players of interludes, and minstrels wandering abroad (other than players of interludes belonging to any baron of this realm, or any other honourable personage of greater degree, to be authorised to play under the hand and seal of arms of such baron or personage). . .

(in Tanner 1940: 485)

13 An important subtext in Lear's insistence on retaining his hundred knights and his daughters' systematic reduction of that number to zero is indicated in Old Irish legal texts which specified how different ranks within nobility were distinguished; the size of the retinue they commanded was a visible encoding of status (Lincoln 1989: 78). Thus to dismantle Lear's retinue is not only to leave him unprotected but also to eradicate his status altogether.

14 This is, unsurprisingly, no idle metaphor. Lincoln reprints a composite of the hall plan from the Feast of Tara, the royal and ceremonial center of medieval Ireland, compiled from detailed descriptions in the twelfth-century *Book of Leinster* and the slightly later *Yellow Book of Lecan*. The plan indicates not only a complex seating hierarchy from the king and queen (the only female permitted at the banquet) down to the satirists, clowns, wall-makers, ditch-diggers, and royal door-keepers, but also the portions of meat to be served to each rank. Carvers and butlers, seated nearest the kitchen, were served the head, the king a tenderloin, the queen a rump steak, and the royal door-keepers the coccyx:

> [Given] the spatial contrast between the top of the diagram/head of the animal/kitchen area, on the one hand, and the bottom of the diagram/coccyx of the animal/doorway on the other, it does not seem too farfetched to suggest that a trip from one end of the hall to the other might well be associated to a similar (and not unrelated) passage through the alimentary canal.
>
> (Lincoln 1989: 80)

15 In an interesting and brief essay, Holland links the botanical imagery in the play with the cycles of legendary vegetation kings. The moving Birnam Wood, he says, visually suggests May Day or midsummer rites in which the celebrants were

> so decked out in sprigs and green branches that it seemed as though a whole forest came marching. The parade signifies defeat for . . . a hibernal giant whose rule comes to an end when the May festival begins. . . . Thus when Birnam Wood moves, Macbeth is killed and Malcolm turns to things "which would be newly planted with the time." The vegetable qualities of the legendary year-king are grafted onto Macbeth's rise and fall.
>
> (Holland 1960: 37–8)

The play abounds in images related to the processes of generation that Macbeth and his wife violate. Shakespeare undoubtedly knew (or knew of) the drawing of the "Banquo Tree," the genealogical tree complete with flowers that accompanied Leslie's 1578 *De Origine, Moribus, et Rebus Gestis Scotorum* (Bullough 1973: VII: 516). Aligned with its iconography, Scotland under Macbeth is a "grave" where "good men's lives / Expire before the flowers in their cups" (IV.iii.166, 171–2) and his defeat figures a ritual cleansing of the Wasteland: the sterile old king is sacrificed and replaced by the virginal Malcolm whose fertility is yet to be verified while Scotland waits for Banquo's scion, James VI.

6 CONCLUSION

1 Derrida elaborates this connection further on in the essay by quoting in full Robin's translation of the passage from Plato that analogizes writing and the vulnerable child:

> And once a thing is put in writing, the composition, whatever it may be, drifts all over the place, getting into the hands not only of those who understand it, but equally of those who have no business with it; it doesn't know how to address the right people, and not address the wrong. And when it is ill treated and unfairly abused it always needs its parent to come to its aid, being unable to defend itself or attend to its own needs. (*Phaedrus* 275e)
>
> (1981: 143)

The reader will note that in this fuller version Derrida follows Robin's translation of the generic "parent" and "child" instead of inserting the masculine "father" and "son" as in the previous extract, and of the phrase "come to its aid" instead of "attend to it." Derrida's changes in the first instance construct "writing" or "logos" as a helpless son in need of specifically masculine protection, whereas Robin's translation constructs "writing" as genderless, ignorant or naive but not necessarily helpless, and needing a parent (again genderless) only when "ill-treated and unfairly abused." Of course it may be assumed that in Plato's discourse gender is normatively masculine; nevertheless, Derrida's alterations signal a specifically infantilized and masculinized context for "logos."

BIBLIOGRAPHY

Unless otherwise indicated, quotations from Shakespeare are taken from the Riverside edition of the *Complete Works*, ed. G. B. Evans, Boston: Houghton Mifflin, 1974.

Adelman, J. (1978) "'Anger's My Meat': Feeding, Dependency, and Aggression in *Coriolanus*," in D. Bevington and J. Halio (eds) *Pattern of Excelling Nature*, Newark: University of Delaware Press.

Adelman, J. (1992) *Suffocating Mothers: Fantasies of Maternal Origin in Shakespeare's Plays, "Hamlet" to "The Tempest*," New York and London, Routledge.

Aijmer, G. (1987) *Symbolic Textures: Studies in Cultural Meaning*, Göthenburg Studies in Social Anthropology, No. 10, Göteburg, Sweden: Acta Universitatis Göthoburgensis.

Albright, E. M. (1927) "Shakespeare's *Richard II* and the Essex Conspiracy," *PMLA* 42: 686–720.

Albright, E. M. (1931) "Shakespeare's *Richard II*, Hayward's History of Henry IV, and the Essex Conspiracy," *PMLA* 46: 694–719.

Alexander, N. (1971) *Poison, Play, and Duel: A Study in Hamlet*, Lincoln: University of Nebraska Press.

Alford, V. (1978) *The Hobby Horse and Other Animal Masks*, London: Merlin Press.

Althusser, L. (1971) *Lenin and Philosophy and Other Essays*, trans. B. Brewster, New York and London: Monthly Review Press.

Aristotle (1961) *Poetics*, trans. K. Telford, Chicago: H. Regnery.

Armstrong, N. and Tennenhouse, L. (eds) (1989) *The Violence of Representation: Literature and the History of Violence*, London: Routledge.

Artaud, A. (1958) *The Theater and Its Double*, trans. M. C. Richards, New York: Grove Press.

Atlan, H. (1988) "Founding Violence and Divine Referent," in P. Dumouchel (ed.) *Violence and Truth: On the Work of René Girard*, Stanford: Stanford University Press.

Averell, W. (1588) *A Mervailous Combat of Contrarieties*, London. (*STC* 981).

Babcock, B. A. (1987) "'The Arts and All Things Common': Victor Turner's Literary Anthropology," *Comparative Criticism* 9: 39–46.

248

Babcock, B. A. (ed.) (1978) *The Reversible World: Symbolic Inversion in Art and Society*, Ithaca: Cornell University Press.

Bachelard, G. (1969) *The Poetics of Space*, trans. M. Jolas, Boston: Beacon Press.

Bacon, F. (1985) *The Essayes or Counsels, Civill and Morall*, ed. J. Pitcher, Harmondsworth: Penguin.

Baker, M. (1974) *Folklore and Customs of Rural England*, Totowa, N.J.: Rowman and Littlefield.

Bakhtin, M. (1968) *Rabelais and His World*, trans. H. Iswolsky, Cambridge, Mass.: MIT Press.

Bakhtin, M. (1981) *The Dialogic Imagination: Four Essays*, ed. M. Holquist, trans. C. Emerson and M. Holquist, Austin: University of Texas Press.

Barber, C. L. (1959) *Shakespeare's Festive Comedy: A Study of Dramatic Form and its Relation to Social Custom*. Princeton: Princeton University Press.

Barber, C. L. and Wheeler, R. (1986) *The Whole Journey: Shakespeare's Power of Development*, Berkeley: University of California Press.

Barroll, J. L. (1958) "Shakespeare and Roman History," *Modern Language Review* 53: 327–43.

Bartels, E. C. (1990) "Making More of the Moor: Aaron, Othello, and Renaissance Refashionings of Race," *Shakespeare Quarterly* 41: 432–54.

Bateson, G. (1958) *Naven*, 2nd edition, Stanford: Stanford University Press.

Bede (1968) *A History of the English Church and People (Ecclesiastical History)*, ed. L. Sherley-Price, revised R. E. Latham, Harmondsworth: Penguin.

Bell, C. (1992) *Ritual Theory, Ritual Practice*, New York and Oxford: Oxford University Press.

Belsey, C. (1985) *The Subject of Tragedy: Identity and Difference in Renaissance Drama*, London: Methuen.

Berger, H., Jr. (1985) "Psychoanalyzing the Shakespeare Text: the First Three Scenes of the Henriad," in P. Parker and G. Hartman (eds) *Shakespeare and the Question of Theory*, New York: Methuen.

Bernal, M. (1987) *Black Athena: The Afroasiatic Roots of Classical Civlization*, 2 vols, New Brunswick: Rutgers University Press.

Berninghausen, T. F. (1987) "Banishing Cain: the Gardening Metaphor in *Richard II* and the Genesis Myth of the Origin of History," *Essays in Literature* 14: 3–13.

Berry, E. (1984) *Shakespeare's Comic Rites*, Cambridge: Cambridge University Press.

Bevington, D. (ed.) (1980) *Complete Works of William Shakespeare*, 3rd edition, Glenview, Ill.: Scott Foresman.

Bloomfield, M. V. (1976) "Quoting and Alluding: Shakespeare in the English Language," in G. B. Evans (ed.) *Shakespeare: Aspects of Influence*, Harvard English Studies 7, Cambridge, Mass.: Harvard University Press.

Boal, A. (1979) *Theater of the Oppressed*, trans. C. A. and M.-O. Leal McBride, London: Pluto Press.

Bocock, R. (1974) *Ritual in Industrial Society: A Sociological Analysis of Ritualism in Modern England*, London: George Allen and Unwin.

Bodin, J. (1606) *The Six Bookes of the Common Weale*, trans. Richard Knolles, London. (STC 3193)

Bohannon, L. (1956) "Miching Mallecho: That Means Witchcraft," in J. Morris (ed.) *From the Third Programme*, London: Nonesuch.

Bonjour, A. (1958) *The Structure of "Julius Caesar,"* Liverpool: Liverpool University Press

Booth, S. (1983) *King Lear, Macbeth, Indefinition, and Tragedy*, New Haven: Yale University Press.

Bourdieu, P. (1977) *Outline of a Theory of Practice*, trans. R. Nice, Cambridge: Cambridge University Press.

Bradley, A. C. (1904) *Shakespearean Tragedy*, Reprinted 1968, New York: Fawcett.

Brecht, B. (1966) *Brecht on Theatre: The Development of an Aesthetic*, trans. J. Willett, New York: Hill and Wang.

Bristol, M. D. (1985) *Carnival and Theater: Plebeian Culture and the Structure of Authority in Renaissance England*, London: Methuen.

Bristol, M. D. (1987) "Lenten Butchery: Legitimation Crisis in *Coriolanus*," in J. E. Howard and M. F. O'Connor (eds) *Shakespeare Reproduced: The Text in History and Ideology*, New York: Methuen.

Bristol, M. D. (1990) *Shakespeare's America, America's Shakespeare*, London: Routledge.

Bristol, M. D. (1991) "In Search of the Bear: Spatiotemporal Form and the Heterogeneity of Economics in *The Winter's Tale*," *Shakespeare Quarterly* 42: 145–67.

Brockbank, P. (1983) "Blood and Wine: Tragic Ritual from Aeschylus to Soyinka," *Shakespeare Survey* 36: 11–19.

Brockbank, P. (ed.) (1976) *William Shakespeare: Coriolanus*, Arden Edition, London: Methuen.

Bucknell, P. A. (1979) *Entertainment and Ritual: 600–1600*, London: Stainer and Bell.

Bullough, G. (1973) *Narrative and Dramatic Sources of Shakespeare*, 8 vols, New York: Columbia University Press.

Burckhardt, S. (1968) *Shakespearean Meanings*, Princeton: Princeton University Press.

Burke, K. (1957) *The Philosophy of Literary Form*, New York: Vintage.

Burke, K. (1966) *Language as Symbolic Action: Essays on Life, Literature, and Method*, Berkeley: University of California Press.

Burke, P. (1978) *Popular Culture in Early Modern Europe*, London: Temple Smith.

Burland, C. A. (1972) *Echoes of Magic: A Study of Seasonal Festivals through the Ages*, Totowa, N.J.: Rowman and Littlefield.

Butcher, S. (trans.) (1951) (first published 1907) Aristotle, *Poetics*, New York: Dover Publications.

Bynum, C. W. (1987) *Holy Feast and Holy Fast*, Berkeley: University of California Press.

Caillois, R. (1959) *Man and the Sacred*, trans. M. Barash, Glencoe, Ill.: Free Press. First published 1939: *L'homme et le sacre*, Paris: Gallimard.

Cantor, P. A. (1976) *Shakespeare's Rome: Republic and Empire*, Ithaca: Cornell University Press.

Cavell, S. (1987) "*Coriolanus* and Interpretations of Politics ('Who does the wolf love?')" in *Disowning Knowledge in Six Plays of Shakespeare*, Cambridge: Cambridge University Press.

Cawte, E. C. (1978) *Ritual Animal Disguise*, Totowa, N.J.: Rowman and Littlefield.

Caxton, W. (1483) (printer and trans.) *The Golden Legend* (*Legenda Aurea* by J. de Voragine), Westminster. (STC 24873)

Chambers, E. K. (1903) *The Medieval Stage*, 2 vols, London: Oxford University Press.

Chambers, E. K. (1933) *The English Folk Play,* Oxford: Clarendon.

Champion, L. (1976) *Shakespeare's Tragic Perspective*, Athens: University of Georgia Press.

Charney, M. (1961) *Shakespeare's Roman Plays: The Function of Imagery in the Drama*, Cambridge, Mass.: Harvard University Press.

Charney, M. (1990) *Titus Andronicus*, Hemel Hempstead: Harvester Wheatsheaf.

Chaucer, G. (1957) *Works*, ed. F. N. Robinson, Boston: Houghton Mifflin.

Cohen, D. (1985) "The Rite of Violence in *1 Henry IV*," *Shakespeare Survey* 38: 77–84.

Cole, S. L. (1985) *The Absent One: Mourning Ritual, Tragedy, and the Performance of Ambivalence*, University Park: Pennsylvania State University Press.

Cox, J. D. (1989) *Shakespeare and the Dramaturgy of Power*, Princeton: Princeton University Press.

Crapanzano, V. (1992) *Hermes' Dilemma and Hamlet's Desire: On the Epistemology of Interpretation*, Cambridge, Mass.: Harvard University Press.

Cressy, D. (1989) *Bonfires and Bells: National Memory and the Protestant Calendar in Elizabethan and Stuart England*, Berkeley: University of California Press.

Da Matta, R. (1984) "Carnival in Multiple Planes," in J. J. MacAloon (ed.) *Rite, Drama, Festival, Spectacle: Rehearsals Toward a Theory of Cultural Performance*, Philadelphia: Institute for the Study of Human Issues.

Danson, L. (1974) *Tragic Alphabet: Shakespeare's Dramaturgy of Language*, New Haven: Yale University Press.

d'Aquili, E. G., Laughlin, C. D., Jr., and McManus, J. (1979) *The Spectrum of Ritual: A Biogenetic Structural Analysis*, New York: Columbia University Press.

Davis, N. Z. (1975) *Society and Culture in Early Modern France*, Stanford: Stanford University Press.

de Gerenday, L. (1974) "Play, Ritualization, and Ambivalence in *Julius Caesar*," *Literature and Psychology* 24: 24–33.

de Grazia, M. (1991) *Shakespeare Verbatim*, Oxford: Oxford University Press.

Delany, P. (1977) "*King Lear* and the Decline of Feudalism," *PMLA* 92: 429–40.

Derrida, J. (1978) "Structure, Sign, and Play in the Discourse of the Human Sciences," in *Writing and Difference*, trans. and ed. A. Bass, London: Routledge and Kegan Paul.

Derrida, J. (1981) "Plato's Pharmacy," in *Dissemination*, trans. and ed. B. Johnson, Chicago: University of Chicago Press.

Dollimore, J. (1984) *Radical Tragedy: Religion, Ideology and Power in the Drama of Shakespeare and his Contemporaries*, Chicago: University of Chicago Press.

Dollimore, J. (1989) *Radical Tragedy: Religion, Ideology and Power in the Drama of Shakespeare and his Contemporaries*, 2nd edition, Hemel Hempstead: Harvester Wheatsheaf.

Donne, J. (1971) *The Complete English Poems*, ed. A. J. Smith, Harmondsworth: Penguin.

Dorsch, T. S. (ed.) (1955) *Julius Caesar*, New Arden, London: Methuen.

Douglas, M. (1966) *Purity and Danger: An Analysis of the Concepts of Pollution and Taboo*, London: ARK Paperbacks.

Douglas, M. (1975) *Implicit Meanings: Essays in Anthropology*, London: Routledge and Kegan Paul.

Douglas, M. (1982) *In the Active Voice*, London: Routledge and Kegan Paul.

Drakakis, J. (1989) "Writing the Body Politic: Subject, Discourse, and History in Shakespeare's *Coriolanus*," unpublished manuscript.

Drakakis, J. (ed.) (1985) *Alternative Shakespeares*, London: Methuen.

Duffy, E. (1992) *The Stripping of the Altars: Traditional Religion in England 1400–1580*, New Haven and London: Yale University Press.

Dumézil, G. (1970) *Archaic Roman Religion*, 2 vols, trans. P. Krapp, revised edition, Chicago: University of Chicago Press.

Dumouchel, P. (ed.) (1988) *Violence and Truth: On the Work of René Girard*, Stanford: Stanford University Press.

Dupuy, J.-P. (1988) "Totalization and Misrecognition," in P. Dumouchel (ed.) *Violence and Truth: On the Work of René Girard*, Stanford: Stanford University Press.

Durkheim, E. (1965) *The Elementary Forms of the Religious Life* (1912), trans. J. W. Swain, New York: Free Press.

Durkheim, E. (1972) *Selected Writings*, trans. and ed. A. Giddens, Cambridge: Cambridge University Press.

Durkheim, E. and Mauss, M. (1963) *Primitive Classification*, trans. R. Needham, Chicago: University of Chicago Press.

Eagleton, T. (1986) *William Shakespeare*, Oxford: Basil Blackwell.

Echols, E. C. (ed. and trans.) (1961) Herodian of Antioch, *History of the Roman Empire from the Death of Marcus Aurelius to the Accession of Gordian III*, Berkeley: University of California Press.

Else, G. F. (1967) *Aristotle's Poetics: The Argument*, Cambridge, Mass.: Harvard University Press.

Evans, M. (1989) *Signifying Nothing: Truth's True Contents in Shakespeare's Texts*, Athens: University of Georgia Press.

Fiedler, L. (1960) *No! In Thunder: Essays on Myth and Literature*, New York: Stein and Day.

Fiedler, L. (1972) *The Stranger in Shakespeare*, London: Croom Helm.

Figes, E. (1990) *Tragedy and Social Evolution*, New York: Persea Books.

Forset, E. (1606) *A Comparative Discourse of the Bodies Natural and Politique*, London (STC 1118).

Foucault, M. (1970) *The Order of Things: An Archaeology of the Human Sciences*, London: Tavistock.

Foucault, M. (1977) "Nietzsche, Genealogy, History," and "What Is an Author?" in *Language, Counter-Memory, Practice: Selected Interviews and Essays*, ed. D. F. Bouchard, trans. D. F. Bouchard and S. Simon, London: Basil Blackwell.

Foucault, M. (1980) "Two Lectures," in *Power/Knowledge: Selected Interviews and Other Writings 1972-1977*, ed. and trans. C. Gordon, New York: Pantheon.

BIBLIOGRAPHY

Foucault, M. (1986) "Of Other Spaces," trans. J. Miskowiec, *Diacritics* (Spring): 22–7.

Frazer, J. G. (1929) *The "Fasti" of Ovid*, 5 vols, London: Macmillan.

Freud, S. (1950) *Totem and Taboo*, ed. J. Strachey, New York: Norton.

Freud, S. (1955) *Group Psychology and the Analysis of the Ego*, in *The Standard Edition of the Complete Psychological Works of Sigmund Freud*, trans. J. Strachey, London: Hogarth.

Freud, S. (1961) *Civilization and Its Discontents*, trans. and ed. J. Strachey, New York: W. W. Norton.

Frye, N. (1957) *Anatomy of Criticism*, Princeton: Princeton University Press.

Frye, N. (1965) *A Natural Perspective*, New York: Columbia University Press.

Frye, N. (1967) *Fools of Time*, Toronto: University of Toronto Press.

Gaines, B. and Lofaro, M. (1976) "What Did Caliban Look Like?" *Mississippi Folklore Register* 10: 175–86.

Geertz, C. (1966) *Person, Time, and Conduct in Bali: An Essay in Cultural Analysis*, New Haven: Yale University Press.

Geertz, C. (1973) *The Interpretation of Cultures*, New York: Basic Books.

Geertz, C. (1983) *Local Knowledge: Further Essays in Interpretive Anthropology*, New York: Basic Books.

Geneva Bible: A Facsimile of the 1560 edition (1969) Madison: University of Wisconsin Press.

Ginzburg, C. (1983) *The Night Battles: Witchcraft and Agrarian Cults in the Sixteenth and Seventeenth Centuries*, trans. J. and A. Tedeschi, London: Routledge and Kegan Paul.

Girard, R. (1977) *Violence and the Sacred*, trans. P. Gregory, Baltimore: Johns Hopkins University Press.

Girard, R. (1978) *"To Double Business Bound": Essays on Literature, Mimesis, and Anthropology*, Baltimore: Johns Hopkins University Press.

Girard, R. (1987) *Things Hidden since the Foundation of the World*, trans. S. Bann and M. Metteer, Stanford: Stanford University Press.

Goldberg, J. (1988) "Hamlet's Hand," *Shakespeare Quarterly* 39: 307–27.

Goldman, M. (1972) *Shakespeare and the Energies of Drama*, Princeton: Princeton University Press.

Goody, J. (1977) "Against 'Ritual': Loosely Structured Thoughts on a Loosely Defined Topic," in S. F. Moore and B. Myerhoff (eds) *Secular Ritual*, Amsterdam: Van Gorcum.

Goody, J. and Watt, I. (1968) "The Consequences of Literacy," in J. Goody (ed.) *Literacy in Traditional Societies*, Cambridge: Cambridge University Press.

Gosson, S. (1579) *The Schoole of Abuse*, London. (STC 12097.5)

Granville-Barker, H. (1927) *Prefaces to Shakespeare*, 1st series, London: Sidgwick and Jackson.

Greenblatt, S. (1981) "Invisible Bullets: Renaissance Authority and its Subversion," *Glyph* 8: 40–61.

Greenblatt, S. (1982) "Filthy Rites," *Daedalus* 111 (3): 1–16.

Greenblatt, S. (1985) "Shakespeare and the Exorcists," in P. Parker and G. Hartman (eds) *Shakespeare and the Question of Theory*, London: Methuen.

Greenblatt, S. (ed.) (1982) *The Power of Forms in the English Renaissance*, Norman, Okla.: Pilgrim Books.

Grimes, R. L. (1982) "The Lifeblood of Public Ritual: Fiestas and Public

Exploration Project," in V. Turner (ed.) *Celebration: Studies in Festivity and Ritual*, Washington, D.C.: Smithsonian Institution Press.

Guy, J. (1988) *Tudor England*, Oxford: Oxford University Press.

Hall, E. (1992) "When Is a Myth Not a Myth? Bernal's 'Ancient Model,'" *Arethusa* 25: 181–201.

Halliwell, S. (1987) *The "Poetics" of Aristotle: Translation and Commentary*, Chapel Hill: University of North Carolina Press.

Hammersmith, J. (1978) "*Hamlet* and the Myth of Memory," *ELH* 45: 597–605.

Hassell, R. C., Jr. (1979) *Renaissance Drama and the English Church Year*, Lincoln: University of Nebraska Press.

Hawkes, T. (1974) *Shakespeare's Talking Animals: Language and Drama in Society*, Totowa, N.J.: Rowman and Littlefield.

Hawkes, T. (1986) "Telmah," in *That Shakespeherian Rag: Essays on a Critical Process*, London: Methuen.

Heffner, R. (1930) "Shakespeare, Hayward, and Essex," *PMLA* 45: 754–80.

Heilman, R. B. (1968) *Tragedy and Melodrama*, Seattle: University of Washington Press.

Heinemann, M. (1985) "How Brecht Read Shakespeare," in J. Dollimore and A. Sinfield (eds) *Political Shakespeare: New Essays in Cultural Materialism*, Ithaca: Cornell University Press.

Helm, A. (1965) "In Comes I, St George," *Folk-Lore* 76: 118–36.

Heninger, S. K. (1977) *The Cosmographical Glass: Renaissance Diagrams of the Universe*, San Marino: Huntington Library.

Herodian (*c.* 1550) *The history of Herodian*, London: William Coplande (STC 13221)

Heywood, J. (1970) *The Four PP*, ed. F. S. Boas, London: Oxford University Press.

Hill, R. F. (1957) "The Composition of *Titus Andronicus*," *Shakespeare Survey* 10: 60–70.

Hobsbawm, E. and Ranger, T. (eds) (1983) *The Invention of Tradition*, Cambridge: Cambridge University Press.

Holland, N. (1960) "Macbeth as Hibernal Giant," *Literature and Psychology* 10: 37–8.

Holleran, J. V. (1989) "Maimed Funeral Rites in *Hamlet*," *ELR* 19: 65–93.

Holloway, J. (1961) *The Story of the Night*, Lincoln: University of Nebraska Press.

"Homilee agaynst Disobedience and wylful Rebellion," in *The Second Tome of Homilies* (1574), London. (STC 13670)

Hooker, R. (1975) *Of the Laws of Ecclesiastical Polity*, ed. A. S. McGrade and B. Vickers, New York: St Martin's.

Huizinga, J. (1955) *Homo Ludens: A Study of the Play-Element in Culture*, Boston: Beacon Press.

Hunter, G. K. (1974) "Shakespeare's Earliest Tragedies: 'Titus Andronicus' and 'Romeo and Juliet,'" *Shakespeare Survey* 27: 1–10.

Hutton, R. (1994) *The Rise and Fall of Merry England: The Ritual Year 1400–1700*, Oxford: Oxford University Press.

Ingram, R. W. (ed.) (1981) *Coventry*, REED, Toronto: University of Toronto Press.

James, E. O. (1961) *Seasonal Feasts and Festivals*, London: Thames and Hudson.

James, M. (1983) "Ritual, Drama and Social Body in the Late Medieval English Town," *Past and Present* 98: 3–29.

Jameson, F. (1981) *The Political Unconscious: Narrative as a Socially Symbolic Act*, Ithaca: Cornell University Press.

Jardine, L. (1983) *Still Harping on Daughters: Women and Drama in the Age of Shakespeare*, Sussex: Harvester Press.

Johnson, R. (1608) *The Most Famous History of the Seven Champions of Christendom*, London. (STC 14679)

Jonson, B. (1965) *Timber, or Discoveries*. In *English Prose 1600-1660*, ed. V. Harris and I. Husain, San Francisco: Holt, Rinehart and Winston.

Kahn, C. (1981) *Man's Estate: Masculine Identity in Shakespeare*, Berkeley: University of California Press.

Kastan, D. S. (1986) "Proud Majesty Made a Subject: Shakespeare and the Spectacle of Rule," *Shakespeare Quarterly* 37: 459–75.

Kastan, D. S. (1987) "'His semblable is his mirror': *Hamlet* and the Imitation of Revenge," *Shakespeare Studies* 19: 111–24.

Kastan, D. S. and Stallybrass, P. (eds) (1991) *Staging the Renaissance: Reinterpretations of Elizabethan and Jacobean Literature*, New York: Routledge.

Keen, M. (1990) *English Society in the Later Middle Ages 1348–1500*, Harmondsworth: Penguin.

Kendall, G. M. (1989) "'Lend me thy hand': Metaphor and Mayhem in *Titus Andronicus*," *Shakespeare Quarterly* 40: 299–316.

Kernan, A. B. (1970) "The Henriad: Shakespeare's Major History Plays," in A. B. Kernan (ed.) *Modern Shakespearean Criticism*, New York: Harcourt, Brace and World.

Kernan, A. B. (1975) "From Ritual to History: The English History Play," in J. L. Barroll, A. Leggatt, A. B. Kernan, and R. Hosley (eds) *The Revels History of Drama in English*, London: Methuen.

Kirschbaum, L. (1949) "Shakespeare's Stage Blood and Its Critical Significance," *PMLA* 64: 523–4.

Knights, L. C. (1937) *Drama and Society in the Age of Jonson*, New York: W. W. Norton.

Kott, J. (1973) *The Eating of the Gods: An Interpretation of Greek Tragedy*, trans. B. Taborski and E. J. Czerwinski, New York: Random House.

Kurtz, B. P. (1910) *Studies in the Marvellous*, Berkeley: University of California Press.

LaFontaine, J. S. (1985) *Initiation: Ritual Drama and Secret Knowledge Across the World*, Harmondsworth: Penguin.

Larner, C. (1981) *Enemies of God: The Witch-hunt in Scotland*, Baltimore: Johns Hopkins University Press.

Laroque, F. (1991) *Shakespeare's Festive World: Elizabethan Seasonal Entertainment and the Professional Stage*, trans. J. Lloyd, Cambridge: Cambridge University Press.

Le Roy Ladurie, E. (1979) *Carnival in Romans*, trans. M. Feeney, New York: George Braziller.

Lévi-Strauss, C. (1966) *The Savage Mind*, Chicago: University of Chicago Press.

Liebler, N. C. (1981) "'Thou Bleeding Piece of Earth': The Ritual Ground of *Julius Caesar*," *Shakespeare Studies* 14: 175–96.

Liebler, N. C. (1992) "The Mockery King of Snow: *Richard II* and the Sacrifice of Ritual," in L. Woodbridge and E. Berry (eds) *True Rites and Maimed Rites: Ritual and Anti-Ritual in Shakespeare and His Age*, Urbana and Chicago: University of Illinois Press.

Liebler, N. C. (1994a) "Getting It All Right: *Titus Andronicus* and Roman History," *Shakespeare Quarterly* 45: 263–79.

Liebler, N. C. (1994b) "Hamlet's Hobby-Horse," *Cahiers Élisabéthains* 45 (April): 33–45.

Lincoln, B. (1989) *Discourse and the Construction of Society: Comparative Studies of Myth, Ritual, and Classification*, New York: Oxford University Press.

Livingston, P. (1988) "Demystification and History in Girard and Durkheim," in P. Dumouchel (ed.) *Violence and Truth: On the Work of René Girard*, Stanford: Stanford University Press.

Long, M. (1976) *The Unnatural Scene: A Study in Shakespearean Tragedy*, London: Methuen.

Loomba, A. (1989) *Gender, Race, Renaissance Drama*, Manchester: University of Manchester Press.

Lumiansky, R. M. and Mills, D. (eds) (1974) *The Chester Mystery Cycle*, EETS, s.s. 3, London: Oxford University Press.

MacAloon, J. J. (1982) "Sociation and Sociability in Political Celebrations," in V. Turner (ed.) *Celebration: Studies in Festivity and Ritual*, Washington, D.C.: Smithsonian Institution Press.

MacAloon, J. J. (ed.) (1984) *Rite, Drama, Festival, Spectacle: Rehearsals Toward a Theory of Cultural Performance*, Philadelphia: Institute for the Study of Human Issues.

Macherey, P. (1978) *A Theory of Literary Production*, trans. G. Wall, London: Routledge and Kegan Paul.

Magie, D. (ed. and trans.) (1921, 1924) *Scriptores Historiae Augustae*, Loeb Classical Library, 3 vols, Cambridge, Mass.: Harvard University Press.

Marcus, L. S. (1986) *The Politics of Mirth: Jonson, Herrick, Milton, Marvell, and the Defense of Old Holiday Pastimes*, Chicago: University of Chicago Press.

Marcus, L. S. (1988) *Puzzling Shakespeare: Local Reading and Its Discontents*, Berkeley: University of California Press.

Marcus, L. S. (1991) "Levelling Shakespeare: Local Customs and Local Texts," *Shakespeare Quarterly* 42: 168–78.

Marlowe, C. (1971) *Doctor Faustus*, in *The Plays of Christopher Marlowe*, ed. R. Gill, London: Oxford University Press.

Maxwell, J. C. (ed.) (1961) *Titus Andronicus*, Arden series, London: Methuen.

Michel, L. (1970) *The Thing Contained: Theory of the Tragic*, Bloomington: Indiana University Press.

Miola, R. S. (1981) "*Titus Andronicus* and the Mythos of Shakespeare's Rome," *Shakespeare Studies* 14: 85–98.

Monter, W. (1983) *Ritual, Myth and Magic in Early Modern Europe*, Athens: Ohio University Press.

Moore, S. F. and Myerhoff, B. G. (eds) (1977) *Secular Ritual*, Amsterdam: Van Gorcum.

Moretti, F. (1982) "'A Huge Eclipse': Tragic Form and the Deconsecration of

Sovereignty," in S. Greenblatt (ed.) *The Power of Forms in the English Renaissance*, Norman, Okla.: Pilgrim Books.

Muir, E. (1981) *Civic Ritual in Renaissance Venice*, Princeton: Princeton University Press.

Muir, K. (1981) "Folklore and Shakespeare," *Folk-Lore* 92: 231–40.

Muir, K. (ed.) (1962) *William Shakespeare: Macbeth*, Arden Shakespeare, London: Methuen.

Muir, K. (ed.) (1972) *William Shakespeare: King Lear*, Arden Shakespeare, London: Methuen

Mullaney, S. (1988) *The Place of the Stage: License, Play, and Power in Renaissance England*, Chicago: University of Chicago Press.

Myerhoff, B. (1978) *Number Our Days*, New York: Simon and Schuster.

Myerhoff, B. (1982) "Rites of Passage: Process and Paradox," in V. Turner (ed.) *Celebration: Studies in Festivity and Ritual*, Washington, D.C.: Smithsonian Institution Press.

Neale, J. E. (1957) *Queen Elizabeth I*, New York: Doubleday Anchor.

Neill, M. (1989) "Unproper Beds: Race, Adultery, and the Hideous in *Othello*," *Shakespeare Quarterly* 40: 383–412.

Nietzsche, F. (1967) *The Birth of Tragedy and the Case of Wagner*, trans. W. Kaufmann, New York: Vintage.

Ogilvie, R. M. (1965) *A Commentary on Livy, Books 1–5*, Oxford: Clarendon.

Oman, C. (1906; reprinted 1969) *The Political History of England*, 12 vols, New York: AMS. Vol. 4: *The History of England from the Accession of Richard II to the Death of Richard III (1377-1485)*.

Orange, L. E. (1976) "Despised Nativity: Unnatural Birth in Shakespeare," *Mississippi Folklore Register* 10: 163–74.

Orgel, S. (1975) *The Illusion of Power*, Berkeley: University of California Press.

Ovid (1931) *Fasti*, ed. and trans. J. G. Frazer, London: William Heinemann.

Palmer, D. J. (1972) "The Unspeakable in Pursuit of the Uneatable: Language and Action in *Titus Andronicus*," *Critical Quarterly* 14: 320–9.

Palmer, G. and Lloyd, N. (1972) *A Year of Festivals: A Guide to British Calendar Customs*, London: Frederick Warne.

Palmer, R. (1976) *The Folklore of Warwickshire*, Totowa, N.J.: Rowman and Littlefield.

Paster, G. K. (1978) "To Starve With Feeding: The City in *Coriolanus*," *Shakespeare Studies* 11: 123–44.

Paster, G. K. (1989) "'In the spirit of men there is no blood': Blood as Trope of Gender in *Julius Caesar*," *Shakespeare Quarterly* 40: 284–98.

Patterson, A. (1989) *Shakespeare and the Popular Voice*, Cambridge: Basil Blackwell.

Pearce, F. (1989) *The Radical Durkheim*, London: Unwin Hyman.

Pecora, V. P. (1989) "The Limits of Local Knowledge," in H. A. Veeser (ed.) *The New Historicism*, New York and London: Routledge.

Pettet, E. C. (1950) "Coriolanus and the Midlands Insurrection of 1607," *Shakespeare Survey* 3: 34–42.

Plutarch (1892) *The Romane Questions*, trans. P. Holland (1603), reprinted edition ed. F. B. Jevons, London: David Nutt.

Plutarch (1967) *Lives of the Noble Grecians and Romans, Englisht by Sir Thomas North, Anno 1579*, 6 vols, ed. G. Wyndham, New York: AMS Press.

Quinones, R. J. (1991) *The Changes of Cain: Violence and the Lost Brother in Cain and Abel Literature*, Princeton: Princeton University Press.

Rabkin, N. (1967) *Shakespeare and the Common Understanding*, New York: Free Press.

Rackin, P. (1978) *Shakespeare's Tragedies*, New York: Frederick Ungar.

Rackin, P. (1990) *Stages of History: Shakespeare's English Chronicles*, Ithaca: Cornell University Press.

Ribner, I. (1957) "Political Issues in *Julius Caesar*," *Journal of English and Germanic Philology* 56: 10–22.

Ribner, I. (1966) (ed.) *The Complete Works of William Shakespeare*, Boston: Ginn.

Ryan, K. (1988) "*Romeo and Juliet*: The Language of Tragedy," in W. van Peer (ed.) *The Taming of the Text: Explorations in Language, Literature, and Culture*, London: Routledge.

Saccio, P. (1977) *Shakespeare's English Kings: History, Chronicle, and Drama*, New York: Oxford University Press.

Schanzer, E. (1963) *Shakespeare's Problem Plays*, New York: Schocken.

Schechner, R. (1988) *Performance Theory* (revised edition) New York: Routledge.

Selden, R. (1987) "King Lear and True Need," *Shakespeare Studies* 19: 143–69.

Seneca (1966) *Thyestes*, trans. E. F. Watling, Harmondsworth: Penguin.

Sharp, C. and McIlwaine, H. C. (1912) *The Morris Book, Part I*, London: Novello.

Siebers, T. (1983) *The Mirror of Medusa*, Berkeley: University of California Press.

Siebers, T. (1988) *The Ethics of Criticism*, Ithaca: Cornell University Press.

Smith, J. Z. (1987) *To Take Place: Toward Theory in Ritual*, Chicago: University of Chicago Press.

Soyinka, W. (1976) *Myth, Literature and the African World*, Cambridge: Cambridge University Press.

Spencer, T. J. B. (1957) "Shakespeare and the Elizabethan Romans," *Shakespeare Survey* 10: 27–38.

Spencer, T. J. B. (1964) *Shakespeare's Plutarch*, Baltimore: Penguin.

Sprengnether, M. (1986) "Annihilating Intimacy in *Coriolanus*," in *Women in the Middle Ages and the Renaissance*, ed. M. B. Rose, Syracuse: Syracuse University Press.

Stallybrass, P. and White, A. (1986) *The Politics and Poetics of Transgression*, London: Methuen.

Stallybrass, P. and Kastan, D. S. (eds) (1991) *Staging the Renaissance: Reinterpretations of Elizabethan and Jacobean Literature*, London: Routledge.

Starnes, D. and Talbert, E. W. (1955) *Classical Myth and Legend in Renaissance Dictionaries*, Chapel Hill: University of North Carolina Press.

Steadman, J. (1971) "'Passions Well Imitated': Rhetoric and Poetics in the Preface to *Samson Agonistes*," in J. A. Wittreich, Jr. (ed.) *Calm of Mind: Tercentenary Essays on Paradise Regained and Samson Agonistes in Honor of John S. Diekhoff*, Cleveland: Case Western Reserve University Press.

Steiner, G. (1961) *The Death of Tragedy*, London: Faber and Faber.

Stevens, M. and Cawley, A. C. (eds) (1994) *The Towneley Plays*, EETS, s.s. 13–14, Oxford: Oxford University Press.

Stirling, B. (1951) "Or Else This Were a Savage Spectacle," *PMLA* 66: 765–74.

Strong, R. (1984) *Art and Power: Renaissance Festivals 1450–1650*, Berkeley: University of California Press.

Stubbes, P. (1583) *The Anatomie of Abuses*, London (STC 23376), reprinted New York: Garland.

Tan, A. (1989) *The Joy Luck Club*, New York: Ivy Books.

Tanner, J. R. (ed.) (1940) *Tudor Constitutional Documents* A.D. *1485–1603*, Cambridge: Cambridge University Press.

Telford, K. (trans.) (1961) Aristotle, *Poetics*, Chicago: H. Regnery.

Tennenhouse, L. (1986) *Power on Display: The Politics of Shakespeare's Genres*, New York: Methuen.

Thomas, K. (1971) *Religion and the Decline of Magic*, New York: Charles Scribner's Sons.

Tiddy, R. J. E. (1923) *The Mummers' Play*, Oxford: Clarendon.

Tillyard, E. M. W. (1948) *The Elizabethan World Picture*, New York: Vintage Books.

Tricomi, A. H. (1974) "The Aesthetics of Mutilation in *Titus Andronicus*," *Shakespeare Survey* 27: 11–19.

Turner, T. S. (1977) "Transformation, Hierarchy, and Transcendence: A Reformulation of Van Gennep's Model of the Structure of Rites de Passage," in S. F. Moore and B. G. Myerhoff (eds) *Secular Ritual*, Amsterdam: Van Gorcum.

Turner, V. (1967) *The Forest of Symbols: Aspects of Ndembu Ritual*, Ithaca: Cornell University Press.

Turner, V. (1969) *The Ritual Process: Structure and Anti-Structure*, Ithaca: Cornell University Press.

Turner, V. (1974) *Dramas, Fields, and Metaphors: Symbolic Action in Human Society*, Ithaca: Cornell University Press.

Turner, V. (1982) *From Ritual to Theatre: The Human Seriousness of Play*, New York: Performing Arts Journal Publications.

Turner, V. (1987) "Are there universals of performance?" *Comparative Criticism* 9: 47–58.

Turner, V. (ed.) (1982) *Celebration: Studies in Festivity and Ritual*, Washington, D.C.: Smithsonian Institution Press.

Underdown, D. (1985) *Revel, Riot, and Rebellion: Popular Politics and Culture in England 1603–1660*, Oxford: Oxford University Press.

van Gennep, A. (1960) *The Rites of Passage* (1909), trans. M. B. Vizedom and G. L. Caffee, Chicago: University of Chicago Press.

Velz, J. W. (1968a) "'If I were Brutus Now...': Role-Playing in *Julius Caesar*," *Shakespeare Studies* 4: 149–59.

Velz, J. W. (1968b) *Shakespeare and the Classical Tradition: A Critical Guide to Commentary, 1660–1960*, Minneapolis: University of Minnesota Press.

Velz, J. W. (1978) "The Ancient World in Shakespeare: Authenticity or Anachronism? A Retrospect," *Shakespeare Survey* 31: 1–12.

Walens, S. (1982) "The Weight of My Name is a Mountain of Blankets," in V. Turner (ed.) *Celebration: Studies in Festivity and Ritual*, Washington, D.C.: Smithsonian Institution Press.

Weimann, R. (1978) *Shakespeare and the Popular Tradition in the Theater: Studies in the Social Dimension of Dramatic Form and Function*, ed. R. Schwartz, Baltimore: Johns Hopkins University Press.

Weinberg, B. (1965) "From Aristotle to Pseudo-Aristotle," in E. Olson (ed.) *Aristotle's Poetics and English Literature*, Chicago: University of Chicago Press.

Welsh, A. (1975) "Brutus is an Honorable Man," *Yale Review* 64: 496–513.

West, G. S. (1982) "Going by the Book: Classical Allusions in *Titus Andronicus*," *Studies in Philology* 79: 62–77.

White, R. S. (1986) *Innocent Victims: Poetic Injustice in Shakespearean Tragedy*, 2nd edition, London: Athlone.

Whittaker, C. R. (trans. and ed.) (1969) *Herodian*, 2 vols, Loeb Classical Library, London: William Heinemann.

Willbern, D. (1978) "Rape and Revenge in *Titus Andronicus*," *ELR* 8: 159–82.

Williams, R. (1966) *Modern Tragedy*, Stanford: Stanford University Press.

Wilson, J. D. (1957) "Shakespeare's 'Small Latin' – How Much?" *Shakespeare Survey* 10: 12–26.

Wilson, J. D. (ed.) (1948) *Titus Andronicus*, Cambridge: Cambridge University Press.

Wilson, J. D. (ed.) (1968) *Julius Caesar*, New Shakespeare series, Cambridge: Cambridge University Press.

Wilson, R. (1987) "'Is This a Holiday?': Shakespeare's Roman Carnival," *ELH* 54: 31–44.

Woodbridge, L. (1994) *The Scythe of Saturn: Magical Thinking in Shakespeare*, Urbana: University of Illinois Press.

Woodbridge, L. and Berry, E. (eds) (1992) *True Rites and Maimed Rites: Ritual and Anti-Ritual in Shakespeare and His Age*, Urbana: University of Illinois Press.

Zeeveld, W. G. (1962) "*Coriolanus* and Jacobean Politics," *Modern Language Review* 57: 321–34.

INDEX